Ilex Foundation Series 27

THE USES OF OPPRESSION

Also in the Ilex Foundation Series

more at www.ilexfoundation.org

THE USES OF OPPRESSION

The Ottoman Empire through Its Greek Newspapers 1830–1862

Marina Sakali, Lady Marks

With a foreword by Bruce Clark

Ilex Foundation
Boston, Massachusetts

Distributed by Harvard University Press
Cambridge, Massachusetts and London, England

The Uses of Oppression: The Ottoman Empire through Its Greek Newspapers, 1830–1862
by Marina Sakali, Lady Marks

Published by Ilex Foundation, Boston, Massachusetts

Distributed by Harvard University Press, Cambridge, Massachusetts and London, England

Production editor: Christopher Dadian
Cover design: Joni Godlove
Printed in the United States of America

Cover image: *Constantinople from the Sea of Marmara, with the Mosque of Sultan Ahmet and Hagia Sophia*, by Edward Lear. © 2006 Christie's Images Limited. The image is shown in a reversed presentation.

Library of Congress Cataloging-in-Publication Data

Names: Sakali, Marina, Lady Marks, author.
Title: Uses of oppression : the Ottoman empire through its Greek
  newspapers, 1830-1862 / Marina Sakali, Lady Marks.
Description: Boston, Massachusetts : Ilex Foundation, 2024. | Series: Ilex
  Foundation series ; 27 | Includes bibliographical references and index.
  | Summary: "The Uses of Oppression follows the development of the
  Ottoman Greek press from its birth in 1830 until 1862, employing the
  reflections of its editors, correspondents, advertisers, commentators,
  and readers as a lens through which to view the everyday lives of a
  generation of Ottoman Greeks-their social aspirations, their reactions
  to political events, their reception of Western-style norms, and other
  contemporary issues"-- Provided by publisher.
Identifiers: LCCN 2024008248 | ISBN 9780674293984 (paperback)
Subjects: LCSH: Greek newspapers--Turkey--History--19th century. |
  Greeks--Turkey--Social conditions--19th century. |
  Greeks--Turkey--Intellectual life--19th century.
Classification: LCC PN5355.T8 S25 2024 | DDC
  079.56109/034--dc23/eng/20240304
LC record available at https://lccn.loc.gov/2024008248

for Alex

Contents

Foreword

I T IS ONE OF THE MOST STRIKING FEATURES of late Ottoman history that the Ottoman Greek minority, despite their inferior civic status, formed a community that crackled with creative energy. They knew how to respond with flexibility, imagination, and resilience to any changes in the local balance of power and in the wider world. In their entrepreneurial flair, in their yearning for education and self-improvement and in their zest for recreation and entertainment, the Greek Orthodox subjects of the sultan embraced life's possibilities to the full.

That is the overwhelming – and perfectly accurate – impression created by this diligent study of the Ottoman Greek world in the mid-nineteenthth century which has been researched by Marina Sakali, Lady Marks, using a remarkable array of Ottoman Greek newspapers as her principal source. Through the prism of the press, she traces the community's collective dilemmas, its internal arguments, its tastes and fads, and its rich network of international connections. The fact that this community came to a bloody end, a century ago, lends poignancy to the story, and makes it doubly important to study the written evidence in a cool and detached way.

The emergence of these lively newspapers was both a telling indication of the community's vigor and a stimulus to its further development. The story starts in 1830 when, as part of a program of cautious reforms, the sultan gave the green light to a written press. More than any other ethnic or religious group in the Ottoman empire, the Greek Orthodox or "Rum" community took advantage of this challenge. Between 1830 and 1862, when a curtain of censorship came down, no less than twenty-seven Greek-language publications appeared, for varying periods. They were distributed in Greek communities across the empire and beyond, and almost all their publishers were based in the great cities known to their Greek inhabitants as Smyrni/Smyrna (Izmir) and Konstantinoupolis/Constantinople (Istanbul). It is always worth recalling that as centers of Greek population, commerce and culture, these two cities still easily outranked any town in the emerging kingdom of Greece, not excluding Athens.

The various Ottoman Greek publications reflect the contrasting atmospheres of the cities in which they emerged: the stylish cosmopolitanism of the great Aegean port and the shadowy power-struggles of the imperial capital. One particularly interesting publisher was Ioannis Skylitses, who shifted his base from Smyrna to Trieste and from there used Austrian-owned ships to dispatch his weekly newspaper,

He Hemera, to places like Athens, Syros, and Alexandria as well as Ottoman towns and cities. Such ventures had a significant effect in knitting together the Hellenic world in the Greek kingdom, the Ottoman empire and beyond.

As well as forging bonds between Greek-speakers in different places, the newspapers read and written by Ottoman Greeks also exposed their ideological divisions and debates. The sharpest of these debates pitted those who wanted to dilute and democratize the monolithic power of the Patriarchate of Constantinople (the supreme religious authority for the Orthodox Christians) against those who preferred the status quo. It could be argued that in this debate the conservative side was the more prescient, anticipating that any dismantling of the patriarchate's power would lead to religious fragmentation (initially between Greek and Bulgarian Christians) and contribute to the messy break-up of the whole imperial system.

With remarkable frankness, the Ottoman Greek newspapers also spell out the contradictory effects of a sweeping reform known as the Hatt-ı Hümayun, which the sultan proclaimed under Anglo-French pressure in 1856. The decree's stated intention was to enhance the rights of the empire's non-Muslim subjects, and over time it did facilitate the establishment of new churches and schools that reflected the Christian minority's collective pride and prosperity. But the immediate effect was to provoke the empire's humbler Muslim subjects, who retaliated with random attacks on Christian lives and livelihoods. The press reflects the Ottoman Greeks' indignation at these attacks – and, significantly, their confidence that the sultan would ultimately protect them.

This highlights something paradoxical, and hard for a modern reader to grasp, in the Ottoman Greeks' self-understanding and world-view during the final century of their existence. As the press makes clear, the community was immensely proud of its linguistic, cultural, and religious heritage – but also, during the period which this book examines, loyal to the sultan. At a minimum, Greek leaders were willing to give some credence to the sultan's promise to hold the ring in a complex and competitive multi-ethnic society.

On the southwestern side of the Aegean, the emerging Greek kingdom, with its irredentist dreams, represented one pole of Hellenism; on the eastern side the Ottoman Greeks, eagerly reaping the benefits of an early wave of globalization, represented another. In the second half of the nineteenth century, it was by no means clear which would prove more successful or on what terms they might eventually coalesce.

Even in the early years of the twentieth century, the future of the Ottoman Greeks – and of Hellenism in general – was a wide-open question. In 1897, a short and humiliating war between Greece and the Ottomans seemed to discredit the whole idea that the Hellenic cause could ever prevail by extending the small Athens-based kingdom at the expense of a ramshackle but still powerful Islamic realm. Among a segment of the Greek elite, inside and outside Greece, a new idea took hold. Instead of directly challenging the Ottoman empire, it would be better to Hellenize it from within by maximizing Greek influence in Ottoman affairs.

As some strategists saw things, this might lead to the creation of a kind of Greek-Turkish condominium, the combined strength of which could keep at bay the spectres of Slavic expansion and Western opportunism. These hopes came to a precarious climax in 1908, when an uprising by junior Ottoman officers in Salonika (Thessaloniki) – the Young Turks – led to a brief surge of optimism. People dreamed of a reformed empire in which all groups (even the Greeks and Bulgarians who were fighting hard over the nearby region's ultimate future) could live in amity. It was also the year in which a pair of strategic visionaries set up a secret fraternity called the Constantinople Organization with the aim of bolstering the Greek cause in the sultan's capital and curbing Bulgarian influence. In the final weeks of 1908, two dozen Greeks were elected to a new Ottoman legislature – fewer than their supporters hoped, but viewed as possibly enough to give the Ottoman Greeks some stake in the fortunes of a reforming empire. The following spring, the Constantinople Organization quietly assisted the Young Turks with the suppression of an attempted counter-coup by conservative supporters of the old Ottoman order.

Yet from that moment on, prospects for the Ottoman Greeks seemed to darken. As the empire frayed (with the loss of Bosnia to Austria, for example) its Young Turk leaders hardened their position and became increasingly determined to impose a kind of ethnic and religious homogeneity on their hard-pressed realm. In Europe, too, a new order of narrowly defined and demographically uniform nation-states was taking hold. In 1912, three of those nation-states – Greece, Serbia, and Bulgaria – joined forces to expel the Ottomans from most of their European territories; the following spring, Bulgaria was reduced in size after a combined attack by all the other parties. Hundreds of thousands of Muslims took refuge in and around Constantinople, and in a climate of rising Christian-Muslim antagonism, the authorities began expelling Ottoman Greek communities from their homes along the Aegean coast. As the first world war unfolded, Ottoman policy focused initially on removing the Greek population from areas near the Black Sea where Russian intervention was feared. The persecution of Ottoman Greeks intensified from late 1916 after the Greek Prime Minister, Eleftherios Venizelos, brought Greece (or at least the part of Greece which he controlled after a public disagreement with the Greek King which resulted in Greece splitting into two parts) into the WW1 conflict on the side of the Entente.

The Ottoman Greek world came to a formal end, it might be said, on January 30, 1923 when the leaders of Greece and the new state of Turkey that emerged from the ashes of the Ottoman Empire put their names to a convention. This fateful agreement provided for a "compulsory exchange of Turkish citizens of the Greek Orthodox religion and of Greek citizens of the Muslim religion" and included the all-important words:

> These persons shall not return to live in Turkey or Greece respectively without the authorization of the Turkish government or the Greek government respectively.

What this meant, in practice, was that at least one million Greek Orthodox refugees who had recently arrived in Greece from Turkey or were still in mid-flight had no prospect of returning to their homelands; meanwhile nearly 200,000 Greek Orthodox who remained in Turkey had to leave imminently.

These numbers raise horrifying questions about the number of Ottoman Greeks who had perished over the previous decade, given that the community's total size has been estimated at just short of 2 million on the eve of the first world war. Even taking into account waves of migration to other places, from the New World to Egypt, it is hard to avoid the conclusion that at least half a million Ottoman Greek lives were lost during the decade of war.

As the convention foresaw, the expulsion of some 350,000 Muslim residents of Greece, with Turkey's encouragement and cooperation, would to some degree make room for the Christian newcomers who threatened to overwhelm a fragile and humiliated Greek state. The Lausanne Convention left a careful loophole for what it called the Greek inhabitants of Constantinople (as well as the Muslims of northeastern Greece) but the exception was narrowly defined, benefiting at most 120,000 of the 300,000 or more Greeks who had lived until recently in the hinterland of the great city. Since then, the city's remaining Greek population has been all but squeezed out of existence by a series of officially-inspired acts: a wealth tax, brutally imposed on all minorities, in the 1940s; a pogrom in 1955; and a round of expulsions in 1964. Only a handful of buildings and institutions still testify to the city's Greek, Christian, and Byzantine heritage: the Ecumenical Patriarchate, the supreme spiritual authority in the Orthodox world; the Cathedral of St. Sophia built by Emperor Justinian in 537 AD (turned recently again into a mosque); and various other churches and monasteries, many of which now lie empty or have been turned to other uses. In August 2022, one of the Greek community's cherished institutions, an old people's home and hospital, was terribly damaged by fire.

The Lausanne accord of January 1923 was a coup de grace, setting the seal of officialdom on a series of disasters which spelled annihilation for the once-flourishing Ottoman Greek world. The most dramatic was the destruction by fire of the Christian quarters of Smyrna, days after the victorious Turkish army entered the city in early September 1922. It has been estimated that at least 15,000 were killed in the fire itself, while in the immediate aftermath 30,000 able-bodied men were deported to the Anatolian interior, supposedly to engage in forced labor, and only a minority survived. A Greek military expedition to the heart of Anatolia had ended in the greatest disaster to befall Aegean Hellenism since it first flourished nearly 3,000 years ago.

Yet the talents of the Ottoman Greeks, recorded in this book, did not dissipate. To a large extent, they were transferred to Greece, where a high proportion of today's industrialists and innovators have roots in what Greeks still call Asia Minor. Also outstanding is the accomplishment of Asia Minor Greeks in the arts and academia. Take two gifted men who originated from the town known as Bursa in Turkish and Proussa in Greek: the theatre director Karolos Koun, and the archaeologist Manolis Andronikos, discoverer of the tomb of King Philip II of Macedonia, Alexander the Great's father, in the province of Macedonia, Northern Greece. Or two accomplished women: an outstanding artistic photographer, known as Nelly, and the novelist Dido Soteriou, who both came to Greece from the Turkish town of Aydin. Ottoman-born Greeks also brought their talents to many other parts of the world. Sir Alec Issigonis, the celebrated designer of the Mini car, applied his engineering skills in Britain; Elia Kazan, a film director whose roots lay in Cappadocia, flourished in the United States; Aristotle Onassis left the ashes of Greek Smyrna for Buenos Aires where he began building his shipping fortune.

It says something about these talented people that they did not spent too much of their time lamenting their lost homelands: whatever their chosen field, they threw themselves into life in their new countries and were generally more interested in the future than the past. Insofar as the Ottoman Greek past has been reconstructed, this has mostly taken place in a literary context, especially in the novels of Ilias Venezis, Nikos Kazantzakis and even Louis de Bernières. These works, for all their beauty, psychological insights, and charm, do not purport to be academically rigorous investigations of the past. That makes it all the more important for scholars to study the Ottoman Greek scene in a more systematic way.

This is what Marina Marks has done. Remote as it seems from our own times, this world existed and flourished; there are people living today who were shaped by it, albeit only through parental memories. If history had taken a different turn, this world might in some form have survived, and it is worth studying carefully to understand why it did not.

Indeed, the rise and fall of the Ottoman theocratic state raises questions which are unresolved and pressing to this very day. Most of the 193 countries making up the United Nations claim to be democracies and at least pay lip service to the modern democratic idea of equality for all under the law. But there are still plenty of tyrannical regimes which give a prevailing role to one religion, relegating others to the status of tolerated minority at best. If anything, the number of such regimes is rising.

Meanwhile, even in the most advanced liberal democracies there are hard arguments about the degree to which religious or ethnic communities should be allowed to self-differentiate, and live by their own norms in matters of say, diet, dress, gender roles and family law. Secular France, for example, imposes more uniformity on its citizens than the Anglo-Saxon democracies generally do.

Precisely because the Ottoman model did, for a certain period of history, seem to function adequately as one form of co-existence, there are people who idealize it. That is a mistake: the world of sultans and sealed-off communities with differing roles and rights cannot be reconstructed, and no sensible person would want to do so. But as the book shows, the Ottoman system did have its own perverse logic; it was something much more interesting than a binary arrangement with one group on top and everybody else down below. In some ways it was more like an eco-system, the constituent parts of which competed or collaborated. A successful Ottoman Greek might easily make alliances with Ottoman Muslim groups or individuals in order to pursue his personal or commercial ends. Yet at certain critical moments, the members of each religiously-defined group or "millet" (nation) would rally together in defence of their respective interests.

This made for a volatile and turbulent but often creative environment. The invaluable research of Marina Marks throws light on a period when creativity, optimism, and a yearning for progress on all fronts was surging among the Ottoman Greeks. Yet in the end it was violence and volatility which tragically prevailed, with consequences that are still palpable today.

Bruce Clark

Acknowledgments

MANY INDIVIDUALS HAVE HELPED ME along the long road to the completion of this study. I would like first to acknowledge the late Leslie Collins, senior lecturer in Bulgarian history and mediaeval land warfare at the School of Slavonic and East European Studies (SSEES), University of London, who as my teacher opened my eyes to the importance of primary sources and taught me always to question received knowledge. His great work on the Crimean Tatars has passed the test of time and still stands as a testament to how historians who fail to examine primary sources can make grave errors of judgement and occasionally – as in the case of the Crimean Tatars – even wipe a whole nation off the map. By reading primary sources in several Eastern languages, Dr. Collins was able to prove that the Crimean Tatars not only did not disappear in 1502, as was asserted, but that at that date their Horde became even stronger than before. His unfailing persistence against all the odds and his mistrust of historians who use only secondary sources for their work became a prime example for me throughout my research.

I hope that, from his resting place, he will be pleased to see this work finally published.

My mentor for this work was Prof. Malcolm Yapp, my supervisor for several years at the University of London. Unfortunately, he retired from the School of Oriental and African Studies (SOAS) and did not oversee its completion. Nevertheless, he continued to support me and inquire about its progress and nag me every year in his Christmas cards. His great knowledge, his magnanimity to his students, his dedication to his work, rivalled only by his dedication to his wife and family, and his constant encouragement will always be treasured. I should also mention here Prof. Tourkhan Gandjei and Dr. Margaret Bainbridge, respectively my Ottoman and Turkish teachers at SOAS, and Hercules Millas, a remarkable Greek civil engineer from Istanbul, who became a well-known writer and translator in both Greek and Turkish, who encouraged me to learn the Turkish language.

I am particularly grateful to Prof. Benjamin Fortna, the Professor of Ottoman History at SOAS (he is now director of the School of Middle Eastern and North African Studies at the University of Arizona), who took over from Prof. Yapp, for agreeing to correct it, for his encouragement throughout, and for recommending it for examination.

I would also like to acknowledge and thank publicly several other people who encouraged me and helped me finish this work: the late Julia Chrysostomides, director of the Institute of Hellenic Studies, Royal Holloway, University of London, for offering valuable advice on the textual presentation; Prof. Anthony Bryer of Birmingham University for facilitating my archival research there and for his general encouragement to complete this work; Prof. Judith Herrin for facilitating my research at King's College, London University; Prof. Paschalis Kitromilides, previously director of the Centre for Neo-Hellenic Studies in Athens and professor of political philosophy at the University of Athens, and currently director of the Asia Minor Research Institute and a member of the Athens Academy of Arts, Letters and Sciences, for facilitating my research in Greece; and Orhan Koloğlu, writer and minister for press and information in the late 1980's, for facilitating my research in Turkey.

I am also grateful to Prof. Şükrü Ilıcak, of the Institute for Mediterranean Studies, and Prof. Nikolaos Panou, of Princeton University, who reviewed the manuscript of this book and offered some valid and useful suggestions.

My family and friends have been a constant source of support and helped me sustain my effort and enthusiasm to the end and bring this work into fruition. I am enormously grateful to all of them. In particular I would like to mention Martin Royalton-Kisch, formerly of the British Museum, for his punctilious editing of this work and his boundless encouragement.

This work would have remained buried among the many other PhD dissertations at the Senate House Repository of London University, had it not been for Prof. Gregory Nagy and Prof. Olga Merck Davidson, who felt that it should be published and become more widely known. I can never thank them enough as this book would not have existed without their resolve, support, and active affirmation.

My thanks also go to Bruce Clark, who very kindly agreed to write a foreword for this volume. His outstanding book, *Twice a Stranger*, is a great contribution to the understanding of the creation of a monocultural modern Turkey out of the ashes of the Ottoman Empire, but also the history of modern Greece, by following the fate of the millions of people who were caught up in the exchange of populations between the states of Turkey and Greece in 1923.

Last but not least, I would like to thank Niloofar Fotouhi, executive director, and Christopher Dadian, managing editor of Ilex Foundation, and their production team for their sterling work in producing this book, the Ilex Foundation for publishing it, and Harvard University Press for distributing it.

Introduction

A dog tethered to a moving cart has two choices: it can either pull on its leash and be roughly dragged along or accept its fate and run along smoothly beside the cart.'

Attributed to Zeno of Citium (c. 334–c. 262 BCE*)*

WHAT SETS HUMANS APART from the rest of the animal kingdom is our unique potential to change our future. From the moment of our birth we are all drawn toward our destinies tied behind life's constantly moving carriage whether we wish to be or not. However, unlike Zeno's dog, which only has two choices, we also have a third: we can jump on that carriage and drive it towards a course that is to our advantage. For those of us who decide to take this third choice and set about finding the right direction toward which to steer our lives, we have at our disposal an important asset: the knowledge and understanding of our past; the choices made by billions of people who came before us to change their lives, recorded faithfully by history.

This book is the result of an effort, pursued over many years, to increase understanding of the social conditions in the Ottoman Empire during the middle years of the 19th century. At that time the Ottoman sultans set out to improve the plight of their Christian subjects, in an attempt to arrest the decline of the Ottoman Empire and update it in a Western European manner. Over nearly fifty years several reforms were introduced in the Ottoman state, usually referred to as the Tanzimat ("reforms").

My goal was to find first-hand accounts by Christian subjects of the Ottoman Empire who were intended to be the chief beneficiaries of the Tanzimat, in an attempt to answer several questions that have not been adequately addressed, such as:

What did the Christians think of the reforms, ostensibly designed to improve their life in the Empire?

How did the Muslims react to the changes brought about by these reforms, which created such a major rupture with the established social and religious order in the Ottoman Empire?

What were the benefits of the Tanzimat for the economy and society of the Empire and especially for its non-Muslim subjects?

My research led me to the mass medium of newspapers published by Greeks in the Ottoman Empire. Newspapers, however, are ephemeral in nature and in this case were produced in a region that underwent violent changes over a long period of time; so the probability of their survival was scant. Nevertheless, I decided to pursue the newspaper trail, for I felt certain that the reward, should I find them, would be well worth the chase.

I began my search for Ottoman newspapers published in Greek in Istanbul, where I spent a whole month looking in library catalogues with little success. I left Turkey disappointed with the results of my search and on my way back to the UK, I spent a few days in Athens. While there I decided to venture to the Newspaper Library of Greece, then housed at the back of the old parliament building of Athens. After my disappointment in Turkey, I had little expectation of faring any better in Greece, but as I was there, I thought I should tick the box. To my great surprise my visit yielded much more than I ever imagined; I found most of the Ottoman Greek newspapers in beautifully bound copies at the basement storage of the library, their rest undisturbed for many decades, forgotten by everyone it seemed, except some resident mice.

To my even greater surprise, as I reviewed their contents, I discovered that the Ottoman Greek newspapers are an astonishing primary source for the history of the late Ottoman Empire and its peoples. Like all primary sources this one sheds light on the period in which it was generated from one direction only, in this case that of the Rum milleti, and in particular those who associated themselves with Greek culture and language.[1] This was exactly what I was looking for and it was something that till then was largely missing from the history books and articles telling the Ottoman story of the period.

Through the well-written pages of these newspapers one can follow the development of a whole generation of Ottoman Greeks caught up in the midst of the most radical social and political changes that ever took place in the empire.[2] In addition, newspapers provide us with a front-row seat to observe how those Ottoman Greeks made use of every possible opening to turn an oppressive situation to their advantage.

This generation of Ottoman Greeks was reaping the benefits of various coincidental developments on the international and domestic stage during the eighteenth and early nineteenth centuries. There were the commercial opportunities given to their fathers and grandfathers by the Habsburgs, the shipping facilities awarded by the Russians to the Ottoman Greeks in the Treaty of Küçük Kaynarca, the re-discovery of classical Greece during the European Enlightenment, and the Porte's attempts to regain control of the empire after sustaining significant losses of European territory and Christian subjects and to strengthen it through a series of reforms, to mention but a few.

1. The Rum milleti, the "Roman Nation," was the community of Orthodox Christians in the Ottoman Empire.

2. More about national identity, the use of the term "Greek" and other national/religious terms later in this introduction.

The Ottoman Greek generation of the 1830s was increasingly concerned with the fabric of its own political and social life and was endowed with the financial power to effect improvements encouraged by the ongoing Tanzimat reforms. Despite living for centuries, in a theocratic supra-national state, where, as far as the state was concerned, people were identified by their religion, the people highlighted as "Greeks" or "Romans" by the Ottoman Greek press were to a large degree aware of their national heritage and traced their cultural ancestry to ancient Greece.

This work follows the development of one of their public expressions – the Ottoman Greek newspapers – from 1830 until 1862, a period that enjoyed considerably more freedom of expression than was possible in later years. The Ottoman Greek press acts as a repository in which survive the vivid reflections of its editors, correspondents, advertisers, contemporary personalities, and readers. They ranged from passionate educators, modish city dwellers, fashionably dressed women, irreverent youth, irate correspondents from the provinces, and upwardly mobile merchants, bankers, and urban professionals. We can follow their everyday lives, their social aspirations, their reactions to political events, and in particular to the reform of the Patriarchate of Constantinople, which combined both the spiritual and the effective political leadership of the Rum milleti. A whole generation of Ottoman Greeks is brought to life again after almost two hundred years, to tell us in their own words about their historical period, their reception of Western-style social norms, their perception of themselves, of the "other," of their life in the Ottoman Empire, and of a plethora of other contemporary issues.

The study begins in 1830, as this year saw the birth of both the Ottoman press and the Ottoman Greek press. Coincidentally, 1830 also marks the birth of modern Greece. In studying the Ottoman Greek press, this coincidence becomes very significant, not least because modern scholars of the history of the Greek press have largely ignored its development in the Ottoman Empire in the nineteenth century. Although the majority of Greeks still lived in the Ottoman Empire during the nineteenth century, most historians show little interest in their story after 1830, concentrating their efforts on the development of the new state of Greece and the Greeks living in Greece.

WHY 1862?

The year 1862 might at first appear a strange date to choose as the cut-off point in a historical study concerning the Ottoman Empire. It could in theory have made more sense to continue until 1878, when the political reforms of the Tanzimat finally collapsed with the closing of the Ottoman parliament by Sultan Abdülhamid (1842–1918), or to follow the fate of the Rum milleti as it gradually broke up into national churches, culminating in the creation of the independent state of

Bulgaria in the same year. My research, however, has revealed that after 1862, the formalization of the relationship between the press and the Ottoman state, effected by a set of press laws and increasing censorship, made it almost impossible to publish articles of a political or critical nature in the Ottoman Greek press. This is not the case for the first three decades of its life, as it evolved around the two imperial reform edicts: the Hatt-ı Şerif of Gülhane (1839) and the Hatt-ı Hümayun (1856). Although one cannot claim that political articles stopped abruptly in 1862, or that after that date there were never brief periods of relaxed censorship, this date is an appropriate terminus for this research as it coincides both with the end of the reform of the Rum milleti and the era of minimum censorship. The extraordinary array of articles, reports, and advertisements published between 1830 and 1862 shed new light on life in the Ottoman Empire and its Orthodox community at a time of marked change, as it imported ideas, goods, and know-how from western Europe.

The period 1830–1862 also coincides with the introduction of state reforms that attempted to alter the long-established status of the *reaya* (subject people) in the Muslim state of the Ottoman Empire. The lens of the Ottoman Greek press offers invaluable information on the reception of and reaction to some of those reforms by members of the Muslim community and members of the Rum milleti. In addition, it records the feelings, hopes, and occasional criticisms of the latter towards their brethren in the new state of Greece.

The Precursors of the Ottoman Greek Newspapers

Gutenberg's innovation of printing in 1439 came at a difficult historical moment for the Greeks. The political and religious upheavals of the period culminated in the total loss of Greek-owned territory, and it was to be another thirty years until Greek books first came off the press.[3] Most of the Greek-speaking intelligentsia moved west to the Italian states, and it was there, in Venice, Milan, and Florence that the first Greek books were printed. The first book in Modern Greek may have been *Erotemata* (*Questions*) by Manuel Chrysoloras, a Greek grammar published in 1471 in Venice. In later centuries, Greek was printed in other parts of Europe following the spread of the Enlightenment. Vienna became a center of Greek

---

3. Emperor Manuel II Paleologos had just signed the union with the Roman Catholic Church in Florence – a political act that was universally repudiated by the population – in order to obtain assistance against the constant loss of territory to the Ottoman Turks. The union failed and with it the hoped-for aid from the Catholics. The eventual fall of Constantinople in 1453 and the loss of the despotate of Mystra in 1460 to the Turks deprived the Orthodox Greek-speaking peoples of the last territory they could call their own. Despite being dispossessed of a state they continued holding on to their identity as constituted by their religion, history, customs, and language.

printing only in the latter part of the eighteenth century, yet it was there that the first Greek newspapers appeared.

Early Greek Newspapers Published in Vienna

Although in the eighteenth century the overwhelming majority of Orthodox Greek-speaking people lived within the Ottoman Empire, it was not an accident that Vienna became the birthplace of the Greek press. Austria-Hungary's commanding position in central Europe in the eighteenth century, its proximity to the Balkans, and its commercial opportunities attracted a number of Greek and other Orthodox Balkan merchants.

The Treaty of Karlowitz, signed on 26 January 1699, concluded the Austro-Ottoman wars of 1683–1697 and put an end to further Ottoman advances in Europe. The treaty marked the beginning of the geographical decline of the Ottoman Empire and made the Habsburg monarchy effectively the dominant power in central Europe, with the Ottomans ceding most of Hungary, Transylvania, and Slavonia to Austria. To maintain its dominant position, which derived not least from its anti-Ottoman war efforts, the Austrian state was constantly in need of funds. As a result, especially since the time of Empress Maria Theresa (1717–1780), opportunities were offered towards the development of any business that promised to generate income. These opportunities attracted a number of Orthodox Christian merchants from the neighboring Ottoman Empire. It is reasonable to suppose that most of them had knowledge of Greek, the lingua franca of commerce in the Balkans and among the Orthodox Christians of the Ottoman Empire. By the beginning of the nineteenth century, some of these people, who had mostly settled in Hungary, had become extremely affluent, and thirty-five of them had acquired the title of baron or count.[4] Financial security, along with a relatively good education and the proximity of the Austrian capital at the crossroads between the Orient and the Occident, with a constant flow of information between the two, created the preconditions for a Greek newspaper among the mercantile Greek-speaking community. Vienna enjoyed the advantage of excellent communications via the Danube, the port of Trieste, and the land routes through Serbia, Moldavia, and Wallachia, making it an ideal center for publishing periodicals for an Ottoman Greek-speaking readership.

The Habsburgs recognized the economic significance of the Ottoman Greek market for books and encouraged Greek printing in Vienna.[5] Similarly, the Austrian government could tax the financial gains generated by the publication of Greek

---

4. Athanasiou 1988, 6–13.
5. See Enepekides 1965, 87.

newspapers, whose readership lay mostly in the neighboring Ottoman Empire. As the Austrian chancellor Thugut noted:

> [If] the [Greek] newspaper ceased publication, Austria would lose six to seven hundred ducats a year income from the postal charges alone.[6]

In fact, between 1774 and 1830 six newspapers and magazines in Greek were published in Vienna. The title of the first one is not known but it is referred to by the name of its publisher, as *Ephemeris tou Vendoti* (Vendotis's Newspaper).[7]

The Ottoman reaction

If for the Austrians the existence of Greek newspapers in their country was merely an economic issue, for the Ottoman government, the potential effect on their readership in the Ottoman Empire was a serious political consideration. In June 1784, the grand vizier summoned the Austrian ambassador, Baron Herbert von Rathkeal, demanding that he stop the publication of the first Greek newspaper in Vienna and arguing that:

> for the Turkish government it is a fundamental principle to keep people in darkness, to divert their attention from state business and to hide from them whatever is discussed in Europe about the Turkish state, its sovereigns and its chief ministers.[8]

But the Ottoman governing elite was not alone in wanting the Greek press of Vienna closed down. The Ottoman Greek elite had equal misgivings concerning a publication in Greek spreading democratic political ideas in the Ottoman Empire. The chief dragoman of the Porte, Constantinos Hypsilantes, repeatedly remonstrated against the arrival of *Ephemeris* in the Ottoman Empire via the Austrian postal system,

> spreading among the Greeks the declarations of Bonaparte and Gentilly, together with other observations and comments that are very dangerous.[9]

6. This statement came in reply to a letter from the Austrian ambassador to the Ottoman state, Baron Herbert von Rathkeal, written in September 1797, relaying Ottoman demands to close down the second Viennese Greek newspaper, *Ephemeris*. See G. Laios 1958, 212.

7. *Ephemeris tou Vendoti* was published in April and May, 1784; *Ephemeris* (Newspaper), December 1790–January 1798; *Hermes o Logios* (Hermes the Intellectual), January 1811–January 1821; *Eidesis dia ta Anatolika Mere* (News for Eastern Places), February 1811–November 1811; *Hellenikos Telegraphos* (Greek Telegraph), March 1812–1836; and *Kalliope*, January 1819–January 1821.

8. Haus, hof, Staatsarchiv, Staatskanzlei, Turkei II Karton 84, Report of Austrian ambassador to the Porte Baron Herbert von Rathkeal to Austrian Chancellor Kaunitz, Constantinople, Büyük Dere 24 June 1784, published in Laios 1960, and Papalexandrou 1972, 19.

9. See letter of Austrian Ambassador Baron Herbert von Rathkeal to Austrian chancellor Thugut dated 24 September 1797, in Laios 1958, 253.

From the start, the publication of Greek newspapers in Vienna became an issue in Habsburg-Ottoman relations and in some instances the Ottomans were in a position to impose their closure on the Habsburgs.

The Viennese press is generally also considered to be the forerunner of the press of the Greek state and for this reason has already been studied extensively by Greek historians and included in all general studies and bibliographies of the Greek press.[10]

Early Greek newspapers from Greece

Ottoman efforts to silence the Greek press of Vienna reveal a full appreciation of the potential power of the printed word. Yet, despite their efforts this power was eventually unleashed during the Greek war of independence in the form of clandestine publications providing the propaganda for the Greek revolution of 1821–1830. Almost as soon as it erupted in March 1821, two hand-written newspapers made their appearance in Galaxidi and Vrachori, near Missolonghi (in western Greece). A few months later, in August of the same year, Prince Demetrios Hypsilantes (1793–1832), who arrived in Greece after the failure of the Walla-chian rising (1821) to organize the struggle for independence, brought with him a printing press and started to produce a newspaper. Two other printing presses arrived soon after, ordered by Prince Alexander Mavrocordatos (1793–1865) and Prince Ioannis Karadjas (1754–1844), respectively. In 1821 and 1822 a number of presses were operating in the rebel territories of Greece, and there were further attempts to publish propaganda newspapers. From 1824 onwards, yet more presses arrived from western Europe. The newspapers that were printed then became less propaganda-oriented, reflecting the gradual establishment of a political structure in what in 1830 was to become the state of Greece. Although they were published in an area that was challenging Ottoman rule, technically these newspapers should be considered to be the first Ottoman newspapers.[11] Between 1821 and 1830 a total of eleven newspapers written in the Greek language were published in the rebel territories.[12]

10. Apart from general bibliographies of the Greek press see, for example, Laios 1961, Laios 1960, Papalexandrou 1972, Laios 1958, Enepekides 1965, Mastoridis 1999.

11. For Greek newspapers between 1821 and 1830, see Mazarakis-Ainian 1970, 6; Philemon 1883b, 3; Papalexandrou 1972; Michalopoulos 1940; Emerson 1826.

12. *Pseudoephemerida* (Pseudo-Newspaper) [nickname], March 1821 (handwritten) in Gal-axidi; *Aetolike* (Aetolian), August–September 1821 (handwritten), in Missolonghi; *Acheloos* (River Acheloos), February 1822 (handwritten), Vrachori; *Salpinx Hellenike* (Greek Trumpet), August 1, 1821–August 20, 1821, in Kalamata; *Hellenika Chronika* (Greek Chronicles), January 1824–August 20, 1826, in Missolonghi; *Telegrafo Greco* (Greek Telegraph), March 20, 1824–December 11, 1824, in Missolonghi; *Philos tou Nomou* (Friend of the Law), March 10, 1824–May 27, 1827, in Hydra; *Ephemeris ton Athenon* (Newspaper of Athens), August 20, 1821–March 15, 1826, in Athens; *Genike Ephemeris tes Hellados* (General Newspaper of Greece), from September 20, 1825 to the present, in

Other Greek Press Activity before 1830–31

One newspaper and two literary magazines appeared briefly in Paris during the Napoleonic period.[13] At the same time two short-lived newspapers appeared in London, where there was a small but significant Greek shipping community.[14] In addition, four newspapers and two magazines were published in the Ionian island of Corfu,[15] first during a period of autonomy under a Russo-Turkish suzerainty after the first French occupation (1798–1799) and then during the second French occupation (1807–1815), and subsequently during the British occupation (1815–1863).[16]

A bilingual newspaper, in Ottoman and Greek, *Vekayi-i Giridiye/Kretike Ephemeris* (Cretan Newspaper) was published in Crete either at the end of 1830 or at the beginning of 1831. This newspaper was the brainchild of Mehmed Ali, who was granted the administration of Crete by the sultan as a reward for his assistance in suppressing the Orthodox Christian revolt in the Morea and South Rumeli. The last number of this newspaper retained in the public records office seems to be that of 7 January 1834. According to the catalogue in the Istanbul University library, sixty issues were published between 23 Muharrem 1248 (1832) and 7 Ramazan 1249 (1834). Bilingual *Kretike Ephemeris* is technically the first newspaper in the Greek language in the Ottoman Empire, although Crete was under the direct administration of Mehmed Ali, governor and viceroy of Egypt.

The main purpose of *Vekayi-i Giridiye* was to publicize the virtues of Mehmed Ali and his government in the island of Crete, but it also contains local news and some foreign items. According to its title page, *Vekayi-i Giridiye* was published weekly, on Mondays. The number of pages varied considerably and occasionally there were extras with encyclicals only in Greek. An annual subscription cost one Ottoman *lira* and a six-month subscription fifty-five *kuruş* (100 *kuruş* equalled one *lira*). Single copies were priced at one *kuruş* and for places outside Crete postal costs were added.

Linguistic Problems

A universal problem for historians is the application of contemporary linguistic usage and perceptions to past eras, such as the nineteenth-century Ottoman Em-

---

Nauplion and then Athens; *L'Abeille Greque* (The Greek Bee), March 31, 1827–March 28, 1829; *Anexartetos* (Independent), July 30, 1827–May 18, 1829, in Hydra and then in Aigina.

13. *Ephemeris tou Stamate* (Newspaper of Stamates) 1798; *Athena* February 28, 1819–May 15, 1819; and *Melissa* (Bee) 1819–1821.

14. *Iris* in 1819; and *Mouseion* (Museum) also in 1819.

15. For the Ionian Islands from 1797–1815, see Mavrogenis 1899.

16. *Gazzetta Urbana* (Urban Newspaper), and *Monitore Corcirese*, January 1, 1808–July 24, 1810; *Ionikos Menytor* (Ionian Herald) 1810–(?); *Mercurio Letterario*, 1805–(?); *Ephemeris Philologiki kai Economike* (Literary and Financial Paper) 1812; *Ionike*, 1811–1869 (official government gazette), first in Zakynthos and then Corfu.

pire. Some terms frequently used in the Ottoman Greek press and employed of necessity in this work require explanation. It is imperative first of all to consider the terms "Turks" and "Greeks" as they were used in the Ottoman Greek press in the period under review.

Today the terms Turk and Muslim define two distinct identities. The first is secular/political, the second religious. In the nineteenth century the line between secular, political, and religious identity was not by any means as clear-cut as it is today. For example, in the Greek press we often encounter the term *Tourkalbanos*, designating an Albanian who was a Muslim. Thus, the word "Turk" could denote religious affiliation. The word "Turk" also carried a religious connotation when referring to Christians converting to Islam, or to mixed marriages between Christians and Muslims. In these instances, the Christians *tourkepsan* (became Turks). The word "Turk" could also signify an uneducated Muslim peasant as opposed to an "Ottoman" (Osmanlı), who might be identified as a bourgeois or upper-class Muslim. "Ottoman" could also refer to Muslims in general, and after 1856 it began to signify a citizen of the Ottoman Empire.

It is worthy of note that the Greek press was aware of the secular nationality of other Muslim ethnic groups, such as the Arabs, Kurds, Albanians, Iranians, and Bosnians, but they never refer to a separate Turkish nation. The Ottoman Turkish language too is seen more as a lingua franca, employed as a second language by many people in the Ottoman Empire and as the official language of the government and the bureaucracy, rather than a language belonging to a particular ethnic group. In 1851, for example, the publishing house Anatole, which belonged to Evangelinos Misaelides and specialized in printing Karamanlı and Ottoman books as well as the long-running Karamanlı newspaper *Anatole,* advertised the forthcoming publication of a Turkish-Greek dictionary. The advertisement pointed out that for their advancement in the bureaucracy the Greeks had to learn the Turkish language, which it described as a mixture of "Arabic and Persian."[17] For the writers and readers of the Ottoman Greek press, the existence of a secular Turkish nation distinct from Islam was not obvious.

The terms "Greek" (*Hellen*), "Rum" (*Romaios*), and "nation" (*ethnos*) are also confused in this period. Greeks in the Ottoman Empire are considered in the press to be those Orthodox Christians who speak Greek – though not necessarily fluently – and claim ancestry from ancient Greece. Those Orthodox Christians who did not speak Greek and did not hail from ancient Greece were usually called co-nationals (*omoethneis*, those of the same nation), the word "nation" here signifying the religious nation or *millet*. Notwithstanding the above, speaking Greek was not necessarily a prerequisite of being "Greek," as articles in the Greek press recognize that lack of education and necessity meant that large chunks of "the Greek nation" had lost their language – a matter that needed rectifying through the vigorous education

17. *Telegraphos tou Vosporou*, no. 378 (March 17, 1851).

of the young, not only in modern but also in ancient Greek. To confuse matters further, the same word, *ethnos*, was also used with its secular connotation. As such, the Greek press recognized that Orthodox Christians, although members of the same religious *ethnos*, were split into secular ethnic groups: Greeks, Bulgarians, Serbs, Vlachs, Albanians, Moldavians, etc. It also recognized the secular ethnicity of the Armenians and Jews, and of all those ethnic groups that formed the Muslim millet in the empire with, as mentioned earlier, the exception of the Turks. The latter were not perceived as one, distinct, ethnic group.

Another ambiguous term in translation is *genos,* which could either refer to ethnic origin, race or family, or indeed a religious family. A frequent phrase, *to genos ton Romaion*, could be translated as "the nation of the Romans." This could either refer to the descendants of the people of the (Eastern) Roman Empire as they were when conquered by the Ottomans, or to the religious "nation" of the Orthodox Christians, the Rum milleti. Yet, it could also mean being of Greek ethnic origin, as some writers in the Ottoman Greek press call themselves *Romaioi* (Romans). During the period of our study all these terms were used interchangeably, although the secular ethnic terms predominated.

In attempting to overcome this problem I have either employed terms of religious nationality or used the way the people describe themselves. In general, I tend to use the broad term Ottoman Greeks when I refer to people who answer to most of the criteria of "Greekness" that I referred to earlier and are living in the Ottoman Empire. I cannot claim, however, that this is an entirely satisfactory solution.

Another problem is posed by the orthographic variety with which writers in the Greek press wrote the same names. For example, the name "Karatheodores" sometimes also appears as "Karatheodore," and very occasionally as "Karatheodorou." After some deliberation I decided to retain this inconsistency in the spelling of Greek, Turkish, and other names, as being more faithful to the original and in order to convey an understanding of the obstacles involved.

When writing about the nineteenth-century Ottoman Empire, I use the names Constantinople and Smyrna instead of Istanbul and Izmir because those were the most frequently used names for those cities in the nineteenth century. The names Istanbul and Izmir were not in official or even in general use at that time. Even the sultan in his letters and *firman*s put next to the date قسطنطينيه (Ḳosṭanṭīnīye), and the first Ottoman newspaper, *Takvim-i Vekayi*, mentioned Ḳosṭanṭīnīye as its place of publication. The names Istanbul and Izmir became the official names of the two cities in 1930.

The titles of foreign newspapers used as sources of information were often translated into Greek by Ottoman Greek editors, and are occasionally difficult to translate into English. Although sometimes one can gather through library searches what the original name must have been, discrepancies remain and corrections may emerge in due course.

DATES

During the nineteenth century, Orthodox nations used the Julian calendar, which was then twelve days behind the Gregorian calendar in use in Catholic and Protestant countries. The Ottoman Greek press also used the Julian calendar, so all dates quoted in this book from the Ottoman Greek newspapers are twelve days behind the corresponding Western European dates. *He Hemera* of Trieste, published in the Catholic Habsburg lands but intended for an Orthodox readership, provided dual dating, with the earlier, Julian date preceding the Gregorian (for example, July 6/18, 1856).

In Greek newspapers Muslim dates were generally converted to the Julian calendar. Following the reform edict of 1839, the Ottoman government started using the Rumi/Roman calendar, which was based on the Julian calendar, for civic matters, until it was gradually replaced by the Gregorian calendar from 1917 and formally abolished by Kemal Ataturk in 1926.

BIBLIOGRAPHICAL MATERIAL

Despite the fact that the Ottoman Greek press is related both to the development of the Greek nation and the Ottoman Empire, the bibliography including it is not large. Greek scholars consider the development of the Greek press after the Greek war of independence purely as an affair of the Greek state. An example of this is *Casting the Greek Newspaper*, by Klimis Mastoridis, published in 1999. Mastoridis paid great attention to Greek newspapers published before 1821 in western and central Europe but once Greece became established as an independent state, despite the fact that the overwhelming majority of Greeks were still living outside its borders, it became the main focus of his attention. He quotes the 1892 *Statistics* (a census of all Greek people) and admits that: "the country where most of the largest circulation Greek newspapers [in the nineteenth century] were produced was Turkey."[18] Yet, the Ottoman Greek press was only worthy of a small mention in a chapter entitled "The Foreign Greek Newspaper": "foreign" for the Greeks because they were produced outside Greece and "foreign" for the Turks because they were produced in a non-Turkish language, the Ottoman Greek newspapers have yet to attract serious interest among scholars in either country. Two exceptions are worth mentioning.

In a 2006 article, Anastasia Falierou set out to examine *Vosporis*, a Greek magazine published in Istanbul at the turn of the nineteenth century and its influence on the Greek diaspora.[19] She refers briefly to the Ottoman Greek press in the nineteenth century but discusses nothing much before 1860, nor does she note

18. Mastorides 1999, 315.
19. Falierou 2006.

the relevant bibliography for that period. She gives the date of first publication of *Neologos* as 1861,[20] although my research places its first publication in 1867.

A book by Ali Arslan, the title of which translates from Greek as *The Greek Press in the Ottoman State Based on Documents of the Period*,[21] concentrates on documents regarding publication permits starting at the end of the nineteenth century. In the first half of the book there is a rudimentary list of most of the Ottoman Greek newspapers, although with some omissions and erroneus dates, and with the Smyrna newspaper *Herigeneia* spelled *Iziyania* (with a question mark). The author's main interest lies in the last years of the nineteenth century up until the end of the Ottoman Empire.

A few general bibliographies and histories include sparse mentions of the Ottoman Greek press. The works of D. Ginis and K. Mayer are the most reliable.[22] In 2008, the National Hellenic Research Foundation published *Encyclopaedia tou ellenikou typou 1784–1996* (*Encyclopaedia of the Greek Press, 1784–1996*) in 4 volumes, for which I contributed most entries on the Ottoman Greek press up to 1862.[23]

More specific studies on the Ottoman Greek press are fewer still. In 1893 the last owner of *Amaltheia* of Smyrna (1838-1922), Socrates Solomonides, published *Hemerologion Amaltheias*.[24] His son, Christos, produced three books with valuable information on Smyrna and its press.[25] Manuel Gedeon, the grand archivist of the Patriarchate of Constantinople during the last two decades of the nineteenth century, published two books that include significant information on the Ottoman Greek press and in particular on the press of Constantinople.[26] Angello Sammarco mentions the Cretan newspaper *Vekayi-i Giridiye/Kretike Ephemeris* (Cretan Newspaper) in his book on the reign of Mehmed Ali;[27] and the historian and one-time minister of press and information of Turkey, Orhan Koloğlu, makes a more detailed study of the same paper, to which I contributed a translation of the Greek version of the newspaper.[28] Koloğlu has also written an article on the journalistic activities of minorities in the Ottoman Empire.[29]

20. Falierou 2006, 39.

21. Arslan 2004.

22. Ginis 1967; Mayer 1960. See also Kalapothakis 1928, by a Greek press and information minister and publisher of the Athenian newspaper *Embros* (1896–1921); Daskalakis 1930; Moschopoulos 1931; Christopoulos 1993, a descriptive list of all newspapers in the library of the Greek parliament by its librarian. See also, Lady Marks 2005.

23. Droulia and Koutsopanagou 2008.

24. S. Solomonides 1893.

25. Ch. Solomonides 1959; 1961; 1970. All were published in Athens, where he moved as a refugee in 1923.

26. Gedeon 1893; 1932.

27. Sammarco 1931.

28. Koloğlu 1989.

29. Koloğlu 1985.

For comparative purposes and additional information, I have used some bibliographies, books, and articles devoted to the Ottoman Turkish and Karamanlı newspapers, French newspapers, and the missionary press published in the Ottoman Empire. I have also found a few books on the history of Greek printing and publishing that refer briefly to the Ottoman Greek press. Finally, I have used some reports of travelers and diplomats that include some information on the Ottoman press. They are all included in the bibliography.

In the chapters that follow we will first investigate the birth, establishment, and function of the Ottoman Greek newspapers, focussing primarily on the circumstances of their publication (publishers, official permits, censorship, techniques, economics of production, etc.). After establishing their credibility as a primary source, we will investigate the contents of the Ottoman Greek newspapers for firsthand information about the political and social life of the Rum milleti in the middle years of the nineteenth century.

Considering the power wielded by the press in any modern society and the primary information that it provides the scholar, it is remarkable that the Ottoman Greek newspapers have not been more fully appreciated, and studied more thoroughly by scholars of the Greek nation and of the Ottoman Empire as a whole.

Chapter 1

The Greek Press of the Ottoman Empire: Birth and Challenges

THE BIRTH OF THE OTTOMAN GREEK PRESS

OFFICIALLY, GREEK NEWSPAPERS began to be published within the Ottoman Empire in 1831, one year after the Ottoman government reversed its hostile attitude toward the press and allowed Greek and other millet newspapers to be printed and circulated in the empire. This change in attitude must be seen in the more general context of the reforms undertaken at the time to modernize the Ottoman state, known collectively as Tanzimat. The Ottoman government began to perceive the press not as a threat but as a means of informing the general public about its actions and developing a favorable attitude to the reforms, especially among those on whose support it counted for implementing the changes, the Ottoman bureaucracy, local government officials, and the army. The Ottoman government also hoped to influence, persuade, and encourage the non-Muslim millets to support the Tanzimat. This rationale underlay the publication of the first Ottoman newspaper, the official gazette *Takvim-i Vekayi*.

The sultanic press initiative, as part of the Tanzimat reforms, came after the Rum milleti had embarked on significant changes of its own already since the late eighteenth century, especially in Constantinople and Smyrna, where the Ottoman Greek press first appeared.

The Rum milleti had its own millet government led by the *millet başı* (Greek *ethnarches*), the patriarch of Constantinople, who combined religious with political duties. The patriarch "was *de jure* free from any encroachments upon his ecclesiastical authority both from Christian laity and the Turks."[1] Among other things, the patriarchate was responsible for appointing the various metropolitans and bishops in the Orthodox dioceses. Since the fifteenth century these positions de facto combined religious with secular authority and in some cases, due to personalities or circumstances, their secular nature superseded their religious nature. Bishops and metropolitans had the power to raise taxes from their flock, some of the proceeds of which they could keep for themselves, since they were not salaried by the government. Custom demanded that upon their appointment, new bishops

---

1. Sokolov 2013, 832.

and metropolitans should pay a sum of money in gratitude to the patriarch. This would ensure that the person appointed had a social standing appropriate to his position as well as providing additional funds for the patriarchate. Appointees also had to pay large sums to the Ottoman government.

The patriarch, too, had to secure his position by paying a sum to the geronts, the eight senior metropolitans and bishops who constituted the electoral body and who also controlled the appointment and transfer of the various metropolitans.[2] In addition both he and the bishops had to pay the annual *haraç* (land tax) like other *dhimmi*s (non-Muslims living in an Islamic state with legal protection). Finally, the patriarch had to pay a set of annual taxes: 33,425 *kuruş* to the state treasury, 5,000 *kuruş* to the dragomans of the Royal Divan, 65,640 *aspra* for the victorious imperial army, 24,060 *aspra* for the royal treasury, and 163,000 *aspra* for the unification of the archbishopric of Ipek (Peć) with the patriarchate.[3] Because of the hefty taxation, which by the nineteenth century had become exorbitant, the patriarchate was seriously indebted and desperate for funds.

At the same time some lay members among the Orthodox Christian population began to assert themselves against the church's authority by virtue of an increasing financial affluence, and demanded a share in the running of the "national" affairs, that is, the patriarchate's political government. These newcomers were from some Orthodox families that had gained prominence since the advent of Greek independence and the near destruction of the old Phanariot order. In order to legitimize their involvement in the political and financial affairs of the millet, hitherto run for centuries by the higher clergy and the Phanariots ex officio, these families attempted to penetrate the religious government of the Orthodox by pushing for a mixed national assembly (religious and lay) that would in addition to the above, also include a number of representatives of this new class of wealth. An early attempt by lay people to control the finances of the patriarchate occurred between 1830 and 1840. This was at a time when the controlling group in the patriarchate was led by Stephanos Vogorides and his son-in-law, Alexandros Photiades. The then patriarch, Constantios, successfully removed control of church finances from the geronts and centralized financial control in one office under one lay official, Ioannis Paspalis. In just two years the latter succeeded not only in erasing the existing national debt completely but in creating a surplus.[4] The geronts regained control from the laymen in 1840, when the laymen failed to manage the finances

2. They were also entrusted with financial control of the income of the monasterial lands, which was collected by the metropolitans. The geronts were also members of the holy synod and held the four sections of the patriarchal seal, all of which were necessary for endorsing the acts and decisions of the holy synod.

3. See Angelopoulos 1865, 258-60, quoted in Sokolov 2013, 1:831–32. 120 *aspra* = 1 *kuruç* = .01 *lira*.

4. Gedeon 1922, 22.

successfully.[5] This struggle became chronic, with the finances switching between lay and geront hands until 1862.

The Ottoman Greek community of Smyrna, which had been prominent in the economy of the port city at least since the eighteenth century, also developed a strong political movement, which challenged the church's political authority. From the period of the French Revolution and the Napoleonic wars, Greeks were already participating on a large scale in the international trade of Smyrna and became the most dynamic sector of the city's economy.[6]

In consequence, the mercantile establishment of the city had been seeking a share of the political power awarded to the Orthodox Church by the Ottoman government. Their struggle culminated in the *Synyposchetiko* (Agreement) of 1785, when the then metropolitan of Smyrna and later ecumenical patriarch, Gregory V, was forced to sign a document considerably curbing his political, financial, and judicial powers in favor of the commercial bourgeoisie.[7] Another example of these political struggles in Smyrna involved the church's less than salubrious efforts to control the education of the Orthodox Christians; the progressive Philologikon Gymnasion, established in 1810, met with the opposition of the metropolitan, the later Patriarch Gregory V, who incited a number of people and some of the most conservative guilds of Smyrna to demonstrate in the streets against the school and its progressive curriculum. It was eventually closed in 1819.[8]

The Ottoman Greek press may also have been considered as part of this struggle by the emerging lay class of merchants, professionals, and intellectuals to enhance their position in society and acquire a share in the political power of their millet.

Seen from this angle, the numerical superiority of the press of the Rum milleti between 1830 and 1862 also reflects the degree of its political development. In that period Orthodox Christians produced forty-one political newspapers (twenty-seven in Greek, two in Bulgarian, three in Rumanian, four in Serbian and five in Karamanlı Turkish), the Armenians seven, the Muslims eight, and the Jews three. If we focus on the Orthodox Christian group, we observe that the Greek speakers and those who identified with them in the Rum milleti produced the overwhelming majority of the newspapers within the millet but also in comparison to all the other millets combined. This numerical superiority was by no means proportionate to the Ottoman Greek population in the empire as a whole, although this may have been the case in Constantinople and was certainly so in Smyrna. In addition to the

5. Gedeon 1922, 22–29.

6. See Frangakis-Syrett 1987.

7. For social struggles in Smyrna in the last quarter of the eighteenth century, see for example S. Karadjas 1958, and for the Synyposchetiko, Eliou 1983, 94–96.

8. For the closure of Philologikon Gymnasion Smyrnes, indicative of the ideological struggles between the followers of the Enlightenment on the one hand and the church on the other, see for example Eliou 1983, 7–45.

twenty-seven newspapers in the Greek language there were five more in the Turkish language but with Greek letters (*karamanlı*). The people speaking and writing in Karamanlı were considered Ottoman Greek despite lacking the knowledge of the Greek language. However, as Evangelia Balta very astutely observed, there was both a class and an ideological division between them and most Greek speakers, at least in the case of Smyrna. The latter belonged to a large extent to the merchant and professional urban classes and were proponents of the Enlightenment, while the former were mostly tradesmen, laborers, and members of the *esnaf* (guilds), and kept close ties with the church. [9]

The Birthplace of the Ottoman Greek Press

The Ottoman Greek press began its life in Smyrna in 1831. The city was by then an international commercial center, with a French cultural accent. The Greek-speaking population of Smyrna in the 1830s numbered approximately 50,000, and it was the biggest and arguably most prominent community in the city. A little less than half that number was made up of citizens of the newly-formed state of Greece, while a small percentage was from other countries.[10] Apart from being a cosmopolitan center, Smyrna had an active intelligentsia and boasted an opera, a theatre, several clubs, and five local French newspapers. Its considerable distance from the capital made it easier for progressive and political innovations, including newspapers, to avoid the close scrutiny of the Ottoman government and the Patriarchate of Constantinople.

The chief catalyst, however, for the creation of the Greek press was the strong presence in Smyrna of Protestant missionaries, who tried to impose their dogma on the local Orthodox population. The missionary activities in Smyrna, their reception, and the development of the anti-missionary movement will be examined in the next chapter.

At the time of its birth, the Greek press was surrounded by optimum conditions for the production of newspapers. Educational and printing activities by missionaries already existed and, as already mentioned, there were five established French newspapers: *Le Smyrnéen, Impartial, Courier de Smyrne* (previously *Spectateur Oriental*), *Journal de Smyrne*, and *Echo de l'Orient*). Their existence influenced

---

9. Balta 2013, 212–13.

10. According to J. Barsigli, Tuscan consul general in Smyrna, as quoted in Oikonomos 1841 (139–43), the population of Smyrna in 1840 was as follows: 45,000 Turks, 55,000 Greeks, 12,000 Catholics and Protestants, 5,000 Armenians, and 13,000 Jews. The French newspaper Impartial of Smyrna, also quoted in Oikonomos 1841, gives for the same period the following numbers: 42,000 Turks, 28,000 Greek *reayas*, 15,000 citizens of Greece, 7,000 Armenians, 14,000 Jews, and 4,500 Latins, plus approximately 13,280 foreign nationals, including 3,500 Ionians holding British passports. If we add the Greek *reayas*, the citizens of Greece, and the Ionians this comes to 46,500 Greek speakers, to which should be added a number of Greek speakers holding other passports.

the establishment of local publishing in Smyrna and meant that there were several printing presses in that town manned by qualified printers.

There was a large paper mill in the village of Artemision (Halkapınar), by the homonymous lake approximately three hours walk from the city.[11] This mill could provide a prompt and cheap supply of locally produced paper. Moreover, in the nearby village of Koryphasion (Kukluca),

> the first private printing press of Ionia was established by merchant Mad-jouranis during the Napoleonic wars.[12]

Furthermore, by an extraordinary coincidence, in 1817 Ambroise-Firmin Didot, of the famous French publishing family, visited Kydoniai (Ayvalık), a town in Ionia only a few hours from Smyrna. Ambroise-Firmin was the eldest son of Firmin Didot (1790–1876), owner of the eponymous French publishing house. When his father retired in 1827, he and his brother Hyacinthe took over the management of the business. They were enthusiastic classicists and learned Greek from Adamantios Koraes. During their careers they published no less than two hundred and fifty volumes.[13] Before 1827, Ambroise-Firmin had pursued a diplomatic career and had been for a time the attaché at the French embassy in Constantinople. He took advantage of his position to visit the Orient and Greece, and was the discoverer of the location of Pergamum.

When Ambroise-Firmin visited Kydoniai, the inhabitants requested a fully operational press. Moved by their request he not only agreed but also invited Constantine Tombras, who was sponsored by the merchant Emmanuel Salteles, to Paris and taught him the art of typography.[14] Upon his return to Kydoniai, Tombras founded a school of typography. After the Turkish destruction of Kydoniai in 1821, these typographers moved to revolutionary Greece, where they became the first printers of the revolutionary press.[15]

For newspaper editors, such as K. L. Hadjinikolaou, the editor of *Mnemosyne* of Smyrna, the press was a political tool that gave

> an opportunity to promote learning, mass knowledge, the discovery of the truth ... and the combating of delusion, which only grows in darkness and by misinformation and rumors.[16]

11. *Ephemeris tes Smyrnes*, no. 60 (June 2, 1850).

12. Ibid.

13. Including the series, *Bibliothèque des auteurs Grecs*, and *Bibliothèque des auteurs Latins*. Their greatest work was a new edition of the *Thesaurus Graecae Linguae*, by Henri Estienne (Henricus Stephanus).

14. A. F. Didot 1826, 388, 399.

15. See Mazarakis-Ainian 1970.

16. *Mnemosyne*, no. 1 (March 9, 1835).

For all these reasons Smyrna was far better positioned than Constantinople to become the birthplace of the Ottoman Greek press. Furthermore, at the outbreak of the Greek revolt, the press of the patriarchate in the capital was completely destroyed by the Janissaries.

> [T]he printed adaptations of the Bible into modern Greek, together with the lexicon *Kivotos* which were being printed at the time, were thrown into a cistern full of water, and the director of the press was hanged together with the Greek notables [and the patriarch].[17]

These actions were indicative of the political importance the Ottoman government attributed to printing. Writing in the 1830s J. Poujoulat, recorded that

> [t]he excessive violence [in Constantinople] against ordinary Greeks in 1821 lasted well into the 1830s. It is understandable that they should not have wanted to attract further violence by publishing a newspaper, which might criticize [the government].[18]

Poujoulat suggested that

> it would be an enormously long time before the periodical press of Constantinople would create some sort of opposition to the Turks.[19]

Poujoulat's observations regarding the development of the Constantinople press were astute. It seems, however, that he was ignorant of developments in Smyrna, where what he called "l'artillerie de la presse" was already in action while he was writing. It is significant that apart from the Greek press, Armenian, Jewish, and Bulgarian press activity also began life in Smyrna.[20]

The Ottoman Greeks of Smyrna had progressive ideas about civil rights and liberties and, as already mentioned, from the last quarter of the eighteenth century their mercantile establishment had succeeded in acquiring a share of the political power in the city. In addition to indigenous political developments, the Ottoman Greek community in general – and in particular that of Smyrna – had encountered the ideas of the Enlightenment and Neoclassicism, especially as these had developed in France after 1789. Being considered in essence a rediscovery of ancient Greek ideas, they were quickly espoused, as is evident in the Ottoman Greek press. Although the editors were frequently critical of their own millet leadership, they were sensible and supportive of the Sultan's efforts to modernize the Ottoman state

---

17. See Mazarakis-Ainian 1970.
18. Michaud and Poujoulat 1834, 1:189-90.
19. Michaud and Poujoulat 1834, 1:246.
20. See S. Solomonides 1959.

in line with those ideas. This becomes clear from their reaction to any suggestions that they should distance themselves from the Ottoman government and give their political allegiance to the Greek state. Such suggestions were promoted by a radical core of Greek citizens who had come to Smyrna because of commercial interests. Their views were opposed in unison by the editors of the Smyrna Greek press, who saw the democratization of Ottoman society as a gradual process that could be brought about through education and secularization at all levels of society. They believed, at least until the late 1850s, that progress was possible in the Ottoman Empire, and called on their readers to support the Sultan's reform program. As early as 1835 the editor of *Mnemosyne*, Hadjinikolaou, commended the Sultan's efforts to stamp out maladministration and pointed out that "the decline in the Empire had its roots in the total absence of democracy and liberal institutions."[21]

In the same article he also reminded his readers that "the revolution of 1820 [he refers to the Greek Revolution], happened only because of the extreme desire of people to live in a democratic state and have the liberty to conduct their lives according to their ancestral values."

Another newspaper editor, Samiotakis, in an editorial entitled "The Political Situation in the Ottoman Empire," wrote in 1847 that:

> the present policies of Sultan Abdülmecid are brave and philanthropic and he is a friend of the people … the new policies of the government towards the subject peoples are objective and constructive, and this new attitude is the direct opposite to [the government's] previous policies.[22]

Because of this dramatic change in the attitudes of the government, Samiotakis urged Ottoman Greeks to co-operate with the government fully so that together they could build a new future for all the inhabitants of the empire, of which after all the Greeks were the most ancient.

Some of these arguments appear to echo ideas originally voiced by Alexander Blacque, a French publisher, who exerted a lasting influence on the Ottoman Greek press, as most of its Smyrna editors had previously been his assistants and trainees. Blacque had arrived in Smyrna from Marseilles with his father, one of the lawyers who had defended Louis XVI. The pro-Turkish, and by inference pro-sultan stance of the Blacque family may have resulted from their history on the losing side of the tumultuous events in France during the revolution. Blacque believed that the Greek revolution delayed the Turkish revolution, and that reforms in Turkey were feasible because Ottoman laws were in fact quite reasonable. He argued that maladministration was a result of the non-enforcement of those laws.[23]

21. *Mnemosyne*, no. 1 (March 9, 1835).
22. *Amaltheia*, no. 428 (April 4, 1847).
23. See Michaud and Poujoulat 1834, 1:246.

THE QUESTION OF GREEK IDENTITY

Frequently discussed in the Ottoman Greek press and of fundamental importance during the fierce anti-missionary movement in the early press years was the question of what constituted the Greek identity. This was often referred to as Hellenism (*Hellenismos*), perceived by the Ottoman Greeks as the sum total of human cultural achievements produced in the Greek language by people who since antiquity had identified themselves with the Greek nation and later embraced the Orthodox Christian religion. Missionary attempts at converting Greeks to Western Christian dogmas attacked what in the nineteenth century lay at the very heart of Hellenism, the Orthodox Christian religion:

> ... they think that if they succeed in dragging the source of all Christianity, the Mother of all Churches, to their society they will shut the Papists up ... but they should have studied the character of the Greek nation ... and they should have learned that Ethnicity and Religion are completely interwoven for us and that the nation as a whole does not move one iota from the dogma of our religion.[24]

Christian dogma as it had evolved in the first centuries of Christianity, ratified by bishops immersed in Platonic, Aristotelian, and Stoic philosophy and expressed in the Greek language, still formed the core identity of the Greek-speaking world of the former Eastern Roman Empire.

The Ottoman Greek press presents this identity as entirely inclusive. To be considered a Hellene depended neither on being the citizen of a Greek state nor of being of "pure" Greek blood, but of consciously subscribing to Greek culture, its language and the Orthodox Christian religion. Hellenism seems to have been based broadly on the Isocratic dictum: "Greeks are those who partake of our education and culture." As such the Greek-speaking peoples of the Ottoman Empire, writing in the Ottoman Greek press, differed both from the French and the German nationalist models that were developing in Western Europe; for them the preservation of the Hellenic identity required neither a pure national lineage nor a revolutionary break from the Ottoman Empire in favor of a national state. Provided they were allowed to identify freely as Hellenes without being penalized or persecuted they were happy to remain in their native land.

EDUCATION AND CULTURE

While the Ottoman Greek press considered living in a national state to be of secondary importance, it regarded retention of one's national identity as a sine qua

---

24. Hadjinikolaou 1837, 62.

non. The key to achieving this was education – a theme that regularly occupied column inches in the pages of the Ottoman Greek press, especially in Smyrna.

Already from the beginning of the nineteenth century Smyrna witnessed a surge in education among the Greek-speaking community. On occasion this even resulted in street fights between conservative and progressive elements. Their arguments revolved around the kind of education that each group wanted Greeks to aspire to: the "conservatives" favored an education based on the classics and religion, while the "liberals" preferred modern languages and science. The rich successfully circumvented the church, which had sole responsibility for the education of the Orthodox, by employing private tutors at home or educating their children abroad. This attitude was resented equally, but for different reasons, both by the church and the editors of the Greek press. The former objected because they lost control over what was taught and the latter because it deprived schools of the much-needed financial support of its affluent citizens. This, they felt, hampered "national progress," which they believed rested on the universal education of all Greeks. Although, as mentioned earlier, efforts to create an independent high school in 1810 failed, Smyrna could nonetheless boast at least one independent school of very high-quality teaching, the Evangelical School of Smyrna (the name does not refer to the Evangelical branch of Protestantism but to the Greek word for the gospels). This establishment was the only one that was not under the authority of the patriarchate by virtue of its founder's will, which placed it under the protection of the British consul. Moreover, following the first official school regulation for Orthodox schools in the Ottoman Empire, which was published in 1846 (probably as a result of the government's law on education, issued in 1845) a number of private schools were opened by Greek or foreign individuals, the latter mostly French or Italian. Some parents preferred to send their children to be educated either in Greece, the Ionian Islands, Malta, or elsewhere in Europe, as can be surmised from school advertisements that appeared in the Smyrna press.

The education of girls, another prominent issue in the press that had important consequences for the standing of women in Ottoman Greek society, is dealt with in detail in a later chapter.

Apart from education, Greek Smyrniots followed other cultural developments in western Europe closely. European and especially French literature was widely read, plays and Italian opera were often performed, and foreign musicians, including orchestras, arrived by invitation. European dancing was practised every week in various social clubs and many people, especially the younger generation, adopted European dress. The editors of the Greek press received these departures from traditional social behavior with mixed feelings. Some, like I. I. Skylisses, editor of *Ephemeris tes Smyrnes* and later of *He Hemera* of Trieste, encouraged the introduction of the French post-revolutionary neo-classical style, believing that it would help create a bourgeoisie that would inevitably establish a democratic political system in the Ottoman Empire. Others, like the editor of *Mnemosyne*, Kyriakos Lambrylos Hadjinikolaou, were equally supportive of French liberal ideas and promoted compulsory public schooling with equal opportunities for all. Hadjinikolaou frequently attacked the mercantile class for failing to share its wealth with the rest of the nation in order to educate its fellow Greeks. He also attacked the new fashion among wealthy Greeks for sending their children abroad in order to see the world, attend finishing school and "learn good manners," as he termed it, before returning to join the commercial establishment. He thought this was an utter waste of money, claiming that much of the "good manners" they acquired at such great expense involved

> spending three hours dressing with great care and attention in front of a mirror, dancing all the new dances with accuracy and skill, playing cards, drinking and socializing with loose women![25]

He also warned parents who sent their children abroad to acquire post-secondary education that, not having the educational background necessary to take advantage of Europe's superior culture, their children would only acquire an industrial society's negative aspects. He found it ironic that western Europeans were learning Greek and reviving the classics while the Greeks themselves neglected their own language and cultural traditions. He viewed their attempts to be fashionable by speaking ungrammatical French to each other and imitating European and especially French ways and dress as lamentable.

This critical attitude towards the superficial adoption of Western habits echoes throughout the early period of the Ottoman Greek press and will be examined in more detail in a later chapter. Similar attitudes toward education and culture began to be displayed about thirty years later by the Turkish journalists of the 1860s, such as İbrahim Şinasi and Agâh Bey, whose newspaper *Tercüman-ı Ahval* was hailed by Greek journalists as one worthy of attention. There are several references to the work of their Turkish counterparts in the Ottoman Greek press, suggesting some interaction and even occasionally collaboration between them. It is still unclear to what extent the Turkish writers and journalists were influenced by the Ottoman Greek press and more research needs to be undertaken in this direction. It seems, however, that while for the Ottoman Greek journalists of the 1830s-50s Western progress was a direct result of its Hellenic cultural origins, it was not until the 1890s that Turkish writers began to accept that the scientific progress of the West could not be divorced from its culture: "A civilization cannot exist with only some branches of knowledge. If the West was deficient in culture, it could not develop its material civilization."[26]

25. *Mnemosyne*, no.28 (September 13, 1835).
26. Şemşedin Sami 1983, 89-90.

Problems

Next to the many positive aspects of the birth of the Greek press in the Ottoman Empire there were several problems. One that was identified by the editors themselves was the slowness of production. Usually, the same individual gathered all the information and wrote the paper. It was then submitted to a printer who, more often than not, worked alone or with only one assistant and was simultaneously engaged in printing books, pamphlets, and stationery. Although there were several printers in Smyrna, the various printing presses used during this period were hand-operated and their maximum capacity was 250 sheets per hour.[27]

Another factor that hampered circulation was the price of the newspapers, which many Greeks considered to be too high in comparison with their European counterparts. I. I. Skylisses viewed it as a chicken-and-egg situation: the high price was due to the restricted circulation, which in turn did not cover the publication costs, which therefore had to remain high:

> We know very well that 800 subscribers paying 40 francs each can barely pay for the costs of the newspaper ... if of course you compare the price of a Greek newspaper published once or twice a week with a European daily you could well say that Greek publishers are taking advantage of their customers ... Think, however, that the English, the French, the Germans, and the Italians offer their newspapers to millions of readers.[28]

Skylisses, publisher of *He Hemera* of Trieste, offered Greek readers "a smaller newspaper containing only political news so that people can afford to buy it,"[29] but it failed to attract a bigger readership.

Whenever Ottoman Greek editors compared their newspapers with the European press, they liked to compare them with national publications, revealing that this was how they perceived themselves and their newspapers within the Ottoman Empire.

European national newspapers, which addressed a linguistically and politically homogeneous society, enjoyed a wide readership. If, however, we compare the Smyrna press with a provincial press, say, that of Birmingham, things look slightly different. The Birmingham press still had the advantage of addressing a population with political and linguistic homogeneity and enjoyed much better transportation facilities than its Smyrna counterpart. Moreover, unlike the Greek press, whose readership was spread over a vast area, Birmingham newspapers were sold within the radius of that city. In 1847 four newspapers were published in

27. Steam-driven presses were in use by some newspapers in western Europe from 1824 with a capacity to produce 1,100 sheets per hour, but did not arrive in the Ottoman Empire until after the period under review.

28. *He Hemera*, no. 303 (June 23/July 5, 1861.

29. Ibid.

Birmingham (population 401,715), of which only two shared similar contents with their Ottoman Greek counterparts, that is, political, literary, and commercial. The other two dealt with commerce, agriculture, trade, and manufacture. All four were published only once a week like the Ottoman Greek newspapers, but not on a subscription basis.

The small circulation of the Ottoman Greek press was also blamed on illiteracy:

> Among the six million who speak the Greek language, how many are
> able to read it, and among those, how many can understand the language
> of the newspapers and among them how many have the money to buy
> them?[30]

Illiteracy continued to be an issue for the press outside the big cities as late as the 1880s. In 1881, Vlassios Scordiles wrote in the literary magazine *Hestia* of Athens:

> In Stenemache of Thrace, every Sunday after the Liturgy, the citizens
> gather in the school, and the schoolteacher reads *Amaltheia* to them, thus
> opening up new horizons to those simple Greeks.[31]

In Anatolia too,

> The unredeemed Greeks were gathering at night around the Greek teacher
> in order to listen to the patriotic and didactic articles of *Amaltheia*.[32]

These quotations are further proof that in the villages, and especially in Anatolia, even at the end of the late nineteenth century, the majority of older people were illiterate and dependent upon the local schoolteachers and priests for reading and writing, and this helps explain in part the restricted circulation of newspapers. Of course, this did not necessarily mean a small readership or that the papers exerted an insignificant influence over the Greek-speaking population within the Ottoman Empire; although unable in many cases to read the newspapers for themselves, they had the papers read to them regularly.

Amaltheia of Smyrna considered illiteracy to be a major obstacle to selling newspapers. Issue no. 401 (October 4, 1846) responded to an article in *Telegraphos tou Vosporou*, entitled "The Three Greek Newspapers of Turkey," in which it was argued that the main obstacle to the spread of the press were the amateurish and profiteering tactics of most publishers and illiteracy among the population:

> Doesn't *Telegraphos [tou Vosporou]* receive, like we do, every week, letters
> and essays from teachers and others in the interior [of the country], which
> are so lacking in orthography and organization, and are so barbaric in

30. Ibid.
31. *Hestia* (August 15, 1881).
32. Solomonides 1959, 26.

style, that one has to change them completely, so that their publication will not shame our paper? ... Didn't *Telegraphos* write, just eight days ago, about the ignorance of some teachers, who are employed by even more ignorant and corrupt *ephors* [school governors]? ... Weren't these your words, when you said that the Great Church must try and close the door to all these embezzlers, so that the money earmarked for education won't be wasted, and our youth won't spend its valuable time worthlessly and harmfully, so that people won't be cheated?

Amaltheia had, in fact, started such a vigorous campaign against semi-literate teachers and the private schools that employed them, that it was reputed to have lost 200 subscribers over that one issue – something it categorically denied.[33]

When comparing literacy between western Europe and the Greeks of the Ottoman Empire, Ottoman Greek editors used an unrealistic yardstick, as literacy in the 1840s in western Europe was in fact comparable to that among the Greeks of the Ottoman Empire or worse. In 1839 in England, for example, ten out of eleven people were illiterate.[34]

The Greek custom of socializing in clubs and coffee shops was also mooted as a cause for the small circulation of Ottoman Greek newspapers:

How often are those who have the money to buy them not content to merely read them in the club reading room or in the coffee shop or in their friend's or neighbor's house?[35]

Greek editors would no doubt have been surprised to learn that reading newspapers in clubs and coffee shops was not an exclusively Greek custom. In Britain, newspapers were bought by almost every coffee-house and by reading-rooms and private clubs. In addition, newspapers were a major feature of ale houses, so much so that, according to *Cobbett's Register*, "[newspapers turned] thousands upon thousands of people ... into sots through the attractions of those vehicles of novelty and falsehood."[36] In these establishments, those who could read would often do so aloud, for the benefit of those who could not.

Xenomania (an incessant desire for anything foreign) is yet another reason cited for the small circulation of Ottoman Greek newspapers:

How many among us do not prefer to read foreign newspapers and look down on our own? ... [T]he total number of subscribers to the Greek press is 6,000, while one European newspaper alone can claim 70,000 subscribers.[37]

33. *Amaltheia*, no. 398 (September 2/14, 1846).
34. Aspinall 1949, 8.
35. *He Hemera*, no. 303 (June 23/July 5, 1861).
36. Aspinall 1949, 28.
37. *He Hemera*, no. 303 (June 23/July 5, 1861).

That number may have been accurate for some European national newspapers but, as mentioned earlier, there were times when even popular papers, like *Cobbett's Register*, could sell only 400 copies a week. Moreover, circulation of British newspapers at the beginning of the nineteenth century was "approximately one paper per 300 inhabitants."[38] If the figure quoted above of 6,000 newspapers for 6,000,000 people, is correct, then considering the conditions prevailing in the Ottoman Empire, the ratio of one paper per 1,000 people is no disgrace beside the figures for Britain.

As in western Europe, among Ottoman Greek speakers purchasing newspapers was predominantly a middle-class habit:

> Most of these 6,000 people are found among the commercial establishment and when business goes well, they are quite prepared to support a paper, but when there is a recession as there is today, especially in the East very few consider that they can spend money on a newspaper. Many times, we saw our readership increase or decrease according to the financial situation.[39]

Ottoman Greek newspapers were sold on subscription and relied heavily on their agents for distribution, being sent all over the Ottoman Empire and abroad. The extent of the operation could create serious financial and distribution problems, often interrelated:

> Don't forget that in Europe, those who buy papers appear daily with ready money in their hands, while there are among us people who delay their subscription for months on end ... Because of the nature of the Greek newspapers, we need agents all over the place and sometimes they either don't bother to register new subscribers or they delay in sending us the money ...[40]

To complicate matters further, Ottoman Greeks appear to have been reluctant to pay annual or six-monthly subscriptions in advance for a newspaper, since a continuous run for the subscribed period was by no means guaranteed. Some editors resorted to a system of IOUs, which guaranteed subscribers their money back should the newspaper cease publication, but this measure was not entirely successful. In another attempt to secure a wider readership, agents were given as much as a 10% commission as an incentive to increase the number of subscribers and send the subscriptions promptly to the editors. Most of these agents had other professions and had neither the time nor the inclination to work exclusively for the newspapers. To make matters worse, some individuals fraudulently posed as

---

38. Aspinall 1949, 7.
39. *He Hemera*, no. 303 (June 23/July 5, 1861).
40. Ibid.

agents, relieved unsuspecting subscribers of their subscriptions and disappeared into thin air, creating havoc between subscribers, editors, and legitimate agents.

Newspaper distribution beyond their local areas and prompt delivery to all subscribers was another headache for editors. Although both Smyrna and Constantinople were well situated as far as transportation was concerned, distribution was often difficult. Bad weather made winter dispatches by sea and land routes unreliable and local disturbances, as well as the Crimean war, greatly disrupted the regular circulation of newspapers outside their immediate areas of publication. Editors experimented with various delivery methods. Skylisses, the editor of *Ephemeris tes Smyrnes*, for example, had a personal connection with the princes of the Danubian principalities of Moldavia and Wallachia (where there was a significant Greek-speaking community) and succeeded in gaining permission to send his newspaper through their diplomatic dispatches.[41]

The logistics of prompt distribution in the first half of the nineteenth century was a problem shared by western European countries as well.[42]

Some people living in the provinces regarded their subscriptions to papers based in the major commercial centers of Constantinople, Smyrna, and Trieste as entitling them to additional dispatching services, and from time to time notices appeared in order to dispel such requests:

> [W]e have neither the time nor the ability to please our friends when they ask us to send them all sorts of different things from our town [Trieste in this case]. We are forced to say this because we are inundated with requests.[43]

CONTROLLING THE PRESS

Although newspapers in the Ottoman Empire were initiated and encouraged by the sultan himself, both the Ottoman government and, to a lesser extent, the Orthodox Church, tried to censor the information provided by the newspapers and the occasional criticisms of their authority.

Censorship was exercised on all printed matter, whether produced in the Ottoman Empire or imported from abroad. Three periods of censorship can be

41. Ibid.

42. In England, for example, although the Turnpike Trusts had spent over £7,000,000 on building and improving roads, travel was slow, hazardous, uncertain, and expensive. Travel from London to Leeds took thirty-three hours, and from London to Manchester twenty-four, etc. Only very few London newspapers found their way to the provinces and even fewer to the colonies and other foreign countries. The difficulty in sending English newspapers abroad or receiving them from abroad was exacerbated by post office restrictions. Domestic destinations were post-free, but when newspapers were either sent or came from abroad, they were treated as letters, and this made them too expensive to buy. See: Aspinall 1949, 8.

43. *He Hemera*, no. 68 (December 21, 1856/January 2, 1857).

distinguished during the Tanzimat era. The first, from the 1830s until 1845, was characterized by a dual censorship executed by the Ottoman government and the millet leadership. It was arbitrary in nature, because there were no clear rules and guidelines on what was or was not printable. Moreover, at the same time foreign nationals (such as the missionaries) could publish without official permission from the government. The second period, from 1845–1856, was a period of liberalization and decentralization, with censorship left to the various millet authorities. In these years the Ottoman press and especially the press of the Orthodox millet enjoyed the greatest freedom of expression. The third period, from 1856 onward, saw a centralization of control by the Ottoman government, which swept away the millet's powers over their own press. It was also characterized by the formalization of the relationship between the government and the press, with increased censorship, mostly affecting the outspoken Christian press, and the limiting of the rights of foreign nationals with regard to printing and publishing.

For the Rum milleti, until the 1850s everything published in Greek, Rumanian, Bulgarian, *karamanlı* Turkish or any other language spoken by the sultan's Orthodox subjects had to submit for censorship both by the patriarchate and the Ottoman government. In the 1840s, for example, a Bulgarian magazine called *Liuboslovia* was published in Smyrna by a Bulgarian, Constantine Photinov. The chief agent for distributing it in Constantinople and parts of Bulgaria and the Danubian principalities was one Ralli Hadji Mavridi. On May 31, 1844 he wrote to Photinov, in Smyrna mentioning the visits from the censors:

> A Turk came to look at *Liuboslovia* and found that it contained no harmful matter; a deacon also came from the patriarchate.[44]

If the newspaper/magazine was not favored by one or another of the governing institutions of the Rum milleti, or even by a particular individual in authority in the area where the newspaper appeared, the censor could delay reading it, thereby delaying its distribution. This inevitably contributed to the short life of some of the earliest Ottoman Greek newspapers. It certainly affected the distribution of *Liuboslovia*. In his letter to Photinov dated February 7, 1845, Mavridi complained about the delay caused to the distribution because of censorship:

> I have received a bundle of *Liuboslovia* but until someone comes from the patriarchate to look at them, I cannot distribute them.[45]

It is important to note that there is no mention of a Turkish censor. My research reveals that this absence reflects the fact that at that time the rules concerning the censorship of publications printed for or by the Rum milleti had changed. In 1845

44. Shismanov 1894, 665.
45. Shismanov 1894, 665.

the Ottoman government handed over responsibility for censorship entirely to the patriarchate. This is confirmed by a letter from Agathangelos, the metropolitan of Vratsa in Bulgaria, to Costantin Photinov in 1845, stating that he had received ten copies of *Liuboslovia* and had given them to the girls' school in that city. He added that he had received an order from the patriarchate and another from the Ottoman government forbidding any books to go into circulation in his province prior to their approval by what he called the *epitrope* (the committee) of the patriarchate.[46] The wholesale transfer of responsibility for censorship to the millets is further confirmed by a prelatical letter read on January 18, 1846 in the churches of the Ottoman Empire; it concerned the implementation by the patriarchate of "preventative censorship in all the publications to be printed."[47]

According to the evidence, it seems that between 1845 and 1856 the Ottoman government granted exclusive responsibility for the censorship of all Orthodox Christian publications to the patriarchate. One can assume that this was also the case with the other millets, though no evidence has been found on this, save for the Pashalik of Egypt, whose ruler Mehmed Ali Pasha had since 1823 exercised his own censorship on all publications produced by the publishing house of Bulak, which he had founded in 1819. Mehmed Ali Pasha's censorship consisted of one single rule: that all publications should be cleared for circulation by the *pasha* himself.[48] During the rule of Sa'id Pasha (1854–1863), censorship in Egypt became more elaborate and the relevant laws fell in line with the practices in the rest of the empire.

The fact that the Ottoman Greek press between 1845 and 1856 was censored exclusively by patriarchal authorities did not mean that Greek newspapers were free to publish whatever they wished. I. I. Skylisses, one of the major figures of this early period of Ottoman Greek journalism, decided to close down his profitable newspaper *Ephemeris tes Smyrnes* in 1854 and start another one in Trieste, in the belief that there he would be able "to write freely about the Ottoman Empire and the European countries, so that the Orthodox Christians of the empire will have a chance to read the truth."[49]

Since at that time it appears that censorship for Ottoman Greek newspapers was exercised exclusively by the Orthodox Church, Skylisses must have been referring to patriarchal and not state censorship. This assumption is further strengthened by the fact that imported newspapers were not subject to patriarchal censorship.

In 1856, after more than a decade of experimenting with the decentralization of censorship, the Ottoman government re-established the authority of the Ottoman censor. It was felt that too much freedom of expression had been allowed,

46. Shismanov 1894, 667.
47. Solomonides 1959, 340–41.
48. See Farah 1977, 165.
49. *He Hemera* no. 1 (September 9/21, 1855).

especially to the Balkan Christians, whose criticisms of the government had been particularly outspoken during this most sensitive period of the reorganization of the state. In October 1856, in a letter to Prince Ghikas (reported in *He Hemera*), the governor of Moldavia, Fuad Pasha, abolished the Prince's law that granted freedom of the press in that principality and demanded that

> no new permits for newspapers should be issued and the editors of existing ones should be ordered to refrain from discussing matters to do with the rights of the Sublime Porte or the kings allied to His Majesty or neighboring countries, otherwise the papers should be banned. A censor will be appointed by the Sublime Porte.[50]

Although in theory the press laws of 1857 and 1865, presented below, were supposed to make it easier to obtain permission to publish a newspaper, in practice it became increasingly difficult to do so. According to the chief archivist of the Patriarchate of Constantinople, Manuel Gedeon, who had also been editor of several Ottoman Greek newspapers and magazines, permission to publish a newspaper was obtained only with great difficulty, unless one was friendly with a minister. Some individuals who could secure newspaper permits through their connections registered them in their names and then rented the permits to people who genuinely wanted to publish a newspaper but lacked the necessary connections. Gedeon cites the example of Evangelos Papadopoulos, known as Vangel Efendi, a low-class individual from Kydoniai, who in the 1870s managed to befriend a government minister and:

> received the Mecidiye medal fifth class for lack of a sixth … He succeeded in obtaining through his connection three newspaper permits … one for a Greek newspaper called *Proia* [Morning], one for a Turkish newspaper called *Sabah* [Morning] and one for a French newspaper called *Matin* [Morning]. He used to rent them for a ridiculously low price. I used to give him for *Proia* (a weekly publication) one Turkish *lira* a month, while the publishers of the other two, which were dailies, 4–5 Turkish *lira*s a month each. He used to receive the money in instalments and sometimes instead of four monthly rents he used to get only three.[51]

Thus far the accepted view by historians was that "the first precedent in Turkey for government suppression of a newspaper was the closing down of *Tercüman-ı Ahval* in 1862."[52] New evidence has emerged, indicating that the first suppression of an Ottoman newspaper published within the Empire took place twenty-one years earlier. In February 1841, *Amaltheia* of Smyrna was closed down by the Ottoman

---

50. *He Hemera*, no. 56 (September 28/October 10, 1856).
51. Gedeon 1932, 57.
52. See for example Lewis 1966, 143.

government "because its liberal articles displeased the Turkish authorities."[53] It remained closed for three months, after which its publisher, Samiotakis, secured permission from the government to resume publication. *Amaltheia* was closed down by the government for a second time in 1844, at the request of the governor of Samos, Stephanake Vogorides. *Amaltheia* had featured a series of articles against Vogorides, whose style of government had created great dissatisfaction among the people of Samos. This time the paper was closed down for four months, but its publisher once more succeeded in resuming its publication.[54]

During the period under review several newspapers – some printed in the Ottoman Empire, some imported from abroad – were suppressed. For example, the newspaper *Tempul* (Time), published in Bucharest, in its March 7/19, 1857 issue printed:

> a program demanding autonomy, the union of the Principalities, a heredi-tary ruler and one representative government, respect for private property, personal freedom, and the right to work. After that the local government closed down the newspaper.[55]

The newspaper resumed publication a little later under the name *Aion* (the closest Greek translation of its Rumanian name).[56] Another Wallachian newspa-per, *Rumania*, was suspended for a month "because of an article touching on the emperor of Russia and the Sublime Porte."[57] The Moldavian newspaper *Star of the Danube* ceased publication altogether in 1856 because of its nationalist articles.[58]

In 1858 the Ottoman Greek newspaper *Vyzantis* (*Telegraphos tou Vosporou kai Vyzantis*) was also suspended for two months by the Ottoman government "because it published some extracts from works by the French philhellenes Saint-Marc Girardine and Mathieu, and some letters from Crete."[59] The French press in the empire suffered too. For example, *La Presse d'Orient* ceased publication for a week in 1857,[60] and was closed down again in 1859.[61]

In the case of the Armenians, Ottoman censorship seems to have been harsher. For example, the publisher of the Armenian newspaper *Arshaluys* (Dawn; published 1840–1844), a man called Hariyan, was imprisoned many times "for his patriotic articles." Finally, in 1844, "his newspaper was closed down and he was condemned to death and hanged."[62]

53. Solomonides 1959, 31.
54. For a description of *Amaltheia*, see the next chapter, page 50.
55. *He Hemera*, no. 83 (April 5/17, 1857).
56. *He Hemera*, no. 87 (May 3/15, 1857).
57. *He Hemera*, no. 104 (September 30/October 11,1857).
58. *He Hemera*, no. 56 (September 28–October 10, 1856).
59. *He Hemera*, no. 149 (July 18/30, 1858).
60. *He Hemera*, no. 98 (July 18/30, 1857).
61. *He Hemera*, no. 215 (October 16/28, 1859).
62. Solomonides 1959, 276–77.

Newspapers from Greece were denied entry into the empire if they contained articles that were perceived to promote nationalism and democracy. For example, the Athenian newspaper *Aion* was barred from the Ottoman Empire in 1849 as a result of articles supporting the Hungarian revolution. It was permitted to circulate again in the empire from September 1850.[63]

A less severe measure employed against newspapers was an official reprimand. In August 1856, *Journal de Constantinople* printed some articles

> against the union of the Principalities and thus created a lot of resentment in Jassy and Bucharest, because it was considered to be speaking for the Porte. Subsequently the Sultan called the editor and reprimanded him severely. The next issue of *Journal de Constantinople* appeared declaring that the offending articles did not represent the official view.[64]

Another newspaper which often received official censure was the French newspaper *Impartial*, published in Smyrna. Its editor, Antonios Edouardos, was "reprimanded by the Ottoman government for being pro-Greek."[65]

Ottoman censorship and, in general, government attitudes towards printing and the press were arbitrary until 1857, when the Ottoman government issued a press law consisting of nine articles. It was addressed to those wishing to start a printing or lithograph press or publish a newspaper, magazine, books, or any other type of publication. Prospective publishers were now required to apply to the ministries of education and the police, who would investigate the application and then send a report to the grand vizier. He would then decide whether to issue a permit or not. For the first time, foreign nationals too, even those who were already operating a printing press, had to apply to the ministry of foreign affairs for a permit. Everyone had to submit their publications to the Ottoman censor, or the publication would be seized and a sum of money had to be deposited as a guarantee before the issue of a permit. On the positive side the law established the principle of copyright, which safeguarded intellectual property and stipulated that, "[t]hose who publish a work have the copyright for life."[66] The press law was issued on January 6, 1857[67] and appeared in the Greek press in its entirety between February and March of the same year.

In December 1857, eleven months after promulgating the press law, the Ottoman government reminded editors that it strictly forbade newspapers to publish articles, correspondence, or any news before the censor had passed them. If the publishers failed to comply, publication would "cease for a period, which

63. *He Hemera*, no. 76 (February 15/27, 1857).
64. *He Hemera*, no. 48 (September 3/15, 1856).
65. Ibid.
66. See Aristarchi 1874, 3:318–26.
67. *He Hemera*, no. 68 (December 21, 1856/January 3, 1857).

will be determined by the seriousness of the crime."[68] By 1862, political articles criticizing the government were few and far between.

In January 1865 the Ottoman government issued a new law about printing, which was considerably more detailed, consisting of thirty-five articles. This simplified the mechanism for obtaining a permit, which was now necessary only for newspapers and magazines with political content. Twenty-five of the articles dealt with the penalties provided for various offences, such as defamation and the spreading of false news.[69] Newspaper owners welcomed the new law because it appeared, at least in theory, that the government had relaxed its grip on the press. Furthermore, it gave new newspapers permission to publish without a monetary guarantee, which had previously been necessary. Also, publishers were not to be punished for publishing false news, provided that they could prove they did so in good faith. Newspapers were to be closed only for reasons of "general security" and only if they were found guilty in court on three occasions. Even when such cases occurred, the government was extremely lenient and usually only closed down the offending newspaper for a limited period.[70] However, the euphoria generated by the new law soon died down. In March 1867, the government published an official notice concerning only the indigenous press. [71] Here the government declared that it reserved the right to take action outside the provisions of the law against those newspapers that harmed the public interest as, of course, the government saw fit. In effect the government was saying that it forbade any public criticism of its actions and that its own previous liberal press laws of 1859 and 1865 were to be applied only to the foreign press, which it aimed to impress by paying lip service to democratization.

From the 1860s onwards (and culminating under Abdülhamid), political journalism was practically non-existent in the Ottoman Empire. The Comte de Persignac gives an interesting account of a discussion that took place in 1907 between the Ottoman censor of Salonica (Thesalonike) and a French editor, who asked what he was allowed to speak of and was told:

> You may speak of everything ... except, you understand, of crowned
> heads, of foreign governments, of nihilism, of socialism, of revolution, of
> strikes, of anarchy, of liberty, of foreign policy, of religion, of churches, of
> mosques, of Muhammad, of Jesus, of Moses, of the prophets, of athe-
> ism, of free thought, of the authorities, of feminism, of the harem, of the
> fatherland, of nation, of nationalism, of internationalism, of republic, of
> deputies, of senators, of constitution, of plots, of bombs, of Midhat pasha,
> of Kemal Bey, of Sultan Murad, of the crescent, of the cross, of Macedo-

68. *He Hemera*, no. 117 (November 29/December 11, 1857).
69. Aristarchi 1874, 320-25.
70. Solomonides 1959, 342.
71. See Aristarchi 1874, 325-36.

nia, of Armenia, of reforms, of grasshoppers, of the month of August [the month Sultan Murat V was deposed], and a few other subjects corresponding more or less to these.[72]

Undoubtedly, this discussion took place in a highly fractious period, when unrest and revolution were anticipated at any moment and censorship was necessarily strict. However, a study of Ottoman newspapers from the late 1850s onwards reveals that there was a gradual decline in the freedom of expression that had been enjoyed in the 1830s, 40s, and 50s, at least with regard to the Ottoman Greek press. Most of the subjects ostensibly banned from the press in 1907 were in fact quite openly discussed in our period.

Strict as it was, Ottoman censorship did not prevent libelous articles from appearing in the Greek press or even in separate pamphlets. The targets were usually Greek personalities: patriarchs, such as Anthimos VI, and prominent members of the national assembly that was convened to discuss the new church regulations. Libelous articles also targeted topics such as the quarrels between the church and lay people, the Bulgarian question, the corrupt and loose life of certain prominent clergymen, arguments between intellectuals about the language controversy, and the Roman Catholic Church. On only a few occasions did the Turkish police take action against the authors of such pamphlets, usually when they attacked the patriarch and his entourage or high officials. In 1841, after a series of attacks against prominent people, including the prince of Samos, Stephanake Vogorides, a personal friend of the sultan, the Ottoman government took steps to "curb the use of phrases unsuitable for the character of a journalist."[73] In 1865 the government made a second attempt to curb this type of attack by decreeing that all newspapers were obliged to publish gratis in their next issue corrections by persons named or discussed in their articles.[74] Press offences and disputes between journalists and private individuals were originally tried in the Sublime Porte by a five-member committee, and from August 1872 in local courts.[75]

Comparison with Greece reveals that Ottoman censorship up to 1862 was far more liberal. Already from the beginning of its life, the Greek state possessed a strong press,[76] which, in the absence of proper parliamentary debate, construed its function as offering opposition to the government. The first constitution of Greece, drafted during the War of Independence by the National Assembly of Astros (1823), included a law giving all the people and the press the right to voice their views on condition that they were not critical of the Christian religion, did not contradict established ethics, and refrained from defamation of character.

72. Persignac 1907, 390.
73. *Aster tes Anatoles*, no. 1 (January 17, 1841).
74. See Aristarchi 1874, 322.
75. Solomonides 1959, 342.
76. By 1837 Athens had 30,000 inhabitants, seven newspapers and six literary magazines.

Nonetheless, soon after the establishment of the Greek state the new government under Count Kapodistrias found that the strong opposition of the press needed curtailing. Thus, Kapodistrias passed a law in April 1831 requiring that a substantial sum of money be deposited as a guarantee for the printing of a newspaper. He also defined the responsibilities of the typesetter in the event of a contravention of the new law. The Bavarian regency of the young King Otto, who became the new head of the fledgling state after the assassination of Kapodistrias in 1831, passed three more press laws, which further curtailed the freedom of the press. Publishers were required to deposit a substantial sum of money with the State Lending Fund in order to be able to pay off any fines imposed by the courts, and the responsibilities of editors, typesetters, and distributors were further defined. In 1837, further laws were passed regarding "abuses of the press." In the 1850s the persecution of the press became exceedingly harsh and several writers were imprisoned or went into hiding. In 1862 the government of King Otto granted a general amnesty for all press violations. Finally, the constitution of 1864 proclaimed the freedom of the press, banned censorship and provided safeguards for the unhindered circulation of the press, under the proviso that the laws were adhered to.[77]

One could draw an interesting analogy between the press and press laws of the young Greek state and the Ottoman Empire. Between the 1830s and the 1860s the Greek state became firmly established and, feeling increasingly secure, could relax its grip on political criticism; while the reverse holds true of the Ottoman Empire. In general, the first thirty years of newspaper publication in the Ottoman Empire suffered little from organized state censorship and therefore offers rich primary source material for examining this exciting period in the history of the Ottoman state.

77. For press laws and censorship see, for example, Dimakis 1977.

Chapter 2
The Greek Newspapers of Smyrna 1830–1862

THE EARLY YEARS (1831–1836):
THE MISSIONARY AND ANTI-MISSIONARY PRESS IN GREEK

THE GREEN LIGHT for the establishment of an indigenous press in the Ottoman Empire in 1830 was noticed first by the Orthodox Christians of
Smyrna. Several factors that contributed to Smyrna becoming the birthplace of the Ottoman Greek press were discussed in the previous chapter. In this
chapter we shall delve deeper into the missionary and antimissionary movements
that dominated the early 1830s in Smyrna and were instrumental in establishing
the first Greek newspapers in that city.

Although there were already some French newspapers being published in
Smyrna, it was the Protestant missionaries in that city that were the catalyst both
in the improvement of the education of the Greeks of Smyrna but also in the
establishment of the indigenous Greek press. These facts, however, did little to
endear them to the Orthodox Christians at that time, who were suspicious of their
links with foreign powers and focused mainly on their "incorrect" religious stance
and their dogmatic differences.

Missionaries were seen as "inferior" Christians by the Orthodox Christians
on several grounds, eloquently listed by K. Lambrylos Hadjinikolaou, publisher
of *Mnemosyne* in 1836. First of all, they were "against the spirit of unity of the
Christian Church,"[1] since they allowed anybody to translate and publicly preach
the Holy Scriptures as he wished. This practice had created "so many heretics,
who, in a most un-Christian manner, attack and excommunicate each other and
are all thrown into eternal hell."[2]

Secondly, it was felt that in order to achieve their purpose of attracting Orthodox Christians to their dogmas they used financial enticements:

> All the people who work for these gentlemen [the missionaries] get regu-
> lar, large salaries, which they could not secure anywhere else. Translators,
> for example, who merely translate one booklet a year, receive 80 *distilos* a
> month. Secretaries or interpreters receive 50 *distilos* a month. People who
> sell or distribute their booklets, teachers and other young people who

1. Hadjinikolaou 1937, 4–5.
2. Ibid.

ΣΜΥΡΝΗ 1835. — ΑΡΙΘ. 6.   ΣΑΒΒΑΤΟΝ 12 ΑΠΡΙΛΙΟΥ

ΜΝΗΜΟΣΥΝΗ.

ΕΦΗΜΕΡΙΣ

ΠΟΛΙΤΙΚΗ ΦΙΛΟΛΟΓΙΚΗ ΕΜΠΟΡΙΚΗ

ΑΙΣΕΤΑΙ ΔΕ ΚΑΙ ΜΟΙΣΑ ΑΙ ΑΓΓΕΛΙΑΣ ΟΡΘΑΙ
ΠΙΝΔΑΡΟΣ ΕΝ ΠΥΘΙΟΙΣ

ΣΜΥΡΝΗ 11 ΙΑΝΟΥΑΡ. 1852   ΕΤΟΣ ΙΕ΄. ΑΡΙΘ. 675.

Η ΑΜΑΛΘΕΙΑ.

ΕΤΟΣ Α΄ ΑΡΙΘΜΟΣ 3.   ΣΜΥΡΝΗ,   ΠΑΡΑΣΚΕΥΗ, ΤΗΝ 30 ΜΑΡΤΟΥ, 1861.

Η ΕΛΠΙΣ,

ΕΦΗΜΕΡΙΣ

ΠΟΛΙΤΙΚΗ, ΦΙΛΟΛΟΓΙΚΗ Κ' ΕΜΠΟΡΙΚΗ.

ΑΡΙΘ. 30   ΠΑΡΑΣΚΕΥΗ ΤΗΝ 15 ΜΑΙΟΥ 1842 ΕΝ ΣΜΥΡΝ.   ΕΤΟΣ Β.

Ο ΑΣΤΗΡ ΤΗΣ ΑΝΑΤΟΛΗΣ,

ΕΦΗΜΕΡΙΣ ΠΟΛΙΤΙΚΗ, ΦΙΛΟΛΟΓΙΚΗ Κ' ΕΜΠΟΡΙΚΗ.

ΑΡΙΘ. 3.   ΠΑΡΑΣΚΕΥΗ, 30 ΑΠΡΙΛΙΟΥ 1819.   ΕΤΟΣ Α΄.

 # ΕΦΗΜΕΡΙΣ ΤΗΣ ΣΜΥΡΝΗΣ

ΕΤΟΣ Α΄.   Σμύρνη, τὴν 28 Δεκεμβρίου 1861.   ΑΡΙΘ. 22.

ΕΥΣΕΒΕΙΑ

ΕΦΗΜΕΡΙΣ ΕΚΚΛΗΣΙΑΣΤΙΚΗ ΚΑΙ ΦΙΛΟΛΟΓΙΚΗ.

teach the abacus, receive 20–30 *distilos* monthly and school cleaners and caretakers, 10 *distilos*. Some who merely speak well of the missionaries in public receive a monthly salary for this service. Others, whose dignity may be questioned, lend the money they receive (from the missionaries), earning 6% a year interest.... Naturally, people of this sort, who know that such huge salaries cannot be found elsewhere, are trying desperately to keep the missionaries [here] and have become their most fervent assistants, their burning zealots, their friends and their prized advocates.[3]

Worse than enlisting the help of mercenary adults was for most Orthodox Christians their attempt "to bring our children up in the spirit of Protestantism."[4]

The last statement refers to the opening of schools by missionaries in the Ottoman Empire. At first, these schools attracted a number of children from the most progressive strata of Ottoman Greek society. These schools appeared to respond to the increasing need for public education, especially with regard to schools for girls, such as the one founded in Smyrna in the 1830s by a missionary named Josiah Brewer. He was one of several Protestant missionaries to arrive in the Ottoman Empire in the early nineteenth century, moving eventually to Smyrna, where he founded and directed a school for girls in the early thirties:

> Lessons were given in ancient and modern Greek, Italian, mathematics, history, and in all kinds of needlework. Fees were 10 *kuruş* a quarter, payable in advance.[5]

Not belonging to the Orthodox dogma, however, missionary schools caused some alarm among the conservative establishment of Smyrna. Several influential people approached the patriarchate expressing worries about the kind of knowledge that was disseminated in those schools. The Patriarchate of Constantinople responded by forming a committee to examine the books and the teaching style in Protestant schools. In his English-language missionary paper *Star in the East*, missionary Brewer, who was also the publisher of its Greek edition, *Aster tes Anatoles*, and a schoolmaster in a missionary school, described this committee as "the nineteenth-century equivalent of the inquisition."[6] In the same issue, Brewer claimed that the ecclesiastical committee of the patriarchate had threatened the girls with bastinado, unless they abandoned the Protestant schools and entered its own. Hadjinikolaou tells a different story. He reports that when he and others informed the Greek community that the missionaries "were mixing their heretical

3. Ibid.
4. Ibid.
5. Advertisement in *O Philos ton Neon*, December 9, 1831, quoted at Ch. Solomonides 1959, 11.
6. *Star in the East*, no. 4 (1836), quoted in Hadjinikolau 1837, 50.

booklets with arithmetic, geography, and history books"[7] they took their children out of the Protestant schools and burned their books, especially the New Testament, which was published by the Bible Society but which had heretical additions not found in the old Greek texts of the Gospels. Then:

> trying to cover their shame [the missionaries] started publishing their newspaper again in order to accuse us and lie about us, but, whereas previously all their arguments were conducted in Greek, now they publish their newspaper in English, so that they can present things as they like ... but they bring only laughter to the Europeans who have occasion to read it.[8]

The missionaries were forced to use different books, vetted by the committee, if they were to remain in operation. The ecclesiastical committee and the Bible Society of Smyrna were entrusted with the task of replacing "the missionary and heretical books" from those schools and then:

> the Bible Society voted for the publication of national books [that is, Orthodox Greek books] for the use of our children and authorized Mr. Venediktos, who happened to own a small printing press, to edit them free of charge and then print them in his printing press.[9]

This policy seems to have anticipated Ottoman government policy towards the missionaries during the Abdül Hamid II era.

Brewer, bitter at the missionary failure to advance the cause of Protestantism among the Ottoman Greeks of Smyrna, accused the Ecclesiastical Committee of having a national policy motivated by profiteering individuals. "The Greek community," he wrote in 1836,

> has collected a few thousand *kuruş* to publish books for children. These books, we hear from well-informed sources, are published in printing presses which are partly owned by some of the most active members of the present opposition. One of them belongs to a member of the Ecclesiastical Committee [and the books are printed] ... in printing presses, which greatly needed to find work.[10]

Brewer's accusations against those who opposed Protestantism as being instigated by financial gain echo Hadjinikolaou's accusations against those who supported Protestantism. The mutual disrespect of each other's spiritual dogmas made both deduce that only material incentives could be behind people's rejection of their

---

7. Hadjinikolaou 1837, 62.
8. Ibid.
9. Ibid.
10. *Star in the East*, no. 4 (1836), quoted in Hadjinikolau 1837, 106.

respective "correct" spiritual positions. In any case Protestantism failed to win the hearts and minds of Orthodox Christians, who remained overwhelmingly faithful to their spiritual position. The reaction to missionary schools and their books had the positive effect of forcing the Orthodox Christian establishment to face the issue of education head on and take action to improve it.

The reaction of the Orthodox Christians of the Ottoman Empire against the missionaries was generally limited to public burnings of their books, public condemnation of missionary activities, and anti-missionary publications. Missionary activity in the newly formed state of Greece produced a more severe reaction. Not protected by their foreign citizenship as they were in the Ottoman state, missionaries had to stand trial in criminal courts. The case of Jonas King, an American missionary, is notorious. King belonged to a Protestant evangelical group, was a friend of Brewer, and worked with him in Smyrna, where, when things became difficult, "he burned all the missionary booklets in his possession in three consecutive pyres in the backyard of the *hani* (hotel) of Yovanoğlu where he was staying"[11] and left for Greece thinking, erroneously as it turned out, that the reaction of people in Smyrna was masterminded by the Orthodox church there. In 1846, however, he was summoned to the criminal court in Athens to answer accusations that: a) he had claimed that Mary should be called "Mother of Christ" and not "Mary, the Mother of God" (the attribute of Mary that had been agreed upon in the Third Ecumenical Synod in Ephesus, in A.D. 431); b) he had criticized the honor given to icons (which had been agreed to in the Seventh Ecumenical Synod in Nicaea AD 787); and c) he had denounced and criticized the Orthodox Christian dogma of transubstantiation. In other words, he was accused of violating Article 18 of the Greek Constitution (laws for the press, slander, etc.), part of which referred to "people who express views, opinions or ideas which are against the basic principles of religion or morality; or are otherwise harmful to religion and morality." The public prosecutor said of King that he was "so full of enthusiasm to change others' religion to his own that he was blinded (to the fact that he was among Greeks) and thought that his mission was on some Indian island among savage natives."[12] King received a sentence of fifteen days in prison, was ordered to pay the legal costs, and was deported from Greece. The trial of Jonas King was the talk of Greece for quite some time. Several books were written about it and were subscribed by the cream of Athenian intellectual society – university professors, the church, a number of lawyers, merchants, and doctors and, oddly, the great freedom fighter and leader of the constitutional movement in Greece, General Makriyannis.[13]

11. Ibid.
12. Antoniades 1846, 17.
13. Ibid..

The First Efforts: 1831–1836

Between 1831 and 1836 three newspapers came out in Greek as a result of the missionary activities in Smyrna. The first two, *O Philos ton Neon* (Friend of Youth) and *Aster en te Anatole* (Star in the East) had a short life, and were connected with the Protestant missionaries in Smyrna. *Mnemosyne* came out briefly in 1834 as a reaction to them and again in 1835 for about twenty-six issues.

O Philos ton Neon, the first Greek newspaper published in Smyrna, was produced in the printing house of the Evangelical School of Smyrna by Antonios Damianos. According to sources cited by Ch. Solomonides, it seems that Avramios Homeroles, who had been the director of the school since 1828, permitted Damianos to share one of the schoolrooms with the printing press of the Manjouranis brothers, who had had a press in Smyrna for some time.[14] In his effort to publish a newspaper in Smyrna, Damianos was supported by the Lutheran Calvinist missionaries Brewer and Lewis[15] and "some European merchants of Smyrna, among whom were Landau, Van Lenep, and Clare."[16]

The contents of this paper were mostly religious but some literary essays also appeared, for example, one on Fénelon, written by P. Romeros (1799–1889).[17] *O Philos ton Neon* had fifty subscribers and, according to Solomonides, its Greek edition ceased publication on December 28, 1831.[18]

The second Greek newspaper of Smyrna, *Aster en te Anatole* was published in Greek by Josiah Brewer, who as we saw earlier felt that by publishing a newspaper he could further the missionary aims and defend the missionary cause better.

To combat missionary propaganda and promote the Orthodox Greek point of view, Avramios Homeroles, the director of the Evangelical School of Smyrna, who had helped Damianos to publish *O Philos ton Neon*, created *Mnemosyne*.[19] Born in Andronico of Kaisareia [Kaiseri] in Cappadocia in 1799, Homeroles's last name was Homouroglou but he later used the Hellenized form, Homeroles. When he was twelve years old his family moved to Smyrna, where he entered the Evangelical School of Smyrna. When he had completed his studies there, he became, for a brief period, a teacher of mathematics in a school in Kaisareia. From 1828 to 1834 he was a master at the Evangelical School, where he also became the director of the school's printing press. In 1833 he brought new type from France in order to publish his book *Dokimion ton Hieron kai Apostolikon Kanonon* (Essay on the

14. Ch. Solomonides 1959, 10–11.
15. Ibid.
16. Ibid.
17. Ibid.
18. Ibid.
19. For Homeroles see Ioannides 1873, 589; also Nikolaides-Philadelpheus 1974, 9; Evaggelides 1936, vol. B, 249; Paranicas 1885, 49.

Holy and Apostolic Regulations), which he brought out in 1834. By the end of 1833 Homeroles had also published all thirty-four issues of *Mnemosyne*. When the young King Otto of Greece visited the Evangelical School in 1833, Homeroles, according to the sources, delivered a most masterly speech of welcome. In 1834 he moved to Constantinople, where in 1839 he died and was given a public funeral.

Among other writers who worked with Homeroles on *Mnemosyne* were the Smyrnaean intellectual I. Latris and a doctor called Marinos Klados, who later with his son Petros published the newspaper *Ionikos Parateretes* (Ionian Observer). The newspaper closed at the beginning of 1834, most probably because of Homeroles' departure for Constantinople. No more information is available about this first series of *Mnemosyne*.

Approximately a year later, in March 1835, *Mnemosyne* resumed publication. According to Solomonides, it was published this time by Antonios Patrikios. This is also confirmed by the credits in the opening number of *Mnemosyne*. "The owners are Ionikon Typographeion of Smyrna" and "… it is also published by Ionikon Typographeion, whose director is Antonios Patrikios".[20] Although there is no mention of the editor in the paper, in issue number 28 of *Mnemosyne* there was a farewell article, apparently written by the editor, who signed it K. L-H. These are the initials of Kyriakos Lambrylos-Hadjinikolaou, the intellectual in the forefront of the anti-missionary movement, who was living and working in Smyrna at that time.

The purpose of the newspaper was set out in the editorial, which appeared on the front page of of the first issue. The editor started by commending public – in the sense of universal – education:

> Without a doubt, public education is a nation's only means of attaining and retaining virtue and gives people the knowledge and enlightenment necessary to improve their thinking. The greatest promoters of public education are those people who, under the protection of the law and with the approval of their government, will strive for knowledge and the discovery of new truths. The wisdom with which people of the enlightened nations of Europe are defending and protecting such things and the happy results of such endeavors prove to us that these are the means [of progress] for which we must strive too. Wise Socrates used to say, as his student Plato attests, that human knowledge must be directed rather to the rebuttal of the lie than to the affirmation of the truth, because the greatest enemy of the truth is not ignorance but delusion. In order for a person to recognize delusion he must be given the means to understand it and fight it. If we want delusion to diminish, we must support and publicize the truth [in our society].

20. *Mnemosyne*, no. 1 (March 9, 1835).

Newspapers were put forward by the editor as that all-important magnifying glass that would show clearly the truth and he argued that:

> a nation has a great need for newspapers and freedom of the press, for they are proof of the degree to which that nation is civilized and that is why we republish *Mnemosyne* ... and we call on all the friends of worthy things to support us and assist us in establishing this newspaper.

In issue no. 26 (September 3, 1835) the newspaper announced that it was running into difficulties:

> We have always done our job as best we could with the funds available. If the funds had been ampler our work would have been better. Our friends and well-wishers encourage us to continue with our publication. We would like to remind them, however, that their contribution alone is not sufficient for accumulating the necessary operational funds and that their financial contribution should be followed up with an introduction to others, inside and outside [the Empire] in order to increase the number of our subscribers. We kindly ask those of our subscribers who wish to continue their subscriptions for another six months to notify the paper-boy.

Issue no. 27 of *Mnemosyne* came out on Monday (September 9, 1835) instead of Saturday "because of a problem in the printing press." Finally, in no. 28 (Friday, September 13, 1835) *Mnemosyne* announced that it was closing down and that all the issues of its second publication would be bound and sold by the Ionian Press at a reasonable price. The reasons for its closure were spelled out in a very long and bitter article by the paper's editor, Kyriakos Lambrylos Hadjinikolaou, entitled "The Second Ascension of *Mnemosyne.*" *Mnemosyne*'s editor said he wrote this article in order to set out the precise facts about the paper and explain the reasons for its closure, so that "people who know nothing about this newspaper will not attribute the wrong reasons to *Mnemosyne*'s re-appearance and its second 'Ascension'." The editor continued by explaining why he used the word "ascension" to describe the closure of *Mnemosyne*: it was "because it is well known that when gods and goddesses abandon human beings they do not die but ascend either to Mt. Helikon or Mt. Olympus." Hadjinikolaou claimed in this article that the failure of *Mnemosyne* to establish itself was due to public indifference and lack of education:

> Those who re-issued *Mnemosyne* believed that the reasons that caused its initial cessation of publication no longer existed and decided to publish it again. They invited the public to subscribe and the intellectuals to collaborate, hoping that their voices would wake people up from their stupor. Unfortunately, very few answered the call; the majority awoke momen-

tarily, only to complain, 'Why are you bothering us?' then turned over on the other side and went to sleep again. Anyone else would have said 'Why bother with such people'? But the publishers of *Mnemosyne*, decided to continue its publication as best they could with their very small resources, in order not to frustrate the hopes of the few. Having quality rather than large profits as their aim, they doubled the size of the paper while keeping the same price. In the beginning they placed the emphasis of the newspaper on moral and literary issues and covered politics very briefly. Then, observing that the public preferred to read about politics rather than other issues, they broadened the political coverage.... Then, hearing that commercial news was uninteresting, they removed it completely and dedicated the paper solely to politics and literature.

Hadjinikolaou claimed that the first time that *Mnemosyne* was published, it intervened a great deal in local affairs and certain people took exception to it and had the paper closed down:

> Some say that *Mnemosyne* should not write about local affairs. This was the main complaint during the first issue of *Mnemosyne*. It created many enemies for our newspaper and they eventually managed to close it down.

That was the reason, the editor argued, why, when it resumed publication, *Mnemosyne* stayed well away from local politics and concentrated on news and politics from outside Smyrna.

> Thus, a reader of *Mnemosyne* who lives outside Smyrna and never comes to Smyrna might say: "Your newspaper is worthy and commendable. Why then is it closing down? One of two things must have happened: either other literary newspapers exist in your city, which are preferred because they are older or better; or the public of Smyrna is uncultured and therefore indifferent." It is very unfortunate that, we are forced, to our great sorrow, to confess that the latter is the reason for our closure. We are not saying this only now that our attempts have failed. We have known it all along but we thought we should try the noble, but as it turned out, useless, task of introducing neophytes [to culture]. To those few who have been supportive in our attempt and who, even now, urge us to continue, we say that every cessation is a sign of regression, or so it seems, for those things that are by nature progressive. Unfortunately, we can no longer take part in such progress because we lack the funds to do so. Your subscriptions have not been sufficient to keep *Mnemosyne* going. So, today *Mnemosyne* ascends to Mt. Helikon, the home of the Muses, her daughters; since in Smyrna, instead of adoring the Muses they prefer the cult of the Fauns and the Satyrs and other spirits that frequent swamps and bogs.

Mnemosyne was the first privately-owned Greek newspaper published in the Ottoman Empire to have a liberal-democratic political outlook. Its articles, which will be analysed in another part of this study, criticized the maladministration of Ottoman officials and named what in its view was the root of the decline of the empire: the absence of democracy and of liberal institutions.

The Newspapers of Petros Klados

After the closure of *Mnemosyne*, the baton of newspaper publishing passed into the hands of an unusual young man, Petros Klados. Between 1837 and 1842, Klados published four newspapers in Smyrna: *Ionikos Parateretes* (Ionian Observer) 1837–1840, *Ethnike* (National) and *Elpis* (Hope) 1841, and *Aster tes Anatoles* (Star of the East) 1841–1842.

Only sixteen years old when he published *Ionikos Parateretes*, Klados, who was born on the island of Chios in March 1821, was destined to become one of the most celebrated bankers of the Ottoman Empire. Soon after his birth his family moved to Smyrna, where his father, a well-known doctor, established a new practice. The young Petros attended the Evangelical School. In 1837, he founded one of the first printing presses in Smyrna, where he published *Ionikos Parateretes* with his father acting as editor. When the newspaper closed in 1840, he published *Ethnike*, and when this too closed down, after only thirty issues, he published his third newspaper, *Elpis*, in May 1841. This too encountered difficulties. In an article entitled "Men and Things," Klados laid the blame for this at the door of the conservative establishment of the city, which was averse to the idea of popularizing knowledge and preferred to keep people:

> blind, in order to suck their blood and grab the fruit of their pains and perspiration with greater ease.[21]

In the same article, Klados argued that the role of the press was to

> open the eyes of the people to what is happening in the world, to new political developments, and to their rights as citizens: as such it should enjoy the support and assistance of everyone. Although it presently enjoys the support of a progressive government, it meets with a multitude of obstacles, which, after a period of great difficulty and distress, it will eventually overcome.

When the press became more established, it would be able to withstand

> the poisoned arrows of lies and slanders cast by those who thrive in darkness against those who desire the truth.

21. *Elpis*, no. 4 (June 6, 1841).

Klados was attacking the conservative establishment of the Greeks of Smyrna, both lay and clerical, which was opposing the spread of democratic and liberal ideas in that city, of which the press and independent schools were seen as the principal carriers:

> Proof of the veracity of our words came … three weeks ago when on our literary horizon appeared two Greek newspapers: ours and *Amaltheia*, which had re-appeared after its three-month suspension. Full of worry they [the conservative establishment] complained openly about the multiplication of newspapers … and labelled our paper as inclined to be degenerate and the other as inclined to be desperate: thus offering to the friends of progress evidence of their reactionary weapons, full of deadly poison.

Klados claimed to be in contact with many foreign journalists abroad, who encouraged him to publish a newspaper. He observed that there were six newspapers and two magazines being published in Smyrna, a number he found inadequate:

> since the number of newspapers and magazines in the USA. is approximately 17,000,000; more than the population of that country:

One of the reasons for not subscribing to Greek newspapers, according to some, was that the European ones had more variety and interest. As Klados wrote:

> We agree with that and we admit that the newspapers that are published in Smyrna, the only city in the Ottoman Empire [where newspapers are published] – are indeed small in comparison [with the European ones] but do not forget that our political life, our civic society, has only just been founded here, and being still in its infancy cannot yet have the luxury of looking down on small things. Secondly, neither our means nor our position allows us to offer more. It is enough, at this stage, to make known to our compatriots the political events of Europe, in translation, so that the majority, who cannot speak a European language, are able to learn about them.

Klados argued that this was an excellent way of making oneself useful to society: "through our words as others do through their deeds." He condemned the

> anti-social behavior of those who are trying to extinguish the patriotic zeal that burns in our hearts and to inhibit the publication of solutions for curing the ailments of our society.

Klados hastened to add that he had no revolutionary desires and that he honored "all our compatriots [in the Ottoman Empire]." His sole desire was

> to publicize the ills of our society and to support truth and justice. We are interested in promoting a progressive society and in order to do that we

must be seen as examples of virtue ourselves in order to impress [on our people] their social duties.

Klados concluded his article by celebrating:

> objective and impartial journalism, which has offered many good things to our society up to now and will continue to do so. It is publicly accepted that the articles and various suggestions of journalists have often been taken up with happy results and have promoted the common interest.

A few numbers later the paper merged with *Herigeneia* (Early Morning Born, an epithet of Eos, godess of dawn). Under the title of the latter, it published only one number before it was closed down by the government, together with

> all the other newspapers of our town except the French press, for failing to obtain a publication license.[22]

Klados tried one last time to publish a newspaper. This time he managed to obtain a *firman* (official permit) allowing the publication of *Aster tes Anatoles* (Star of Anatolia), which lasted for one year (1841–42).

Klados was the first Greek publisher to take some measures to allay subscribers' fears of possibly losing their money. Having pre-paid the subscriptions for other publications, either for six months or a year, many people lost out when those publications failed. Klados' idea was to persuade people that a subscription to the newspaper was not a waste of money, displaying early on the qualities that would later make him one of the greatest bankers of the Ottoman Empire.

In its first issue, he pledged to send *Aster tes Anatoles* to subscribers of other Smyrnaean newspapers who had lost out in this way. He wrote that he had come to an agreement with their publishers. The agreement, although he does not mention it, probably involved purchasing their lists of subscribers. In no. 2, Klados announced further reassuring measures; he would issue IOUs to all his subscribers, signed by himself. Although reassuring to those willing to pay, these measures were not enough to persuade more people to pay their subscriptions. In no. 14, the editor re-printed an article from the Smyrnaean magazine *Ichnographike Apotheke* (Repository of Sketches), entitled "To the delaying [to pay] subscribers":

> A strange idea is nestling in the heads of some people. This idea is the following: they believe that the owners of magazines and newspapers, the paper producers, the printers, the press operators, and all the other warm-blooded animals that take part in the publishing business are like the chameleon, which allegedly survives by eating fresh air.... This unfortunately is not so and I can assure you that all the above-mentioned people are following the same natural laws as the rest of humanity, and require

22. *Amaltheia*, (August 2, 1841), quoted in Ch. Solomonides 1959, 134.

solid food. This misapprehension made by some who owe us money might seem quite insignificant when compared with the following: those same people think that publications are like a lower species of plant, which once planted flourishes and grows all alone, and then drops its flowers and fruit outside their front door, without any attention or cultivation on their part. It is very difficult for us to grasp how it is that such enlightened people who read newspapers and magazines have developed such idiotic beliefs!

When Klados later, in 1842, left the paper to pursue a banking career, the new editor, Kalligeris, who took over from issue no. 23, announced that no. 24 was going to be given away free, but anyone who took a copy and kept it would be considered a subscriber and would be expected to pay the six-monthly subscription in advance.

Aster tes Anatoles was Klados's fourth and last attempt at publishing a newspaper in Smyrna. This time, as we read in his publishing declaration,[23] he managed to get an imperial *firman* for his newspaper, something that he had failed to do previously. Klados claimed in his declaration that *Aster tes Anatoles* "was new only as far as the name is concerned" and "old as far as the spirit and the style of publication." This newspaper, exactly like the others before it, was intended to

> enlighten our co-nationals in the East about everything beneficial to the public at large, and to praise the good deeds of the government. It will enlighten the government about maladministration in the various parts [of the empire]. Although not the normal practice in the Empire, maladministration is considered as such by those who generalize and accuse the entire state of being thus inclined, rather than singling out individual cases of proven corruption among officials. Finally, it will enlighten our fellow Orthodox [*homoethneis*] in the east [eastern Ottoman Empire] about our foreign policy and the interests of our state." Klados added that he remained "faithful to the beliefs that we supported from the beginning," and added that "our banner will be the well-being of the people, and the exposure of their problems through this newspaper to the common father and good guardian of all, our most respected ruler.

Klados then touched on an issue that had been a thorn in the side of Smyrnaean society for some time, the personal attacks on prominent people through the press and various other publications. Klados re-assured the public and the government that

> not only are we not going to interfere in the private lives of any citizen, even among our fellow Orthodox, but we are not even going to infect our columns with paid essays of such a nature.

23. *Aster tes Anatoles*, no. 1 (January 17, 1841).

According to him, the situation had recently got out of control because of those people who were

> sitting in the journalist's chair … degrading the press, and turning it into an organ for the passions, the self-interests, the curses, and finally the moral assassination of some of our most respected citizens and fellow Orthodox.

The publisher of *Aster tes Anatoles* declared that he was prepared to confront any newspaper of Smyrna which might use derogatory language "against the government or our co-nationals," but would not stoop to use the same derogatory style of argument. Thus, he felt that he would add the weight of the newspaper to that of the government, which

> recently has taken all the measures necessary to curb the use of phrases unsuitable to the character of a journalist.

Finally, Klados hoped that the public would

> welcome *Aster tes Anatoles*, since they know well the mild and peaceful spirit of all those involved in its publication.

However, Klados left the paper to other publishers after only twenty-three issues. Two of them were Avlonites and Kalligeris, who published *Heregenia* and with whom he had previously collaborated. Having struggled to establish himself in Smyrna as a newspaper publisher, Klados turned to commerce and banking and soon became one of the most successful bankers in the Ottoman Empire, with offices in Smyrna, Constantinople, and Paris. Among the Greeks he also became famous for his generous donations to various Greek charitable foundations. Klados died in Smyrna in May 1887, and was buried with great honors.[24]

Amaltheia (1838–1924)

While Klados was trying to establish his newspapers, another newspaper made its debut in Smyrna. *Amaltheia*, which was to become the longest-running Ottoman-Greek newspaper, appeared in Smyrna in 1838. It was first published by Constantine Rodes, a man of Greek and Swedish origin (his father was Swedish and his mother a Greek from Constantinople). He was educated in the Phanar and then in Florence. He arrived in Smyrna in February 1838 from Constantinople, where he had established a printing press on the Bosphorus at Neohorion called Aghios Taphos (Holy Tomb). According to Solomonides – a later owner of

---

24. Ch. Solomonides 1959, 130.

Amaltheia and the major secondary source for all Smyrnaean Greek newspapers in our period – he arrived in the city penniless. Again according to Solomonides, Rodes presented himself to the Philologicon Mouseion, a literary and scientific club created by the Evangelical School of Smyrna, where Smyrnaean intellectuals of the time presented and discussed their works. There, he "made exhibitions of chemical experiments, and acquired admirers and patrons."[25] His dream, however, was to own a printing press and publish a newspaper. He managed to do this with the financial assistance of several Smyrnaean notables, especially Perakis Vernardos and Kyriakos Lambrylos Hadjinikolaou. In February 1839, J. Kallergis became the editor of *Amaltheia*. Approximately two years later ownership of the paper passed to Vernardos and Lambryllos Hadjinikolaou, though we do not know why these two men decided to take over, or what happened to Rodes. The new owners offered the editorship to P. Vitorides, the brother of E. Vitorides, who was then the director of the printing press of *Amaltheia*. In 1840, P. Vitorides employed as assistant editor, the lawyer Iacovos Samiotakis, who four years later in May 1844, became the owner and editor of *Amaltheia*. Samiotakis sold the newspaper to Socrates Solomonides a few months before Samiotakis' death on 7 June 1882.

Samiotakis was one of those interesting and talented characters who flourish in adversity. He was the son of the Chian notable, Nicolaos Samiotakis, who fled the island of Chios to Tenos during the Ottoman massacres of 1822, in the wake of the Greek revolution. His wife fled to Hydra, while his seven children, including Iacovos, were taken prisoner. Only four years old at the time, Iacovos managed to escape, first to Psara, and then to Tenos, from where he was sent to his uncle in Smyrna (all his brothers and sisters were bought back from the Turks by their mother's uncle, with the exception of Ioannis who died in captivity). In Smyrna, young Iacovos was placed as an assistant to Alexander Blacque, the merchant and publisher of the *Spectateur d'Orient*. Later he was sent to Basle in Switzerland to complete his high school education, and after that to the University of Heidelberg, where he graduated with honors and obtained a doctorate in law. His brilliant academic career brought him to the attention of King Ludwig of Bavaria, who invited him to his palace in Munich. The king offered him an introduction to the Greek court by entrusting him with a gilded book to bring to his son, King Otto of Greece, in Athens. Arriving in Greece, he took the examinations of the Areios Pagos [the supreme court of Greece], and obtained permission to practice law in Athens. In 1839, he entered the judiciary and was appointed public prosecutor at Patras. But the legal profession in the fledgling Greek state did not offer the young man the challenges he wanted, so at the age of only twenty-three, he abandoned his practice and returned to the more cosmopolitan life of Smyrna, becoming the editor of *Amaltheia*. In 1849, Samiotakis was invited by the admiral of the

25. Ch. Solomonides 1959, 29.

Ottoman fleet, Halil, son-in-law of the Sultan, to the fleet's flagship, where he was presented with a gold cup inlaid with precious stones for his services to the Ottoman Empire.

He was appointed correspondent for several German newspapers, including *Die Kölnische Zeitung*, and *Die Algemeine Zeitung*. He was also appointed judge in the Greek consulate in Smyrna. In 1856, he published *Triton*, a commercial supplement to *Amaltheia*, which was circulated twice a week, edited by Evangelinos Georgiannopoulos.

In 1839 *Amaltheia* was published in about fifty copies, which, according to Solomonides, was "unheard of before that in Smyrna." According to the same source, in 1846 subscriptions increased to 580.[26] *Amaltheia* itself stated that, "after increasing the number of our subscribers, we can now boast approximately 500."[27] It was remarkable that this newspaper successfully appealed to the Greek-speaking communities outside Smyrna, and not just in my period of research, but later on too. In 1845 it was sold in Constantinople, Athens, Syros, Mytilene, Bucharest, and Jassy. In later years and until the Balkan Wars "thousands of copies were circulating in Macedonia, Epirus, the Aegean Islands, and between the Greeks of Romania, Egypt, America, and elsewhere."[28]

The early content of *Amaltheia* focused largely on domestic and foreign news, and it was only after Samiotakis took over the paper in 1840 that it was enriched with commercial news, currency exchange rates for Smyrna and Constantinople, and a supplement called "Pinakeion," which serialized various foreign novels. Samiotakis also translated and published foreign poetry and had a column dedicated to literary criticism of recently published Greek books. Yet, his main contribution not only in the context of *Amaltheia* but also to the whole of the Ottoman press, was his publication of political articles critical of the government, its officials and its functions. To some degree Samiotakis followed in the footsteps of *Mnemosyne*, although his articles twice caused the paper's closure, as mentioned earlier. The first closure followed a series of articles concerning the free election of the local notables (February 1841), and the second came after another series criticizing the authoritarian government of the governor of Samos, Prince Stephanaki Vogorides (February 1844). On both occasions Samiotakis managed, through the mediation of the personal physician of Sultan Abdülmecid, Stephanos Karatheodori, to gain permission to re-issue the paper.[29] These closures are the first instances of censorship exercised against a newspaper published in the Ottoman Empire by one of its subjects.

26. Ch. Solomonides 1959, 26.
27. *Amaltheia*, no. 398 (September 13, 1846).
28. Ch. Solomonides 1959, 26.
29. Ch. Solomonides 1959, 28.

The aims of *Amaltheia* were spelled out in an article by Samiotakis,[30] replying to accusations from various Greek readers that the paper was insufficiently pro-Greek. He re-iterated the aims of the newspaper and summarized the difficulties encountered by an Ottoman publisher from the non-Muslim millets, whose readership had a developed sense of national identity. Samiotakis' unenviable task was to try to please all sides in order to protect and promote his newspaper. First, he had to satisfy the government that his newspaper would not instigate thoughts of national independence or support separatist tendencies among the Orthodox people or risk the closure of his newspaper. Secondly, he had to strike a fine balance between promoting the progressive social ideology advocated by the majority of his readers and appeasing the conservative institution of the patriarchate. Thirdly, he had to contain extreme nationalists among his Greek readers, who having lost patience with the Ottoman government and seeing the potential of a national state just across the water, were expecting a Greek newspaper to be supportive of such aims, otherwise considering it to be a traitor to the national cause. Finally, he had to cater to the majority of Orthodox Christians who, far from dreaming of national independence, were trying to survive and develop both individually and as a society within the Ottoman reality and who comprised the majority of his current and potential subscribers:

> The subscribers of each paper must know exactly the principles, the means, the position, and the aims of the paper, if they are to give their subscription to it, not just as an act of charity, but as an exchange for the purchase of something of personal benefit…. Some subscribers, and many among the readers of *Amaltheia*, have as their yardstick for judging a newspaper the language in which it is written and not the country in which it is published, thus criticizing, unfairly, the contents of *Amaltheia*…. But what is *Amaltheia*? It is a newspaper, which is published with the permission of the Ottoman government, written in the spoken Greek language, for the use of Greeks who reside in the Empire. This answer describes exactly the circle of activities and duties of the newspaper. Because it is published with the permission of the Ottoman government, it goes without saying that, at least as much as possible and according to the circumstances, it has to work for the benefit of this government. Moreover, because this newspaper is published mostly for the use of Greeks within the empire, it has to publicize to them the aims and goals of the government. These are currently brave and philanthropic and must be explained but also compared with its previous policies, which were exactly the opposite. It should also assist in the promotion of good and just feelings towards the government by the Greeks, thereby helping the success of its benevolent aims towards them.

30. *Amaltheia*, no. 428, (April 11, 1847).

Moreover, it should protect the Greek subjects of the Sublime Porte from the sad results of idiotic provocations and ineffectual hopes, and teach that nations do not live by memories of the past and hopes for the future alone, but that it would be preferable for them to accept their present condition and to try to improve it without violent changes and destruction, but rather through submitting themselves to the will of God and by being faithful subjects to the presently fatherly government of the friend of the people, Sultan Abdülmecid. So, our newspaper will be able to report to the government expressions of the true feelings of gratitude of the subject people for the, currently, impartial attitude of the government towards our nation, and to submit to the representatives of this government some just and humble requests. Finally, to contribute, as much as possible, to the enlightenment and intellectual maturity of the people. These are the duties of *Amaltheia*, which we fulfil with a clear conscience and with the highest moral hopes. It is not that we do not know that a broader type of journalism is practiced today, but our duties in Turkey during the present circumstances are these. And we hope that we are doing our best to serve both the government and the nation.

The last owner of *Amaltheia* was Socrates Solomonides, who bought it in 1882 and produced it until the end of the Greek presence in Smyrna in 1922, even continuing to publish it for a short while after emigrating to Greece. He paid 500 gold sovereigns for the newspaper rights and 150 gold sovereigns for the typographic letters and the hand-operated press. This seemingly high price might be explained by the fact that during the reign of Abdülhamid, no *firman*s were issued for the publication of new newspapers in the Ottoman Empire.[31] Newspaper publishing rights became a rare and highly desirable commodity and commanded a high price.

The Period 1839–1849

Between 1839 and 1849 several papers attempted to establish themselves in Smyrna but failed to do so either because they could not obtain a *firman*, or because they were closed down by the government, or even because they could not attract enough subscribers. These newspapers and the essential information about their editors and contents is presented below in chronological order.

Argos (1839–1840) was published by the first editor of *Amaltheia*, the Greek intellectual, Constantine Rodes,[32] after he had quarreled with the financiers of *Amaltheia*, K. Lambrylos Hadjinikolaou and P. Vernardos, and had resigned from that newspaper.

31. Kalapothakis 1928, 11.
32. For biography, see the description of *Amaltheia* above, page 50.

Ionike Melissa (Ionian Bee, 1839) was published and edited by Ioseph Magnes, who had owned a printing press and a bookshop in Smyrna.

Herigeneia (Early Morning Born, 1840–1841) was published and edited by Spiro Avlonites at the press of Ioannis Kalligeris, who, according to Solomonides, was a teacher in the school of Aghios Dimitrios, which was financed by the guild of Lampadouchoi (Torch bearers). The same guild may also have financed the press.

Hesperinos Keryx (Evening Messenger, 1842). Source: Solomonides.[33] No copy is known.

O Philos tou Laou (Friend of the People, 1842). Source: Solomonides.[34] No copy is known.

Orion (1843). Source: Solomonides.[35] Nothing is known about this newspaper except that, according to Solomonides, it was edited by Rodes[36] and published by Argyres Karavas. Solomonides provides us with a short biography of Karavas, relating that he was born in Chios and then moved to Syros, where he was educated by the renowned intellectual Neophytos Vamvas. He then went to Montpellier in France for a university education. During the Greek revolution, he returned to his country, where he fought and was awarded the highest military honor for bravery. After the cessation of hostilities in 1829, Karavas, who had an excellent knowledge of ancient Greek, modern Greek, French, and Italian, was invited by the University of Modena to teach ancient Greek. In 1833, he moved to Smyrna, where he settled, and married the daughter of the shipowner Nomicos, who was also the cousin of Andreas Syngros, a vastly wealthy businessman and banker, founder of the Banque de Constantinople, and one of the greatest benefactors of modern Greece. In Smyrna, Karavas published *Dokimion tes Stichourgias* (Essay on Versification); *To Psalterion* (Psalm Book); *Ekdikesis tou Achilleos* (Achilles' Revenge) (1847); and *Sirena: Erotica Asmata* (Siren: Love Songs) (1844). Together with I. I. Skylisses, he published the short-lived magazine *O Philologikos tes Hellenikes Glosses* (Manual of the Greek Language). He also taught ancient Greek at the Evangelical School of Smyrna. Later, he was appointed headmaster of the high school in Chios, and continued to publish various essays, as well as a second volume of the *Manual of the Greek Language*. In this, he included a poem dedicated to Sultan Abdülmecid, who, a few years earlier, had issued the Hatt-ı Hümayun. He also tried to publish another newspaper *O Philalethes* (Lover of Truth) (1845), which was closed down immediately by the authorities as he had not obtained a *firman* to publish. Karavas died in Chios in 1878.

33. Ch. Solomonides 1959, 135.
34. Ibid..
35. Ch Solomonides 1959, 136.
36. See section on *Amaltheia* above, page 50 and following.

Ephemeris tes Smyrnes, no. 85 (November 24, 1850).

O Melisegenes (September 1844–January 1845) was published by the intellectual Rodokanakes, and printed by his own press. The contents consisted of foreign and domestic news, commercial news, the price lists of various commodities, and the currency exchanges in Constantinople and Smyrna. Rodokanakes failed to attract sufficient subscribers, and eventually had to abandon publication at the beginning of 1845, so that he could concentrate on the translation of *The Wandering Jew* by Eugène Sue. In 1846, he attempted to publish another newspaper, *He Aletheia* (The Truth), but he failed to obtain the necessary *firman*. For a while, in order to bypass this problem, he tried to publish it ostensibly as a supplement of the newspaper *Ionikos Parateretes* (which had in fact ceased publication eight years previously), but it was closed down by the authorities after only a few months.

Ephemeris tes Smyrnes (1849–1854) one of the most important newspapers of the period, was published in Smyrna by Ioannis Isidorides Skylisses. From 1855 it continued life in Trieste as *He Hemera* (1855–1862).

Skylisses,[37] was born in Smyrna in 1819. His father was a Chian merchant, while his mother came from an established Smyrnaean family, the Homerides. He received his elementary education on the island of Kythera, where his family had sought refuge from the massacres of Chios. Returning later to Smyrna he was enrolled at the Evangelical School, and continued his further education at the Commercial School of Chalke. He apparently knew French from an early age and at the age of fifteen translated into Greek "La Thébaïde" of Racine. Upon the completion of his education, he returned to Smyrna, where he became deeply interested in journalism and began to collaborate with the various periodicals and magazines published there: *Argos* (1839), *Ionikos Parateretes* (1837–1840), *Mnemosyne* (1834. 1835–6), *Apotheke Ophelimon Gnoseon* (Repository of Useful Knowledge) (1837–1844), and *Amaltheia* (1838–1922). He published his first magazine in collaboration with his teacher Argyrios Karavas in 1841, called *O Philologikos Kepos tes Ionias* (The Literary Garden of Ionia), which lasted only a few issues. At the same time, he composed the poem "The Love of Hero and Leander," imitating the style of Alfred de Musset, and wrote a verse translation of *The Death of Socrates* by Alphonse de Lamartine (Smyrna 1841). Together with another Smyrnaean intellectual, Nicholaos Salteles, he published a collection of poems entitled *Evanthia* in 1844.

In 1843, Skylisses left for Paris, where he entered the University in the Faculty of Physics. At the same time, he developed an interest in politics and became a regular visitor to the French Parliament. In 1844, he publicly criticized Article 3 of the proposed Constitution of Greece. This was proposed by a number of MPs, whose initial aim was to remove some of King Otto's advisers – Greeks who hailed from the Ottoman Empire and the Greek communities of Western Europe and

37. Biographical source Solomonides 1959, 147, 151, 152, 154–158, 290, 341.

Russia. The article divided the Greeks into *autochthones* (those born within the newly-established kingdom of Greece) and *heterochthones* (those born outside Greece) and limited Greek citizenship, and its concurrent rights to the first group. Skylisses' immediate response was to write and send to the parliament of Greece a poem in which he expressed his bitterness at the division of the Greek people into first- and second-class citizens. He argued that during the Greek revolution, all the Greeks fought together and that, at that time, nobody had made the distinction between the *autochthones* and *heterochthones* Greeks. Indeed, nobody cared where Greek fighters had come from.

Immediately after this, at the end of 1844, he bought, with the assistance of a friend, Constantine Varsamis, a printing-press with which he promptly left for Smyrna. His dream of publishing a political newspaper was not to be realized until 1849, but in the meantime, he began his publishing career with a libelous book attacking the professor of the Evangelical School of Smyrna, Venediktos Konstantinidis. The book, entitled *The Man of Smyrna*, ridiculed the professor and was so offensive that it brought upon Skylisses a patriarchal reprimand. Later regretting the incident, Skylisses wrote and published a second book, entitled *Calendar*, as a kind of apology to Konstantinidis (who had meanwhile replied to Skylisses with a book called *The Donkey of Smyrna*). Skylisses named his press The Press of the Paris Mysteries after the famous novel by Eugène Sue,[38] which he published in two volumes in 1845. He also published *Memoirs of a Doctor* by Alexandre Dumas in three volumes (1846); *Leon Leoni* by George Sand (1847); *The Wandering Jew* by Eugène Sue (1846); *The Forbidden Fruit* by Octave Feuillet (1848), and a collection of his own poems called *Moments*, as well as his verse novel called *Myth* (1846).

By 1849, he had decided to fulfil his dream of publishing a political newspaper in Smyrna. He traveled to Constantinople in order to obtain permission from the minister of the interior, Âli Pasha. Despite his promises, Âli kept postponing the day of the *firman* issue, so that Skylisses was forced to attend his office every day for months until, one day, meeting the minister on his way out of his chambers, he rushed forth to remind him of his promise. The minister answered him: "Votre affaire marche, marche," to which Skylisses retorted "Oui, mon excellence, elle marche toujours comme le juif errant, sans jamais atteindre le but!'[39] Pleased by this answer, the minister then issued the necessary permits. There was, however, one important restriction, namely that the newspaper should not contain articles of a political nature. *Ephemeris tes Smyrnes*, first appeared on April 15, 1849. On its first page it stipulated that it was going to be a mixture of news and "interesting" items – the latter being, according to the words under the title, in the sphere

38. Eugène Sue (1804–1857) was translated in Greek and was very much loved by the Greeks of the Ottoman Empire, as is made clear by the new books published in serial form in the newspapers of the time. Sue was a naval doctor who took part in the Battle of Navarino in 1827.

39. Solomonides 1959, 151.

of "literature, poetry, music, sciences, and the arts." The paper also informed its public that it was printed with imperial permission and published the relevant documents to prove it.

From the start, the paper employed agents in many places. Besides Smyrna, where "subscriptions should be paid at the newspaper's printing house,"[40] they were based in Constantinople, Mytilene, Athens, Syros, Vraila, and Jassy. Skylisses offered his agents a 10% commission, and he advertised in the paper for new agents. In issue no. 20 (August 26, 1849) he advertised for agents in Alexandria and Salonica. By no. 66 (July 14, 1850) agents were recruited in Bucharest, Galatz, Salonica, Patras, and Alexandria. To facilitate communications all the agents were sited in ports, except Bucharest, which probably qualified for its own agent not because it had a considerable Greek-speaking community, but because it was the center for censorship in Wallachia. In fact, Skylisses complained bitterly about the delays in that region "even from Vraila, the newspaper had to be sent to Bucharest to be censored." He pointed out to the censor that *Ephemeris tes Smyrnes* "belonged to the category of completely harmless publications" and asked him to move the censorship office for the Greek press to Vraila, which was the entrance to Wallachia, but to no avail.[41]

Censorship was not the only problem that delayed the distribution of newspapers in the Danubian principalities. "During the winter months, postal services were not prompt."[42] The icing up of the Danube caused many problems, and the number of subscribers failed to rise in that area. Skylisses was compelled to visit the area in the late spring of 1850 to see what could be done about boosting the numbers. He came to an agreement with the *hegemon* (prince) of Wallachia, "who embraced anything to do with the spread of education with eagerness," that *Ephemeris tes Smyrnes* could be sent "from the capital [Bucharest] to the provinces of the principality together with the dispatches from the Ministry of the Interior to the local governors." Thus, Skylisses was able to reassure the "people, who know the Greek language in the province of Wallachia, and who desire to have regularly some Mediterranean newspaper – something almost impossible before, because of the irregularity of the dispatch, and postal difficulties [in winter]," that they could now obtain *Ephemeris tes Smyrnes*. In addition, he announced new agencies in Bucharest, Vraila, and Galatz, which were to cover the provinces of Moldavia.[43] That Skylisses went to such great pains to attract the mainly merchant Greek communities of the principalities is quite understandable if we consider that out of "approximately 6,000 subscribers to Greek newspapers, the overwhelming

40. *Ephemeris tes Smyrnes,* from the title page.
41. *Ephemeris tes Smyrnes*, no. 17 (August 5, 1849).
42. *Ephemeris tes Smyrnes*, no. 48 (March 10, 1850).
43. *Ephemeris tes Smyrnes*, no. 63 (June 23, 1850).

majority are merchants."[44] Of these, more than 10% became subscribers. In 1850 *Ephemeris tes Smyrnes* had "620 subscribers and rising"[45] although Skylisses insisted that "the newspaper must reach 1,000 subscribers," and urged his compatriots to subscribe, not necessarily to his newspaper, but to any Greek one:

> When one hears that in Europe fifty newspapers are published in one and the same city, of which each has between 3,000 and 50,000 subscribers, one would think that 1,000 for an area stretching from Bucharest and Jassy to Alexandria of Egypt should not be difficult to find.

He largely blamed the low subscription level on poor communications within the Ottoman Empire, which delayed both the arrival of news at the publishing houses and the delivery of papers to their readers, with the result that many people refrained from subscribing to it. However:

> The Ottoman Steamship Company line, which is being established between Smyrna, Chios, Samos, Syme, Kos, Rhodes, and Crete – see announcement at the back [of the paper] – would make the spread of the press more ample, and speedy.[46]

Another means of delivering the paper was via the French postal service. This covered Alexandria, Beirut, Constantinople, the Hellespont (Dardanelles), and Smyrna. On July 1, 1849, however, the French postal service reduced the transport price of letters under 7.5 grams but doubled the cost of the rest of the post, including the carrying of newspapers.[47] As a result:

> This measure of the French Post, which reduces the cost of sending a letter and doubles that of a newspaper, forces us to abandon the honor of exchanging our newspaper with Athenian publications, as we have been doing so far. We ended up paying 80 *kuruş* a year per issue, in transport charges alone, for each publication we exchanged. We shall, therefore, only continue our exchange with those Greek newspapers that are vital to us for our news from Greece.[48]

Although his newspaper was both popular and successful, as is clear from its high readership and the attestations of other rival papers, Skylisses decided to close it down in 1854[49] and move from the Ottoman Empire to Trieste in order to publish another newspaper aimed at the same public, namely the Greeks of the

44. *He Hemera*, no. 303 (June 23/July 5, 1861).
45. *Ephemeris tes Smyrnes*, no. 48 (March 10, 1850).
46. Ibid.
47. *Ephemeris tes* Smyrnes, no. 16 (July 29, 1849).
48. *Ephemeris tes Smyrnes*, no. 17 (August 5, 1849).
49. *He Hemera*, no. 1 (September 1/12, 1855).

Ottoman Empire. The full reasons behind the move are not clear, but the public explanation was:

> so that I would be able to write freely about the Ottoman Empire, and European countries, in order for the Orthodox Christians of the Empire to have the chance to read the truth'.[50]

We can assume that Skylisses felt restricted and frustrated in Smyrna both with the restriction on his publishing license regarding political articles and with the patriarchal censorship that had exclusive responsibility for Greek publications printed in the Empire between 1845 and 1856. Publications entering from abroad were subject only to Ottoman state censorship, which Skylisses presumably believed was preferable.

He Hemera (The Day, 1855–1862) was published in Trieste from September 1855 until September 1862 and briefly in Vienna from September 1862 to June 1863, returning to Trieste from July 1863 until December 1873. It continued publication in Trieste under the title *Nea Hemera* until 1912 and then moved to Athens, where it came out until 1936 and again after 1945 under the same title. Until 1863 it was published by Ioannis Isidorides Skylisses,[51] and can be considered a continuation of his earlier newspaper, *Ephemeris tes Smyrnes*.

Judging from the paper's distribution agencies in the empire and elsewhere, *He Hemera* enjoyed a wide readership. By 1860 it had 800 subscribers, most of whom were merchants.[52]

From its first number, *He Hemera* had agencies in Athens, Patras, Syros, Constantinople, Smyrna, Salonica, Mytilene, Chios, Alexandria, Corfu, Bucharest, Vraila, and Galatz. By 1856 agents for Adrianoupolis, Philippoupolis, Jassy, Serres, Volos, Varna, Beirut, and Cephalonia were added. One more agency, for Craiova, was added in 1857. By 1859 Cyprus and Cairo joined the ranks, and by 1862 Kydoniai and Vidin obtained their own agents. *He Hemera* could also be obtained in other areas by the agents of Austrian Lloyd Steamship Company.[53] Indeed Austrian Lloyd seems to lie behind Skylisses' decision to publish *He Hemera* in Trieste. At least it seemed to Skylisses a promising idea in 1861: "the quickest way (to distribute the paper) appeared to be via Austrian Lloyd to the Ottoman Empire."[54] But apart from Austrian Lloyd's steamships, Trieste, being part of the Austrian Empire, offered several attractions to a Greek wishing to publish a newspaper there.

---

50. *Ephemeris tes Smyrnes* was re-published for a short period in 1857 by G. D. Lambissis (see *He Hemera*, no. 70 (January 4/16, 1857).
51. Publisher of *Ephemeris tes Smyrnes*. See above, page 58 and following.
52. *He Hemera*, no. 303 (June 23/July 5, 1861.
53. Ibid.
54. Ibid.

As mentioned earlier, the publishing of foreign newspapers in the Habsburg lands was not only tolerated but encouraged, as a source of much-needed income. The location of Trieste between the Ottoman Empire and Western Europe, offered ideal opportunities for gathering news from the latter and distributing to the former. Finally, there was an affluent, albeit small Orthodox community scattered in the various cities of Austria-Hungary. For the setting up of the paper Skylisses managed to secure the assistance of Baron von Sina, an import-export merchant from Epirus, who had amassed a great fortune and a title in the Habsburg Empire, and Amvrosios Ralles, of the great Chios family, which fled to the West after the Turkish invasion and occupation. The choice of Trieste was a good one, for in the first year of its publication *He Hemera*

> not only covered its expenses but put Skylisses one thousand florins in the
> black – which he subsequently sent to Smyrna in order to enrich its local
> government's educational efforts with a physics laboratory and instru-
> ments.[55]

Skylisses continued to publish *He Hemera* in Trieste until 1861. Printed on Friday, it was loaded onto a Lloyd steamship on Saturday and arrived in Constantinople the following Thursday.[56] Areas where the steamship anchored before reaching Constantinople, like Syros, received the newspaper earlier.[57] As yet we lack information about how long it took for *He Hemera* to reach other destinations, such as Alexandria, but presumably it was as long as it took the Lloyd's steamship to get there. In 1861 Skylisses discovered that the Vienna post took just four days to reach Constantinople via Constantia on the Black Sea. The imminent creation of the new railroad between Ruschuk and Varna would make the trip even quicker and Skylisses calculated that sending the newspaper via this route would benefit most of *He Hemera*'s subscribers. On the November 1, 1861,[58] he announced the move of the newspaper to Vienna and explained:

> The Salonicans will receive it via Constantinople, the Ionian islands,
> Patras, the Albanian shores, Epirus, and Egypt would still receive it via the
> steamship service (from Trieste) and Chios, Mytilene, Smyrna, Crete and
> other places in the Mediterranean will receive it via the quickest way. So
> far the fastest way is via Trieste, but the creation of the new railroad be-
> tween Ruschuk and Varna will make the Vienna to Constantinople route
> even quicker.

55. For biography of Skylisses see Solomonides 1959, 36, 138, 147–154, 161, 282, 284, 286, 312.

56. *He Hemera*, no. 320 (October 20/November 1, 1861

57. The average time between Trieste and Constantinople by steamship (with a three hour stop in Syros and a few hours in Corfu) was 114 hours. From *He Hemera*, no. 35 (May 4/16, 1856).

58. *He Hemera*, no. 320 (October 20/November 1, 1861).

There may have been other incentives for the move to Vienna, including a chance for Skylisses to acquire his own printing house, since until 1860 *He Hemera* was printed by Austrian Lloyd. From November 8, 1860 the newspaper was printed at 782 Wollzeile Strasse in Vienna. But immediately after the move, serious problems arose over distribution. That month the Danube's waters were so low that navigation was impossible and the post had to get to Constantinople via the land route, thus lengthening instead of shortening the delivery time. The new printing-house was apparently also unsuitable, because a few months later, in April 1862, he moved *He Hemera* to a new address at 481 Reisnerhof Strasse. Because of the move only an "extra" two-page sheet appeared, no. 344. Skylisses apologized to his subscribers, describing the difficult circumstances in which he found himself: "Everything here is in disarray and many things went missing, which is very upsetting, but we will get over these difficulties soon." Despite his optimism, Skylisses could not overcome various obstacles: problems with the new printing house, difficulties in the posting of newspapers, and rising expenses. For the next six months he kept urging his subscribers to pay promptly. In no. 322 he informed the agents of *He Hemera* that the newspapers would now be sent to the agents without the name of the subscribers on each envelope, to save time and effort. "Only where there are no agents will the name of the subscriber appear on the newspaper's envelope." But things didn't work out as expected and by the end of 1862, tired and disillusioned, Skylisses came to the conclusion that moving to Vienna had not been advantageous. He abandoned both *He Hemera* and Vienna, and moved to Paris to publish the magazine *Myria Osa*, which ran for two years. Although homesick, as he admitted to a friend:

> The idea that I don't have any political or human rights in my own
> country, in my own place of birth, is unbearable. If things were different,
> Smyrna is of course the place where I would like to end my days.[59]

Yet despite these misgivings, he returned to Smyrna in 1870, and began to publish articles in that other famous Smyrnaean newspaper, *Amaltheia* (1838–1922). In 1873 he was taken ill, suffering from depression, and was advised to recuperate in Alexandria. Returning in 1886, he gave several lectures at the "Homer" club, of which he had been made an honorary member. But on his relapse with the same malady in 1890, he left for Monte Carlo and died upon his return to Smyrna in the same year.

In addition to the works mentioned earlier, Skylisses also translated *The Miser*, *The Misanthrope*, and *Tartuffe* by Molière (1851); *Fernand Duplessis* by E. Sue (1852); *Lucretia Borgia* by Victor Hugo (1852); *The Janissaries* by Rose; *The Seven Deadly Sins* (1843), and *Adalbert* by E. Sue (1850); *The Memoirs of a Doctor* by

59. Ch. Solomonides 1959, 27.

Piton (1851), and the *Hugolic* passage from Dante's *Inferno*. Under the pseudonym Cleon Gelon (literally, "crying, laughing"), he published a poem in 1868 entitled "God listen to the voice of your sorrowful people," dedicated to Crete, which was in revolt against Ottoman occupation. Under the same name he also published an essay entitled "Le Russisme Grec," a poem addressed to the historian Fallmerayer and a political poem "Greeks and Greek Citizens" (*Hellenes kai Helladitai*). In the latter, he accused the Greeks of Greece of impudence, as he thought that all Greeks should be allowed to participate in the government of their country and not only those born in the state of Greece. He also wrote a comedy, frequently performed in Smyrna, entitled *You are Mad* (*Eisai Trelle*).

Together with *Vyzantis* (1854–1857), *Amaltheia* (1838–1922), and *Anatole* (1850–1922?; in Karamanlı Turkish), *Ephemeris tes Smyrnes* is among the most noteworthy of Ottoman newspapers of its time.

The Years 1851–1861

Between 1851 and 1861, three more attempts were made to publish newspapers in Smyrna but they all failed. *Iris* appeared in 1851, *Emporikos Tachydromos tes Smyrnes* (Commercial Post of Smyrna) in 1856 and *Telegraphos tes Smyrnes* (Telegraph of Smyrna) in 1859.

Our information regarding *Iris* comes from an announcement in *Amaltheia* (May 1, 1852), which describes it as divided into two parts, the first dedicated to commercial news (*emporikes eideseis*), and the second to literature (*philologike stele*). Works by Byron and *Orlando* by Ariosto, both translated by Lambyses, appeared in the literary section. Solomonides,[60] writes that *Iris* was published by P. Ioannides and D. Christoyannopoulos but it did not last long. Nothing else is known about this newspaper.

Emporikos Tachydromos (Commercial Post), was also advertised in *Amaltheia* (1 January 1856), which mentions that "a commercial newspaper called *Emporikos Tachydromos tes Smyrnes* is being published twice a week." Solomonides mentions that it was a short-lived paper. This newspaper is also mentioned by Mayer, who gives the date of publication as 1857.[61] Nothing else is known of this paper.

We know from Solomonides[62] that *Telegraphos tes Smyrnes* was published by N. Stamelos, former printing manager of *Amaltheia*. He left that paper in 1849, and opened his own printing house in the Schoinadika (rope makers' area) of Smyrna, where he published his own and other books. He also had a bookshop in

---

60. Ch. Solomonides 1959, 161.
61. Mayer 1960.
62. Ch. Solomonides 1959, 331.

Yol Bedesteni, where he founded the first "lending library in Smyrna, and everyone who wishes can apply and register."[63] Ginis gives the year 1859 as the publication date of *Telegraphos tes Smyrnes*[64] and Solomonides the years 1859–61. The latter also mentions that in 1863 *Telegraphos tes Smyrnes* attempted to publish again but failed to obtain the necessary *firman* and was closed down immediately. Nothing else is known about this newspaper.

The Years 1861 and Following

From 1861–1870, *Euseveia* (*Piety*) was published by Archdeacon Ignatios at the printing press of P. Makropoulos. Between no. 3 (23 February 23, 1861) and no. 4 (August 24, 1861) there is a gap of six months. The reason for this was again that the newspaper was first published without a *firman* and was consequently closed down. However, the publisher, after a six-month stay in Constantinople, managed to obtain one.[65]

The publisher, Ignatios, archdeacon of the metropolis of Smyrna and later bishop of Xanthoupolis and metropolitan of Libya, explained in issue no. 1 (February 9, 1861) why he had decided to publish a religious newspaper. In a declaration aimed at "the holy clergy of the Orthodox Church of Christ and our pious Christian fellow nationals" (the word used is *homogeneis* 'of the same nation or fellow countrymen') the archdeacon claimed that:

> with great sorrow I observed that although our nation ... is daily enriched
> with beautiful and most beneficial works of a religious, scientific, and po-
> litical nature, it has suffered from a very harmful omission: the absence of
> an ecclesiastical newspaper. I noticed that a newspaper that takes no part
> in politics, but occupies itself solely with ecclesiastical and moral studies
> ... defending our clergy and our church against attacks; a newspaper that
> encourages and builds piety for the people, and upholds the patristic
> and Holy traditions, both by advising and telling the true history of our
> Church, does not exist. Our newspaper will publish the minutes of our
> Holy Church in general, and the God-pleasing actions of our clergy, and
> will describe the donations and other actions beneficial to the public, the
> progress of schools or our other institutions ... and wherever they do not
> function properly, will bring it to the attention of the public, so that this
> can be corrected by public scrutiny and pressure.

He also wrote that he would publish important speeches by the clergy and explain

63. Advertisement in *Ephemeris tes Smyrnes* (March 9, 1851).
64. Ginis 1967.
65. See *Euseveia*, no. 4 (August 24, 1861).

to the general public some difficult passages in the scriptures. He mentioned that he undertook this task of publishing a newspaper fully cognizant of the great difficulties, and of the time and money needed in order to fulfil this need.

In Sum

Euseveia was the last paper to be started in Smyrna within our period of study and already in its contents we can observe the focus of the press beginning to deviate from political issues to cultural and religious content. Greek newspaper publishing in Smyrna, which was begun by Protestant missionaries and followed by the Greek reaction to them, soon passed into the hands of editors who were imbued with the new liberal democratic ideals that were gathering strength in the city. These editors were a well-educated, idealistic group of people, full of ingenuity and courage, and dedicated to the freedoms of democracy. They believed they could improve their compatriots' lives through the medium of the press. Few of the Smyrna newspapers were successful or long running. Most were short-lived ideological expressions of their editors. One of them, however, *Amaltheia* withstood the test of time and even endured the expulsion of Greeks from their ancestral homeland in 1922. Although the Smyrna press did not possess the appearance and greater political gravitas of that in Constantinople, it was entertaining, imaginative, and educational, and remains a valuable source of information for the political, private, and public life of the Greeks and other nationalities living in that city during the period under review.

Chapter 3

The Greek Newspapers
of Constantinople 1843-1862

THE OTTOMAN GREEK PRESS had already been established in Smyrna for twelve years before the first newspaper appeared in Constantinople. Some possible reasons for this significant delay were outlined earlier in this study and chiefly reflected the attitudes of the conservative establishment of the Ottoman Greeks in the capital with their cautious approach to innovations of a political nature that might draw a negative response from the government. It can be affirmed that in contrast to the Ottoman Greeks of Smyrna, the Ottoman Greeks of Constantinople were considerably less enthusiastic about newspaper publishing throughout the period we are examining. In fact, a Greek from the Ionian Islands, Demetrios Xenes, became the most prominent newspaper publisher in Constantinople, shielded as he was by his powerful British passport.[1]

The cautiousness of Constantinopolitan Ottoman Greeks towards publishing their own newspapers suggests that they had yet to be convinced of the true intentions of the Ottoman government towards the subject peoples. In the next chapter, evidence is offered from Constantinopolitan Ottoman Greeks who were privy to the thinking of Ottoman officials that the situation of the Rum following the Greek revolution remained, in their opinion, tenuous. On the other hand, the audacious approach of the Smyrnaean Ottoman Greeks towards establishing a political presence through the press could also be seen as supporting the notion that outside the capital the control and influence exercised by the Ottoman government at that time was minimal.

Five newspapers were published in Constantinople from 1843 to 1862. Copies of almost all of them are in the Benakeios Collection, in Athens. Among the five I have included *Othomanikos Menytor* (Ottoman Messenger), the Greek translation of *Takvim-i Vekayi*, published by the Ottoman government for the benefit of the Rum milleti.

All the surviving newspapers are described in depth using, in addition to the newspapers themselves, any secondary information available. Where newspapers have not survived, I was restricted to secondary sources.

---

1. The Ionian islands were a British protectorate between 1815 and 1863.

TELEGRAPHOS TOU VOSPOROU 1843–1857

The first publisher of *Telegraphos tou Vosporou* (Telegraph of the Bosporus) was Constantine Adosides, who had been an employee of the Porte since 1841.[2] His father, Atos Ağa, was a sculptor from Asia Minor. According to Gedeon, Constantine's father was a good Christian. Adosides knew little Greek but had an excellent command of Ottoman Turkish. In 1850, Adosides published a book entitled *Elements of Ottoman Grammar,* which he dedicated to Sultan Abdülmecid. Because of his difficulties with Greek, he employed Constantine I. Photiades as the editor of *Telegraphos.* Photiades was an intellectual hailing from an important Phanariot family. His son, Ioannis, married in December 1852 the daughter of Prince Stephanake Vogorides Domnitsa. The Photiades-Vogorides family alliance was considered so powerful that the Sultan himself attended the wedding. Two assistant editors worked with him on *Telegraphos tou Vosporou*: I. I. Skylisses and Elias Tantalides. As we have seen in the previous chapter, Skylisses later became the publisher of *Ephemeris tes Smyrnes* (Smyrna, 1849) and *He Hemera* (Trieste, 1855). Tantalides was a well-known Constantinopolitan poet and orator.

After running *Telegraphos* for seven years Constantine Photiades felt that changes and improvements should be made. In issue no. 339 (June 1850) we read:

> We would like to make our newspaper worthy of our city and contribute towards the intellectual maturity of our nation in everything good, great, and sincere. We have the zeal to improve ourselves. Thus: a) our pages will be larger than before; b) the contents will have even more variety; c) each number will carry a serious article relating to the major event of the week and will include analysis and criticism [and] will also carry a political review; d) because we have (already) established correspondents in all the major Ottoman cities and are gradually establishing others in European cities also, we will publish the latest and most important news as soon as we receive it from the steamships and through the post and by any other means; e) in order that the public may be informed of Government Acts, we will frequently translate [passages] from the Official Section of *Takvim-i Vakayi.* Also, for the various items of internal news, we shall read all the other local papers; f) in order for this to be worthy of the public and able to satisfy the curiosity of our muse-loving nation, from time to time we shall publish literary reviews and report on education and its progress in Constantinople; g) we will also publish book-reviews and a critique of every new book published …; h) every week we shall translate half a page of the most interesting foreign novels … which will come out in the form of a supplement … which eventually will be bound into a book; i) commercial news will have a place in our paper, as well as [news of] the

2. Gedeon 1932, 42.

movements of goods in every major domestic and foreign port; j) the latest discoveries and archaeological finds will always be mentioned. *Telegraphos* will continue to come out every Saturday so that it can be transported on the Trieste steamship, which on its way to Trieste first passes through the Dardanelles to Smyrna, Mytilene, Syros, etc., and Salonica, so that all our subscribers will receive our newspaper promptly…. *Telegraphos* will not act merely as a telegraph of news … but will enter into fierce debate and argument: … our intention is to correct lies and one-sided views … our reporting will be completely impartial … and we hope that the public will recognize our contribution and subscribe to it.

In 1853 Adosides sold the newspaper to Demetrios Xenes. It is not clear why he gave it up after ten years. Perhaps, the continuous struggle to collect subscriptions became too much for him. Reminders to subscribers to pay their subscriptions appeared constantly in the paper.

The new owner of *Telegraphos* was an unusual man. Born in the Ionian islands he had managed to obtain high rank in the Ottoman civil service, yet had prudently kept his British passport, which gave him extra protection.

Xenes was a flamboyant character, who had attracted the faithful friendship and admiration of some powerful Turks. Among these were the grand vizier, Âli Pasha and the minister of police, Hüsnü Pasha. According to Gedeon, Xenes was the only Greek journalist in Constantinople who owned a horse and employed a footman who followed him through the streets of the capital. Because of his friendship with powerful individuals, he was often able to mediate in favor of his fellow Orthodox, Russian as well as Greek. Gedeon mentions some events that explain the high regard in which Xenes was held both by the Greeks and the Russian Embassy. For example, 1867 saw the arrival in Constantinople of a ship full of prisoners taken at the Battle of Vaphai in Apokorona, Crete. Among them was the nephew of Manolakes Argyropoulos, sometime first secretary at the Russian Embassy in Constantinople. Argyropoulos and the Russian Embassy decided not to involve themselves directly in attempts to free his nephew and the other prisoners, but instead asked Xenes to help, since the prisoners were all from good families. Xenes acquiesced. When the ship docked,

> the prisoners saw Xenes, a man unknown to them, embarking with four or five soldiers and two officers. He then showed the captain a document he was carrying with him and took all the Greek prisoners, most of them officers in the Greek army, to a hotel in Galata. There he dismissed the Turkish soldiers and told the marveling prisoners that they were to be the guests of Sultan Abdülmecid until they left the country.

According to Gedeon, also in 1867, Xenes managed to persuade the sultan to extend his hospitality, in the grandest manner, to the famous Greek chieftain, Hadji Michali, and to the Greek colonel who was his companion and aide-de-camp. They lived as the sultan's guests in great luxury in the Hotel des Anglais in Constantinople, and were seen accompanying Xenes to the patriarchal church for various services. Gedeon remembers how:

> we children gathered round in the church courtyard to see this chieftain, with his heroic appearance [he had killed an unspecified number of Turks] and his long black beard.[3]

Xenes belonged to the "democratic" group in Constantinople, which sometimes

3. See Gedeon 1932, 45.

challenged church authority and, on several occasions, took a stand against the autocratic ways of the patriarchs, especially Anthimos VI. For example, during the months of August and September 1873:

> there were several small demonstrations against the unbearable rule of the Patriarch Anthimos VI.... At that time, in his house in the Phanar, Dr. Theodoros Georgiades (the democrat in opposition to Anthimos) created the "Committee of the Greek Nation" (*Epitrope tou Romaikou Ethnous/ Rum Milletinin Komisyonu*). Although there was already a National Mixed Council (that is, lay and clergy) having meetings in the Patriarchate, which had been authorized by the Sublime Porte, the then Minister of Foreign Affairs, Reşid Pasha, once received Georgiades' committee as the representatives of the Rum milleti.[4]

This act, which went against the government line, shows the influence Xenes and some other individuals exerted on Ottoman ministers. Further evidence of this is contained in the following report:

> [S]ome members of this committee used to go into the Patriarchal Church and shout, "Down with the Patriarch!" The Patriarch would have them arrested by the police, but then Dr. Georgiades would inform Xenes. He would immediately tell the first Dragoman of the Russian Embassy, Michael Onou, who had them released at once.[5]

Although Xenes opposed the patriarchate many times, accusing it of maladministration, he was still highly respected by that establishment. In 1868 and 1869 he was invited "by the most senior metropolitans to accept a position in the Mixed National Council of the Patriarchate. Patriarch Gregory VI also wanted him to be a national councilor." Xenes, however, persistently refused. In 1876 the Holy Synod and the mixed national council decided to honor him by naming his newspaper *Vyzantis* as the official ecclesiastical newspaper, "because it had corrected the lies and rumors that had circulated against the Great Church and was publishing, free of charge, all the articles contributed by the Patriarchate" (Gedeon was probably referring to the struggle which led to the creation of an independent Bulgarian Church and to the Pan-Slavist movement, which led eventually to the foundation of Greater Bulgaria in 1878). Moreover, "all the senior clergy were subscribing in the years 1876 and 1877."[6]

Xenes was a Russophile all of his life, even "during the difficult years 1874–

---

4. Ibid. The Committee of the Greek Nation was an unofficial group created by political opponents of the established system to oppose the patriarchate, whereas the national mixed councils were official decision-making bodies of the patriarchate, approved by the Ottoman government. For further discussion of national councils, see below, page 111, note 113.

5. Ibid.

6. Ibid.

1877,"[7] His support earned him the high regard of the Russian Embassy, which always came to his assistance. But he became alienated from those Greeks who harbored pro-Western sympathies; Demetrios Aristarches, for instance, "publicly and in writing had called him a despicable gazetteer, a sick mercenary who rules with his money, and a mare-rider."[8] Other Greeks, including Gedeon himself, who honored and respected the Russians, remained friends of Xenes until he died, at the end of the nineteenth century.

The Ottoman government also supported Xenes, until September 1871, when his great friend Âli Pasha died and Hüsnü Pasha, as a consequence, fell from power. An investigation was made into the expenses accrued during the time that Hüsnü was in charge of the police and:

> they found in the accounts that thirty Turkish *lira*s a month had been given to Xenes Efendi. When the Chief Inspector of accounts asked Hüsnü why the money had been given, he answered that it was because "it had been demanded by his office" (that is, his superiors).[9]

When Xenes first took over *Telegraphos* in Jan. 1853, he announced his policy for the paper on the front page:[10]

> I am going to make this paper equal to the other Greek newspapers of Turkey. *Telegraphos tou Vosporou* is the only newspaper in the Capital that is published in our language. Through the quality of our newspaper, I shall persuade those Greek citizens of our Capital who already buy foreign newspapers to subscribe to *Telegraphos tou Vosporou* also. I have asked scientists and intellectuals to contribute articles. I shall frequently publish the Official Acts of the Imperial Government as well as those of the Great Church of Christ. I shall add a commercial page and publish new, high quality French novels in the literary supplement. I shall retain an unreserved respect for the Government and for the Great Church of Christ but if some authority is guilty of embezzlement or bad government, I shall expose it, in order to force Central Government to take action; a deed, which will accord with the philanthropic and courageous sentiments of HM the Sultan. I shall defend our Holy Religion against the malpractice of its enemies and the false accusations of paid agents of other religions. Finally, I shall attack any bad behavior among senior clergy.

After a year at the helm of *Telegraphos tou Vosporou* Xenes succeeded in increasing its popularity and readership. In an article in no. 520 (12 December 1853),

7. Ibid.
8. Ibid.
9. Ibid.
10. *Telegraphos tou Vosporou*, no.471 (January 3, 1853).

almost a year after he had bought the newspaper, he wrote about the importance of journalism and the success of his paper:

> Public opinion, whose wider expression is independent and prudent journalism, is the refuge of honesty, the terror of criminals and the invincible shield of the true interests of every nation. Through journalism nothing remains secret and nothing interesting remains hidden. From the smallest anecdote of social life to the most important political event, everything is publicized in newspapers of every color. The most important task of the newspaper is constantly to enlighten people about their real interests, to expose fraud and maladministration, and point the way to improvement. This newspaper has been under our direction for almost a year and the large number of new subscribers has, on the one hand, reassured us that we have not been considered by all to be of no use to our nation, and, on the other, has encouraged us to remain and indeed to continue to progress in the future along the lines we have set out.

By November 1856 *Telegraphos tou Vosporou* was going so well that Xenes announced that it would be published twice a week.[11] The previous July "the imperial government allowed Mr. Xenes to publish a second newspaper in Constantinople."[12] This was *Vyzantis*, which soon after merged with *Telegraphos tou Vosporou* to create *Telegraphos tou Vosporou kai Vyzantis*.

In 1863 *Telegraphos tou Vosperou kai Vyzantis* changed its name to *Vyzantis*. It kept this name until the death of its publisher, Xenes.

ANATOLIKOS ASTER 1861–1894

According to Gedeon, the main source for this newspaper, *Anatolikos Aster* (Eastern Star) was published by three teachers from the Megale tou Genous Schole (Great School of the Nation): Ioannes Philalethes, Constantine Photiades, later governor of Samos, and Vassilios Kalliphron. They employed several editors; among them were, between 1862 and 1864, Stavros Voutyras, a well-known Constantinople intellectual, who later became editor of the newspaper *Neologos* (Constantinople); between 1862 and 1865, Demetrios Nikolaides, later editor of *Constantinoupolis* (Constantinople) and *Pericles Hen*, who also translated novels. *Anatolikos Aster* marks the beginning of a new era in Ottoman Greek journalism, in which political news and criticism were gradually replaced by personal and partisan attacks within the Rum milleti. According to Gedeon, *Anatolikos Aster* "under the influence of Sophronios, metropolitan of Arta, scathingly attacked the old patriarch Ioakeim

---

11. *Telegraphos tou Vosporou*, no. 671 (November 10, 1856).
12. *Telegraphos tou Vosporou*, no. 656 (July 28, 1856).

II, and corrupted the minds and hearts of Orthodox Greek youth by teaching them unbridled bad language ... and because of this, Philalethes and Photiades withdrew quite early on and Kalliphron remained the sole owner."

The paper's public arguments with another publication, *Omonoia* (Concord, 1862–1871), are legendary and exemplify what journalism was reduced to from this period onwards. Although just beyond the period covered in this book I will discuss them briefly as an example of the kind of journalism that prevailed in the 1860s and 1870s.

According to Gedeon, Demetrios Katselides, the publisher of *Omonoia* was from Samos:

> an ex-merchant, who was unlucky in his commercial enterprises but who could not have been more fortunate in his choice of a wife, for he married the niece of the Metropolitan of Chalkedon, Gerassimos, a man very powerful in the Church. He supported *Omonoia* because it belonged to a relative and also supported (his friend) the Patriarch Ioakeim II. It is said that Ioakeim gave a lot of money to Katselides for *Omonoia*.[13]

The patriarch and the synod, in an encyclical of May 1862 to all monasteries, recommended the purchase of *Omonoia*. In July 1863 *Omonoia* lost its protector, Ioakeim, and a little later began to be published in a smaller format. "From time to time it would be closed down by the Turkish press office; then it would appear again, either to replace a paper that had closed down or to unite with another, such as *Neologos*, or it would come out in a small size. In 1870, *Omonoia* was taken over by the famous journalist Vlassios Gavrielides, who had just arrived in Constantinople.[14] After only a year, however, *Omonoia* closed down permanently.

In its introductory article (9 May 1862) *Omonoia*[15] promised to try to

> avoid discussion and criticism, so that people are able to reach their own conclusions. Also, we shall avoid any personal insult, attack, quarrel, or slander, but we shall not be afraid to attack anyone who speaks against the actions of the government or who insults our Holy Church ... always, of course, in pursuit of the truth.

Although *Omonoia* had pledged not to quarrel with anyone, it could not entirely keep to this resolution. To be fair, it was provoked into conflict by *Anatolikos Aster*, whose publishers had declared war on the great protector and benefactor of *Omonoia*, the patriarch Ioakeim. By association, hostilities with the paper became inevitable. On Friday 18 May 1862, *Anatolikos Aster* published the minutes of

---

13. Gedeon 1932, 18-19.
14. Ibid.
15. *Omonoia*, no. 1 (May 9, 1862).

the mixed national council, at which, apparently, a great deal of time had been devoted to *Omonoia. Anatolikos Aster* concluded that:

> [*Omonoia*] is not an official ecclesiastical paper, neither is it well known to the public as such, at least at present. It does not have the credentials of an ecclesiastical newspaper, nor does the Council know about the way it was created or its means of support. Because of this, the matter of *Omonoia* [in the national council] was tabled. It was agreed that it would be discussed at a later date.

The following Wednesday, *Omonoia* published what it considered to be ample proof "for the unbiased" that it was indeed an ecclesiastical paper:

> His Holiness the patriarch, a year and a half ago, conceived the idea of creating an ecclesiastical newspaper, for which the National Council had already made provision, but which had not yet come into being because their resolutions had not been implemented. They needed a paper which would, simultaneously, set right remarks made by enemies of our church against our clergy, publish essays about the intellectual, moral, and religious capacity of the nation, and tighten the bonds that bind the holy clergy to the nation by publicizing the official Acts of the Holy Synod and the National Mixed Council. By publishing those Acts we shall prove, to those who do not consider *Omonoia* an ecclesiastical paper, what its true mission is. The future course of *Omonoia* will persuade anyone who is unbiased that *Omonoia* is not only as well known, but also has the credentials of an ecclesiastical newspaper.[16]

This answer did not fully repudiate the accusations of *Anatolikos Aster* that *Omonoia* was "not an ecclesiastical paper," but rather revealed the special relationship with the patriarch, who in supporting the publication of *Omonoia* as an ecclesiastical paper did so of his own accord without the knowledge or agreement of either the synod or the mixed council (as the grand archivist of the patriarchate, Gedeon, in his mention of *Omonoia*, recorded).[17] This fact appears to have been known to the editors of *Anatolikos Aster*, who used it to attack *Omonoia* and, indirectly, Ioakeim II, at every opportunity.

In July 1862 *Anatolikos Aster* claimed that the chief editor of *Omonoia*, G. Polychroniades, was providing political [that is, "inside"] information about the Great Church and the government to foreign newspapers. Polychroniades answered in an article entitled "*Anatolikos Aster*," in which he wrote:

> [T]he three professors of the Great School of the Nation ... consider jour-

16. *Omonoia*, no. 5 (May 23, 1862).
17. Gedeon 1832, 18-19.

nalism their monopoly and instead of fulfilling their sacred mission to the
public are involved in slanderous remarks and such-like. The public knows
who the editors of this newspaper are … and how slanderous were their
remarks about me in their last number… and that neither the government
nor the Holy Church would believe such things…. These gentlemen concluded that I pass on information to various foreign newspapers because
I am the agent of various foreign newspapers (in Constantinople). This
is something that goes against the grain of my character. It is well known
that I have a great respect for the government and I call on these people to
prove their slanderous remarks; otherwise they will be regarded by me and
by the public exactly as the law regards slanderers…. [W]e are not going
to get involved in the delirium emanating from the teachers of the Great
School of the Nation and will continue to fulfil our duty to the nation.[18]

Polychroniades stopped short of threatening *Anatolikos Aster* with a libel action,
which might indicate that the accusations against him, but also indirectly against
Patriarch Ioakeim, could have some substance. Ioakeim was allegedly passing
information to "enemy agents."

In October 1862 *Anatolikos Aster* again attacked *Omonoia* and its patron,
Patriarch Ioakeim, as being "harmful to the national interest." *Omonoia* tried to
refute this by claiming the accusations were merely a rhetorical exercise with no
substance. Both the moderates and the reformists among the Greeks despised
Ioakeim, who was widely considered a supporter of the senior clergy and stood
accused of embezzlement and other criminal acts. He was also instrumental in
enraging the Bulgarian delegates in the mixed national council, which eventually
brought about the schism with the mother church.[19] In July of 1863 *Omonoia*'s
protector, Ioakeim, was deposed and it closed down, although a little later it began
to be published again in a small format.

Anatolikos Aster closed down permanently in 1891, a few months before its
owner, Kalliphron, died at the age of 73.

OTHOMANIKOS MENYTOR 1834–1840 (?)

There are indications by certain Turkish scholars, such as Selim Nüzhet,[20] Server
Iskit,[21] and Orhan Kolloğlu,[22] that this newspaper was the Greek version of *Takvim-i
Vekayı*. I have been unable to find any copies of this newspaper and am therefore
compelled to rely on Manuel Gedeon for information:

18. *Omonoia* no. 25 (August 1, 1862).
19. See Christovitz and Karatheodori 1860. See also Collins 1983.
20. Nüzhet 1931, 32, 33.
21. Iskit 1937, 1.
22. Kolloğlu 1989; Kolloğlu 1981, 38, 41.

Eight years before the publication of the *Telegraph* (probably in 1835) the newspaper *Othomanikos Menytor* began publishing in small size in the Greek language. Its editor was Ioannis, or Yangos,[23] Mousouros. In 1867 this man became a member of the Council of the (Ottoman) State, as he was fluent in both Greek and [Ottoman] Turkish. It seems that *Othomanikos Menytor* was an official, or semi-official, newspaper of the [Ottoman] Turkish State. A letter from the Metropolitan of Chios, Sophronios, in 1840, informs us that this newspaper was imposed [by the patriarchate acting for the government?] on the Metropoles and Bishoprics belonging to the Patriarchate of Constantinople and perhaps on the other Patriarchates in the Empire, but with some restraint. For example, in the whole of Chios, only three issues were ever imposed. [*Othomanikos*] *Menytor* lasted for about six years, since as far as I have been able to ascertain it was in existence in 1840. I have seen some numbers in the personal collection of old newspapers and magazines belonging to my friend, the bookseller George Ladas, who allowed me to have a look at them. I have found no other information on this paper.[24]

There is one more reference that might either be referring to *Othomanikos Menytor* or to *Takvim-i Vekayı*:

> The patriarchate was required to find Greek subscribers for the newspaper of the Turkish government. Carrying out this command, in 1842 the patriarchate submitted to the Porte the money of 130 subscribers.[25]

Both the above quotations show that the Ottoman government tried, at least for some years, to impose the reading of and collecting money for its official newspaper from the millets. Although our information relates solely to the Rum milleti, it seems unlikely that the Ottoman government tried to impose this measure only on them and not on the other millets.

In Sum

The journalists of Constantinople appear to belong to a different breed to those of Smyrna. While the latter's publishers and editors came from the rising commercial or intellectual classes, most of the Constantinople journalists were hommes des affaires connected either with the Ottoman or the patriarchal establishment, or both. Yet, despite their standing and connections, the individual who dominated

---

23. When he was a student at the Megali tou Genous Schole, under the schoolmaster Logadis, sometime before 1830, Mousouros signed his name as "Yangos."

24. Gedeon 1932, 49–52.

25. Sokolov 2013, 359.

the Constantinople Greek press was Demetrios Xenes, an Ionian island-born Greek with a British passport. This passport and his friendships both with Âli Pasha and the Russian Embassy enabled him to produce a group of political newspapers with impunity. The only other newspaper from outside what became the Xenes group of newspapers during our period of review was *Anatolikos Aster*. Despite its grand entrance in the sphere of journalism and despite being manned by several highly erudite individuals, *Anatolikos Aster* marked the beginning of a new era in Ottoman Greek journalism, in which political news and criticism were gradually replaced by personal and partisan attacks, mostly within the Rum milleti. This kind of journalism, which began in the 1860s, reduces the credibility of the Ottoman Greek press as a primary source for charting the political development of the Ottoman Empire and in particular of the Rum population. Yet, it remains useful for the study of the social and cultural development of the Rum milleti and as such merits further study.

Chapter 4

Reforms in the Ottoman Empire through the Lens of Its Greek Newspapers

SULTAN SELIM III (1789–1807) is credited with initiating an era of reform, which lasted for most of the nineteenth century. His aim was to regenerate the empire by shifting the locus of state control back into the hands of the Sublime Porte, chiefly by centralizing the administration, eliminating the opposition of entrenched elites, and reforming the army. The Treaty of Jassy (1792) persuaded Selim III that the improvement in the position of the Christian population in Turkey was paramount. As soon as he came to the throne, he issued a *hatt* in which he explained the defeats at the hands of the Russians by the general "unhealthy atmosphere" in the empire at the time, and instructed everyone to reassess their behavior particularly in state and military matters:

> The Sultan was helped in his reforming work by several members of the Greek aristocracy. Among those deserving mention are the names of Prince Alexander Hypsilantes and his son Constantine, who not only supported the Sultan in his humane undertaking, but helped him by both advice and action, inspiring him with the ideas of Empress Catherine's famous "Greek project." Following the Russo-Turkish war Alexander Hypsilantes even drew up a project of social and political reform for Turkey, which he presented to the Sultan. Under this project the Christians were to be given equal status in all respects with the Sultan's Muslim subjects and to be made full citizens of the empire, enjoying all rights.[1]

Although Selim could not implement these reforms, as they went against Islamic practice, the well-being and interests of the non-Muslim subjects of the Porte became an important aspect of the reform program in the nineteenth century. There were several reasons for that. As a result of the Treaty of Küçük Kaynarca (1774), and Treaty of Jassy (1792) the Ottoman government had had to accept interference in the internal affairs of the Ottoman state by conceding to Russia the role of protector of the Orthodox Christians in the empire. In addition, the Orthodox Christians, arguably the most dynamic and politically developed group in the empire, were becoming increasingly dissatisfied with their political situation.

1. Philimon 1859, I:13, 261, quoted in Sokolov 2013, 154.

79

An offer of improvement in their conditions could both negate the pretexts for Russian interference and keep the Orthodox Christians on board. Mahmud II's efforts began a sustained period of change continued by his successors, Abdülmecid and Abdülaziz, known as Tanzimat (Reordering/Reformation).

The eighteenth century was a landmark for the Ottoman Greek society as well. Several groups of Orthodox Christians began to challenge the absolute authority both of their immediate leadership and of the Ottoman state leadership. The political struggles between the upwardly mobile strata of Ottoman Greek society and the Patriarchate of Constantinople in its political guise were discussed in the first chapter of this study. To these should be added the demands for political independence formulated on behalf of the Orthodox Christians by Regas Pheraios (1757–1798), writer, political thinker, and member of the Greek Enlightenment, in the 1790s, culminating in the Greek War of Independence in 1821. The reforms, already under way during the Greek Revolution, would not prevent the establishment of the Greek state in 1830; but its establishment dispelled any doubt among the Ottoman leadership that serious reforms of both the Ottoman army and Ottoman political institutions needed to be undertaken.

THE TANZIMAT

Tanzimat (Arabic for reforms) is the collective name given to a series of reforms revolving around two main imperial decrees, known as the Hatt-ı Şerif of Gülhane (1839) and the Hatt-ı Hümayun (1856).[2]

The former established the necessary preconditions for the creation of a new political order in the empire, which would guarantee the security of life, honor, and property of all the sultan's subjects, irrespective of their religion. The decree also announced the establishment of a regularized system for assessing and levying taxes in order to combat corruption, and introduced a new system of conscription and training for the Ottoman army. The second decree, the Hatt-ı Hümayun, was promulgated after the Crimean War, in 1856, and is believed to have been largely dictated by Great Britain and France. The decree opened the doors of the civil service to all citizens of the state. It also made possible the establishment of community schools independent of religious authorities by placing their teachers under the control of a mixed council whose members were appointed by imperial decree. In addition, legal reforms dealt with equality in the courts, which were commanded to accept the evidence of both Muslims and non-Muslims as equally valid. Judges of commercial, common, and criminal law courts had to be drawn from all religious backgrounds and laws had to be promulgated and translated

2. See, for example, Lewis 1966, 75 ff.

into all the languages spoken in the empire.[3] Torture in prisons was forbidden and the police force was to be reformed in order to offer equal protection to everyone. Following the conscription laws of 1839, the new decree ordered that it should be indiscriminate. Several articles dealt with the formalities of buying, selling, and inheriting property. Banking was established as an institution and the improvement in communications became a major concern of the government. Trade was mentioned as being of paramount importance to the state and every government restriction that jeopardized trade or the development of agriculture was lifted. Embezzlement by civil servants and local governors became severely punishable. Although a free trade agreement with Great Britain was already signed in 1838, the Hatt-ı Hümayun's penultimate article (no. 39) opened its doors wide to Western capitalism by affirming that "the Ottoman state would do everything in its power to attract Western science, arts, and capital."[4]

The Tanzimat also aimed at breaking the power bases of entrenched elites, mainly in the provinces, which had taken control of the state away from central government. At the same time, it hoped to gain the support of the non-Muslim populations by providing them with opportunities for employment and social mobility. The redefinition of the legal status of non-Muslims was also part of the effort to regain control over the population. Some of the articles of Hatt-ı Hümayun reaffirmed promises made in 1839 regarding the security of the individual from the high-handedness and corruption of state officials. It dealt, moreover, in much greater detail with the position of non-Muslim communities, especially the Orthodox Christian community, in the new Ottoman society. For the first time the subject peoples (non-Muslims) were officially invited to comment on the decisions made by the government that affected their lives, and to suggest alterations. In particular, the new decree included seven articles devoted exclusively to the Rum milleti, which altered the status quo ante established after the conquest of Constantinople by the Ottomans. Although the tenure of the patriarchal office for the duration of the incumbent's life was re-affirmed, a review of the election regulations was ordered. Further taxation would be imposed in order to pay for a salaried clergy, whose remunerations were to be determined by the grade of each clergyman and the current income enjoyed by the patriarch and community leaders. Christian religious property was declared inviolate, but the governing bodies of such property were henceforth to consist of both clergy and laymen. Other articles permitted the restoration of churches, schools, hospitals, and cemeteries, provided that all the inhabitants of the place were Christian and the buildings

---

3. Article 21 of the Greek translation of the Hatt-ı Hümayun, published in its entirety (forty articles) in *Telegraphos tou Vosporou* on February 6/18, 1856.

4. Ibid, article 39.

were old. For new buildings the permission of the sultan, the patriarch, and the local bishops were necessary. Freedom to worship publicly was to be permitted in areas where no other religious group lived. The Hatt-ı Hümayun also promised complete religious equality and forbade the cursing, belittling, or any degradation of any persons of a different religion. Forced conversions were also forbidden.

Reception of the Announced Reforms by the Ottoman Population

There was great variety in the way the Ottoman population at large received the announcement of these reforms. Greek speakers, through the press, had been provided with considerable information relating to the reform measures emerging after the issue of the *hatt* in 1856 and the reaction of the various millets to aspects of it. At the same time, the press gave them the opportunity to read the Hatt-ı Hümayun itself in translation as well as a number of public documents and official letters related to it. They also had the opportunity to read lengthy quotations from a number of public speeches, political commentary by the press, and private letters on a variety of subjects arising from the promised reforms. They were supplied with information about how the reforms were being received and implemented and how successful (or not) they were.

Between February and April 1856, the Ottoman Greek newspapers published all forty articles of the Hatt-ı Hümayun. A report from Philippoupolis in *Telegraphos tou Vosporou*, on March 13, reprinted in *He Hemera* on March 23, described the reaction of the Ottoman Christians as being:

> like an electric spark that ignited Christian enthusiasm all over Turkey and lifted the hearts of the Christians. In Philippoupolis after the reading at the Governor's house on February 27, the mass of people who were gathered outside cried enthusiastically "Hurray," and then moved on to the Metropolitan Church of the Virgin Mary with their Bishop Chrysanthos. There, he wore his sacred clothing and after a liturgy of thanks he delivered with eloquence a short speech full of meaning. After that the Hatt-ı Hümayun was read again. This was followed by a second, more detailed speech by our preacher, Mr Gogos.[5]

At the same time the readers of the Ottoman Greek press were informed that the issuing of the Hatt-ı Hümayun could also mean that the various privileges that were given by the Ottomans to the Orthodox Christians might have to be exchanged for the new rights imposed on the Porte in the Treaty of Paris by its own Western allies. They were also informed that Russia was trying to ensure that the status quo

5. *He Hemera*, no. 29 (March 23/April 4, 1856).

ante regarding the privileges of the Orthodox Christians should remain and that the new rights given to the Rum should be in addition to their existing privileges. In May 1856, *He Hemera*, in an article reprinted from *Nationale Zeitung* (National Newspaper) of Berlin, published a memorandum by Âli Pasha to the other signatories of the Treaty of Paris on the privileges of the Christians in the empire. In this memorandum, the Ottoman minister of foreign affairs argued that these privileges should not be reiterated in the treaty, as Russia insisted:

> The Sultans in their customary philanthropy and in the spirit of Islam, from the moment of the conquest and in the peak of their powers, offered to the Christians of the Ottoman Empire their first privileges, voluntarily. No material difficulty prevented those leaders from using their unlimited powers against the religion of the defeated; on the contrary they used their powers in favor of that religion, offering privileges never since then violated. If in the interior of the state of Osman suppressions similar to those in other countries occurred, this should be attributed to the ignorance of the times, the differences of race, and to the still vivid memories of the struggles and the conquest. The Ottoman state went through this process in a similar way to any other state, and can confirm without fear of being proven wrong that at times of ignorance and religious hatred some powers destroyed the whole of Europe and that happened in areas outside the Ottoman Empire … where the tolerance of the Sultans is almost unprecedented in history. The inhabitants of the areas that were conquered by the Ottomans retained their national character, their laws, and their religion; and while in other places the mixture from which most modern peoples exist is violently mixed, in Turkey those various elements were preserved intact, living till today under the auspices of the Muslim law which was so unjustly accused by the infidels.… One would search in vain to find how in this day and age of progress the privileges of the Christians in the Ottoman Empire would be endangered without the auspices of foreign protection unless one considers the recent events by a permanent enemy of Turkey, Russia, which actively, and for a long time successfully, conspired to twist the European public opinion in this matter and, under the pretext of religious protection, tried to realize her political ambitions: gradual dismemberment and eventual destruction.

Âli Pasha concluded that Russia was the defeated power, after all, and should not be dictating terms that would constitute a disgrace for the Ottoman Empire.[6] Nevertheless, three years later, in 1859, Âli Pasha confessed to the Russian ambassador, Prince Lobanov-Rostovsky, that "the Hatt-ı Hümayun was an edict which

6. *He Hemera*, no. 36 (May 11/23, 1856).

contained poetry rather than truth, thanks to Lord Redcliffe's evil spirit; it had not been adapted to local conditions or to the culture of the Turkish provinces."[7]

Reports of the Sublime Porte's intentions concerning the Orthodox Christians were followed by a variety of letters, articles, and reports presenting the general reaction of the country to the proposed reforms. Some articles of the Hatt-ı Hümayun, for example those that equalized the social and political status of non-Muslims and Muslims, were perceived as unacceptable by the latter, who, on many occasions, reacted negatively to the reform program. Many Muslims viewed the promotion of equality between Muslims and non-Muslims, one of the cornerstones of the Hatt-ı Hümayun, as contrary to Koranic law and as a "betrayal of the Faith."[8] Muslims from all over the empire were shocked to learn the contents of the imperial edict. Outraged at what they perceived as an irreverent attack on their religion and customs, many turned their anger against the sultan, since it was he who had initiated the Hatt-ı Hümayun and "he and his ministers were determined to implement it"[9] while he simultaneously claimed to be the Muslim Caliph! This contradiction was first acted on by the sherif of Mecca, who led a revolt in outrage against the sultan. He claimed that "the Sultan did not have free will as he was surrounded by infidels,"[10] and his call for a revolt against the Sultan "was answered immediately by 50,000 men."[11] The Ottoman army reacted and "asked the pasha of Egypt to send armies to Mecca and Neapolis (possibly Nablus in Palestine) to put down Muslim opposition to the Hatt."[12] The revolt spread from Mecca to the Yemen province, where the Porte sent "the Kurd Ahmed Pasha, who left immediately"[13] to crush it. There were, according to the Greek press, several attempts against the life of the sultan in later years. The official Ottoman newspaper, *Takvim-i Vekayi,* in a report of March 1857 that was reprinted in the Greek press, stated that "Mehmed Bey, a man in charge of the Imperial Treasury in Topkapı Palace, had thrown several sacred garments [of the prophet Muhammad] into the sea and into wells"[14] in order to express the feeling, common among many Muslims, that the sultan was unfit to be caliph. After almost two years the Greek press printed information about two attempts against the sultan's life. The first was by forty Circassian conspirators (1859)[15] and the second was by pashas reacting to the Tanzimat, including Jaffer Demo Pasha from Albania.[16]

7. Sokolov 2013, 427.
8. *He Hemera,* no. 35 (May 4/16, 1856).
9. *He Hemera,* no. 38 (May 23/ June 6, 1856).
10. *He Hemera,* no. 46 (July 20/August 1, 1856).
11. *He Hemera,* no. 35 (May 4/16, 1856).
12. *He Hemera,* no. 36 (May 11/23, 1856).
13. *He Hemera,* no. 40, (June 8/20, 1856).
14. *He Hemera,* no. 79 (March 8/20, 1857).
15. *He Hemera,* no. 211, (September 18/30, 1859).
16. *He Hemera,* no. 46, (July 20/August 1, 1856).

But by far the largest and easiest targets of Muslim outrage were the Ottoman Christians. Desperate, angry, and humiliated people described in the Greek press their painful experiences at the hands of their Muslim compatriots, including their local governors and the police, and recorded the widespread hostility against the Christians and overwhelming violence all over the empire. The Ottoman government appeared willing but, in most cases, powerless to restore order. Ottoman Greek readers could observe that the patriarchate was rather more effective, at least, in bringing culprits to justice, although in most cases Ottoman justice failed to satisfy the Christian victims. The Greek press reported several cases when local bishops had Muslims arrested for various offences and brought to court, but Ottoman justice rarely imposed a punishment on them.[17]

It was thought possible that the extremely negative reaction to the *hatt* was exacerbated by the fact that the tool of communication used by the government, the official Ottoman language, was unknown to most ordinary Muslims. As a correspondent of *He Hemera* in Elmalı of Pamphylia in Asia Minor (today near Antalya in Turkey), wrote:

> The Hatt-ı Hümayun is hardly understood by the Ottomans here, who are, anyway, scarcely different from beasts in their ignorance. The *kadı* read it in the governor's house and the notables heard it. But what the [Muslim] people [who were ignorant of Ottoman in which the *hatt* was written] understood was that they were forbidden to call the Christians "*Giaur*" and "*Kaffir*." After that, these very curses became even more common.[18]

This report from Elmalı, and others similar to it, showed Greek readers the obstacles which the government had to face in implementing the promised reforms: Muslim officials and the Muslim masses were generally unsympathetic to both the spirit and the letter of the reforms. There is ample evidence for this in the Greek press, in letters and reports from all over the empire. The people of Elmalı were lucky to escape with a few curses, something that, according to the correspondent, "they had in any case become accustomed to during the Ottoman occupation." Christians in other parts of the empire were not so lucky: "Letters from Rumeli, Macedonia, Epirus, Thessaly, and Syria refer to attacks by Muslim fanatics."[19] In Ikonio [Konya] of Karamania in April 1855, "Muslims attacked Christian houses, robbed them and raped the women. The Christians had to flee to the mountains. In Amassia the same thing happened."[20] A letter from Sarajevo in Bosnia related news about the "Latin" (Roman Catholic) church there, which was besieged for a

17. See for example *He Hemera*, nos. 40 and 41 (June 1856).
18. *He Hemera*, no. 46 (July 20/August 1, 1856).
19. *He Hemera*, no. 38 (May 23/June 6, 1856).
20. *He Hemera*, no. 31 (April 6/18, 1856).

whole month by the local "Ottomans" (that is, Muslims) trying to burn it down. "Only the intervention of Hurşid Pasha from Bosnia, who protects Christians everywhere, is stopping them from doing so."[21] A letter from Smyrna written in April 1856 described how "Muslims were very upset about the Hatt ... which resulted in a great unrest in Karaburun."[22]

These unnerving reports were balanced to some degree in the Greek press by reports that the Ottoman government was trying to restore order and protect the Christians. The Greek press frequently mentioned the government's attempts to impose the *hatt* by dispatching Muslim armed forces to fight Muslim opponents of reform.

When in the autumn of 1856 an imperial *firman* was issued, giving provincial governors in Rumeli authority over the life and death of the people in their jurisdiction:

> some said that this measure was the prelude to the implementation of the Hatt there, because, especially in Albania, it is necessary to present a strong government in order to frighten the unruly people.[23]

A letter from Shkodër, northern Albania to the *Newspaper of Agram* (the historic name of Zagreb in Croatia) informed Greek newspaper readers that "Ottoman armies have arrived to punish Ottoman [Muslim] violence against the Catholics."[24]

Yet, while the Ottoman government could do relatively little in the face of such popular dissatisfaction, the British and French contingents that were still stationed in the Ottoman Empire following the end of the Crimean War were apparently both able and willing to defend Christians from Muslim reprisals. Throughout 1856 Ottoman Greek readers learned of attempts by the Christians, following the promises of the imperial edict, to install bells in their churches with the support of French and British commanders. In Nikomedia, in Asia Minor, for example:

> the local Muslims reacted [to bells being put in churches] by killing the priests of the village, but the [in this case] British officer ordered an attack on the Muslim mob, which resulted in the arrest of the Ottoman Governor and quite a few other Muslims, who were sent to Constantinople.[25]

While:

> parts of the Ottoman Empire were occupied [*sic*] by the Christian powers in the wake of the Crimean War the Ottoman government thought that it was an opportune moment to print the Hatt-ı Hümayun and exhibit it

21. *He Hemera*, no. 45 (July 13/25, 1856).
22. *He Hemera*, no. 32 (April 13/25, 1856).
23. *He Hemera*, no. 53 (September 7/19, 1856).
24. *He Hemera*, no. 54, (September 14/26, 1856).
25. *He Hemera*, no. 30 (March 30/April 11, 1856).

publicly. The magnitude of the encountered opposition by the Muslims, however, and the imminent departure of Christian armies from Turkey, made the Government change its mind.[26]

Soon after this article Muslims were reported as "attacking Christians in Varna, Valdjik, and Smyrna,"[27] and the situation of the Christians was reported to be gradually worsening. The Beys of Bosnia led the reports of Muslim atrocities by "using Christians [alive] either for bayonet practice or for hunting – using them like hunted animals."[28] In Jeddah the chief of police and the head of the "Adramutlu" (most probably it refers to the Hadramaut) organized the massacres of hundreds of Christians, as reported in several issues of the Greek press. Consequently, "the Ottoman government arrested them [the chief of police and the leader of the Adramutlu] and condemned them to death."[29] News of this brought a wave of unrest in Arabia, where they were hailed as heroes and martyrs of the Islamic faith.[30] Scores of letters with similar stories arrived in the Greek press from all over the empire.

The Christians sympathized with the Ottoman government's problems in implementing the reform program and when speaking about "Muslim atrocities" always made a point of distinguishing between the sultan and his government in Constantinople, who were regarded as agents of progress, and its provincial employees and the Muslim population at large, who were overwhelmingly opposed to reform. In August 1856, for example, a letter from Sarajevo (to the *Österreichische Zeitung*) praised the good intentions of the government but commented that, the Hatt-ı Hümayun is impossible to implement because the Turks are and insist on remaining backward."[31]

A letter writer from another side of the empire, Pamphylia in Asia Minor, was of the same opinion:

> No one among the Christians wants to diminish the excellent intentions
> of the Government but its employees are so prejudiced and unenlightened
> … and we are here so far away from the eye of the capital that the orders
> of the Sublime Porte reaching here either remain unimplemented or are
> used against the poor *reaya*s.[32]

It might have been small consolation to the correspondent from Pamphylia to know that even under "the eye of the Capital" things were not so different. Readers were informed by an irate gentleman writing from Constantinople in June 1856 that

26. *He Hemera*, no. 40 (June 8/20, 1856).
27. *He Hemera*, no. 42 (June 22/July 4, 1856).
28. *He Hemera*, no. 163 (October 17/29, 1858).
29. *He Hemera*, no. 178 (January 30/February 11, 1859).
30. *He Hemera*, no. 182 (February 27/March 11, 1859).
31. *He Hemera*, no. 48 (August 3/15, 1856).
32. *He Hemera*, no. 46 (July 20/August 1, 1856).

the Ottoman people have become intolerable in Constantinople. Every day they commit murders and robberies and beat people up, even in the middle of the day, in front of everyone and no one [in the government] cares. We all walk the streets with the *Kyrie Eleison* in our lips.[33]

A single Muslim voice was raised in September 1856 in defense of Muslim aggression. *He Hemera* reprinted in translation a letter written in French signed by "a Muslim," which had appeared in the *General Newspaper of Augusta* [of Belgrade], trying to explain to Christian readers the havoc caused in the empire by the Hatt-ı Hümayun "in the Turkish [*sic*] provinces." The writer seems well educated – his knowledge of French suggests a French education, perhaps in a military academy. His choice of newspaper may indicate a Muslim who lived near the Serbian border, perhaps a Bosnian or an Albanian. His own explanation for the massacres of Christians in the empire was that foreign intervention stopped the implementation of law and order. The current violence was blamed on "consular agents who are limiting the powers of the Pashas."[34] *He Hemera* commented sharply on this letter:

> We believe the agents of the Christian powers … interfering with the activities of powerless and stupid Pashas, are not the ones that deprive the provinces of progress and the flourishing of commerce, or, indeed, those who put hurdles in the path of the Ottoman peoples' progress. In other sources must one search for the backwardness of the Ottomans [Muslims].[35]

The government's relentless pursuit of centralizing control of the state through these reforms and the negative reaction to the Hatt-ı Hümayun by their Muslim compatriots created deep concerns within the Orthodox Christian population. A large number of Orthodox Christians were skeptical about the long-term wisdom of the reforms and their suitability for a fundamentally Islamic state. Yet, despite these concerns, the Greek press of the empire, and especially the Smyrna newspapers, supported (with a few exceptions) the reform program for a few years, and in 1856 a number of them endorsed the reform of the patriarchate.

The curbing of church power and its confinement to spiritual and cultural matters was perceived by some Ottoman Greeks as hailing the introduction of democracy in the Ottoman state. This view was already evident in the Greek press in the 1840s. In 1847 the editor of the newspaper Amaltheia of Smyrna, Samiotakis, wrote an article defending his newspaper from extreme nationalists from the Kingdom of Greece, who had accused him of failing to take a more nationalistic pro-Greek line. Samiotakis argued that the Ottoman Greeks had a vested interest in the Ottoman state since they were, after all, its oldest inhabitants, and urged

33. *He Hemera*, no. 40 (May 8/June 20, 1856).
34. *He Hemera*, no. 52 (August 31/September 12, 1856).
35. Ibid.

his Ottoman Greek readers to support government reforms as a very positive step for the future of the Ottoman Empire. According to Samiotakis, before the nation should seek a different way of political life it should seek "intellectual maturity of the people which should be achieved through, among other things, education and the free press."[36]

But by 1858 both the editors and the readers had realized, as we shall see later, that the Ottoman Empire would not become a Western European democracy like France and England. As one anonymous Ottoman Greek letter writer put it in March 1858, "All the subjects of the Sultan are considered equal in front of the law, a law, however, that doesn't exist."[37]

Such feelings among the Ottoman Christians were reinforced by Muslim comments like the following by Abdi Pasha of Grasatch, who in 1861 was quoted in the press as saying that "the Christians are made to be the slaves of the Ottomans [Muslims] forever."[38]

Such reports in the press outlined the general climate in the empire following the imperial edict, as the government strove to carry out the task of implementing the promised reforms. Three aspects of political reform were extensively covered in the Greek press: conscription, judicial reforms, and the reform of the patriarchate.

Conscription

Military reform was aimed at centralizing control of the army, which was appropriately renamed Asâkir-i Nizamiye-i Şahane (The Ordered Soldiers of the Sultan).

Already Selim III and Mahmud II had made serious attempts to modernize the Ottoman army – Mahmud II in particular. Having the entire Janissary corps eliminated in what may have been the bloodiest massacre of the nineteenth century, Mahmud II restricted enrollment into his "new army" to "born Muslims and loyal Turkish lads."[39] In 1841, the army was divided into provincial commands, each led by a *müşir* (field marshal) appointed by and answerable to the *serasker* (commander in chief) in Constantinople.

Thus, the provincial governor's control of the military, which nearly caused the de facto partition of the Ottoman state, came to an end.[40]

36. *Amaltheia*, no. 428 (April 4, 1848).
37. *He Hemera*, no. 316 (September 22/October 4, 1861).
38. Ibid.
39. Virginia Aksan, in Aksan and Goffman 2007, 129.
40. The Ottoman forces were divided into six armies. Two were based in Istanbul, one for the control of northwestern Anatolia and Thrace and the Hassa Ordusu (Imperial Army), responsible for southwestern Anatolia. Other armies were based in Scutari (for control of Rumeli and Albania) in Sivas (for control of Anatolia), in Damascus (for control of Syria, Cilicia, Iraq and the Arabian peninsula), and in Baghdad (after 1848 for Iraq and the Arab peninsula). Each army was divided into the infantry, cavalry, artillery, and reserves. Infantry and cavalry regiments were divided and run in the European manner. The artillery provided seventy-two cannons for each regiment, half mo-

In accordance with the equality of duties as well as rights, propagated in the Hatt-ı Hümayun, the Ottoman government contemplated the universal conscription of non-Muslims as well as Muslims. The participation of non-Muslims in the Ottoman army had in fact occurred before, both in the land forces and in the navy. As early as in the time of Sultan Bayezid II (1481–1512), Christian aristocrats who sided with the Ottomans as they conquered new lands were granted large pieces of land (*timars*) and serfs. *Timars* were not hereditary and service in time of war was compulsary. At times Christians comprised more than one half of the timariots. Although Christian timariots gradually disappeared, Christian Albanians customarily joined Ottoman campaigns under their own chieftains and most Ottoman sailors were taken from the Greek islands and coastal towns. There was an attempt in 1839, after the Hatt-ı Şerif of Gülhane, to recruit some Christians, such as Armenians and Bulgarians, who had never before fought in the army, but the communities resisted strongly.[41] In 1833–34 an attempt was made by Mahmud II to introduce Christians into the army reserves (*redif*), but it became merely a tax-collection exercise, as all the Christians took up the option to pay the tax necessary to avoid conscription.[42]

In 1855, despite the fact that Christians were paying a tax exempting them from military service, the Porte nevertheless decided to recruit them to fight the Russians during the Crimean War.

On 10 May 1855 Patriarch Anthimos wrote to Metropolitan Stephen of Larissa that the rumor about this recruitment was true and the Porte had notified all the peoples' leaders about this. Anthimos thanked the Sultan who "granted the subject peoples [the honor] to become a part of his military forces" … although he had made an exception for the citizens of Epirus and Thessaly, who had suffered from the recent mutinies. On 6 June the Patriarch addressed the bishops of the dioceses of Epirus, Thessaly, and others – Ioannina, Larissa, Dimitsana, Dryinoupolis, Arta, Grevena, Phanariophersala, Velegrada, Paramythia, Bosnia, Nyssa, Zvornik, Erseke, Raskoprezrena, Vidin, Rhodes, Mytilene, Mithymni, Chios, Lemnos, Imvros, Kos, Crete, Maroneia, and Patmos – with a circular declaring that Sultan Abdulmecid favored the Greek people with his trust and had announced the recruitment of suitable people to the royal army in order that the Greeks could share triumphs, ranks, and honor with the Muslims. This pleasing order should be fulfilled. But since the above-mentioned dioceses [of Epirus and Thessaly] had suffered from insurgency, the Sultan

---

bile and half fixed. Some 65,000 irregular troops (mostly Cossacks, Tatars, Turcomans, and Kurds) completed the armed forces. Soldiers conscripted into the Ottoman army had to serve in the reserve forces for another seven years after their regular service. (Information from lectures by Dr. Leslie Collins, SSEES, University of London).

41. Moreau 2007, 22.
42. Moreau 2007, 23.

magnanimously decided to exempt their citizens from recruitment at this time. The Patriarch asked the bishops to inform their people about the trust shown towards them by the Sultan, and to console them with this new expression of his royal mercy in allowing the recruits to stay at home, and he encouraged the people to pray for the Sultan.[43]

The ecumenical patriarchate was indeed stepping on eggshells during the Crimean War.

> Both the Turks and the western diplomats demanded that the Patriarch declare the Russians to be schismatic, in order to arouse the Greeks against their common enemy, Russia. Anthimos was bold enough to refuse this demand. Nevertheless, the Porte did obtain the Patriarch's signature to its missive, commanding people not to mistreat the French soldiers who were there to protect the government "against the cunning intentions of Russia, which it was trying to accomplish under the pretense of Orthodoxy." The Greek people, however, realized this was a forced lie and did not ascribe this missive to the Patriarch.[44]

However, the participation of non-Muslims in the Ottoman Army became institutionalized in 1856.

Some Muslims were equally resistant to serving as regulars, including the Muslim Albanians and the Muslim population of Bosnia–Herzegovina, "who were ferociously opposed to conscription."[45] In the end, only "the Turks of Anatolia and Rumeli were recruited into the regular army."[46] According to article 24 of the Hatt-ı Hümayun, conscription became indiscriminate, but it was again possible to avoid it by paying a fee. Moreover, article 16 also allowed the indiscriminate admission of all religions to the military school. The school was an earlier creation of Mahmud II, established in 1834 following an earlier foundation, the army medical school, founded in 1827.[47]

The Hatt-ı Hümayun ostensibly institutionalized the privilege of military service for non-Muslim subjects like Mahmud II's earlier attempts in 1833–43, but in practice it became another way of collecting money. It is clear from the press reports that the heads of the non-Muslim millets were aware of the true intentions of the Ottoman government and navigated their situation carefully. A similar situation had arisen in 1840 following the declaration of the Hatt-ı Şerif the previous year.

The government replaced the humiliating *kharaj* (tax on agricultural land and

43. Sokolov 2013, 420.
44. Sokolov 2013, 421.
45. Karal 1988; cited in Moreau 2007, 354–55.
46. Ibid.
47. Karal 1988, 19; cited in Moreau 2007, 354–55.

produce) with a military tax (*bedeli askerie*), payable by all Christians aged between 14 and 60. *Kharaj* was abolished so far as the letter of the law was concerned, but in fact only its shameful name was changed while the tax itself remained in place, still accompanied by the ways of levying that humiliated the Christians.[48]

In March 1856, as the representative of the Rum milleti, "the Ecumenical Patriarch was invited to discuss the implementation of the Hatt with the relevant ministries."[49] When he was told that Orthodox subjects from all over the empire would have to serve in the army, he retorted that:

> it may be so, but it should not apply to the citizens of Constantinople, who were from ancient times exempted from military service. The majority of Ministers agreed that the privilege should continue.[50]

A few months later, however, the Sublime Porte

> summoned the Ecumenical Patriarch and announced to him that there was going to be conscription of non-Muslim Ottomans, beginning with 16,000 men in the Capital, who would serve under the Ottoman flag.[51]

From those 16,000, only 3,000 would have to serve in the army. The rest would have to pay 5,000 *kuruş* each in lieu of service.[52] In June 1856 after some deliberations,

> the non-Muslim Ottoman national leaders opted for all 16,000 men to be conscripted rather than pay the money.[53]

But if they were to have no choice in the matter, the Armenian patriarch is quoted as having advised the other patriarchs that before conscription became law, they should first ascertain how the money was going to be collected, and secondly what the rights and duties would be of those who were going to serve in the Ottoman army, because until then "only Muslims were promoted."[54] To the Christian reader of the Greek press it became clear that he was soon going to pay yet another tax.

The above information concerning conscription of non-Muslims presents firm evidence that the issue here was not the voluntary military service of the Christians, which existed from "ancient times" and from which "only the citizens of Constantinople were exempted," but merely a question of proper advancement in the army.

A second issue that arose from the conscription of non-Muslim subjects was

48. Byzantios, 1851, 3:241–42; cited in Sokolov 2013, 340.
49. *He Hemera*, no. 27 (March 9/21, 1856).
50. *He Hemera*, no. 39 (June 1/13,1856).
51. Ibid.
52. *He Hemera*, no. 40 (June 8/20, 1856).
53. Ibid.
54. Ibid.

whether the conscripted Christians were to serve in separate units under their own Christian officers or be dispersed among Muslim units. It was reported that the grand vizier Reşid Pasha, the minister of finance Saffet Pasha, and the minister of defence Rıza Pasha all supported the creation of separate units, because "this was going to create competition between the various army units, which in turn would be good for the state."[55] Other ministers held the view that, "equality meant exactly the opposite and Christians should be dispersed in the Ottoman army units."[56]

The editor of *He Hemera* commented that, "of course, if the Christians were asked, they would prefer to be separated and led by Christian officers because thus they would avoid the mistreatment and beatings they would certainly suffer, being so few among so many Ottomans [Muslims]."[57]

In the next number of *He Hemera,* following a report from the *Journal des Discussions* on conscription in the Ottoman Empire, the editor commented that:

> mixing a few Christians with a lot of Ottomans would risk the "Turkification" of Christian customs and language and I cannot see how this would benefit the culture of the Ottoman Empire and civilization as a whole.[58]

Another issue that concerned Greek readers was the question of the *bedel-i askeri,* the sum of money payable by those exempted from conscription. Already in June 1856, with a speed uncharacteristic of the Ottoman government, the orders about the distribution and levying of the military tax were translated from the Ottoman language and sent to the governors of the provinces:

> The religious and secular leaders of the non-Muslim communities gathered in the capital of every province and together with the Ottoman governor decided about the number of conscripts.[59]

The state planned "to collect 62,500,000 *kuruş*, which were to be paid by the non-Muslims of the empire"[60] according to the number of conscripts in each province who would not serve in the Ottoman army. "In Smyrna the military tax amounted to 565,000 *kuruş* and the burden was shared among the non-Muslim communities of Smyrna."[61] "In Rumeli it came to 60,500 kuruş."[62] Some Christian letter writers lamented the loss of opportunity to "improve our situation by conscription into the army," instead of which they had to pay this enormous tax,

55. *He Hemera*, no. 76 (February 15/27, 1857).
56. Ibid.
57. Ibid.
58. *He Hemera*, no. 77 (February 22/March 6, 1857).
59. *He Hemera*, no. 44 (July 6/18, 1856).
60. Ibid.
61. *He Hemera*, no. 46 (July 20/August 1, 1856).
62. *He Hemera*, no. 53 (September 7/19, 1856).

but "… it is well known that Reayas will be always Reayas despite the declared equality."[63] The fear that the collection of the tax might cause ill treatment of the *reayas* by tax collectors, as was the case with many other taxes, forced the patriarchal synod to appoint a committee which would form regulations regarding how the exemption money from conscripted Christians was to be collected.

Greek readers were asked to address the question: what did equality mean with respect to the military reform? Non-Muslims would have to be conscripted, though most of them would not serve but instead, without having any choice in the matter, would have to pay for the privilege of not serving. Moreover, the imposition of a separate tax on the non-Muslims was clearly in direct contravention of article 28 of the Hatt-ı Hümayun, which stated categorically that all Ottoman subjects would have to pay the same taxes.[64] A correspondent from Constantinople seems to voice the general opinion of the Ottoman Greeks regarding the implementation of the reform measures:

> The Ottoman government is solely occupied with the collection of the military tax and that is all it has done about implementing the Hatt-ı Hümayun.[65]

While the patriarchate was taking measures to protect the rather peaceable population of the Balkans, the *armed* Christians of Albania and the *armed* Muslims of Albania made their attitude to conscription stridently clear. The Christians would not countenance being exempted and paying for the privilege, while the Muslims were not interested in being conscripted. Many of these Albanians, both Christian and Muslim, had long been accustomed to serving in the Ottoman army as volunteers and the advent of conscription was considered an insult to them:

> Such was the outrage of the Albanians against the *nizam* (conscription) and against an additional order to disarm, that it succeeded in uniting Christians and Muslims in one body. It was reported that Hanzağa, a well-known leader of the fanatical party, is inciting the Christians of upper Albania to rebel against the implementation of conscription and disarmament, promising to respect their faith if they did so. It is doubtful as yet if the Christians will rebel with those Turks [that is, Muslims].[66]

Another reason for the Albanians' reluctance to join the new Ottoman army as conscripts was its new uniform, which did not compare favorably with the elaborate Albanian dress. A letter from Shkodër informs that:

63. Ibid.
64. "All subjects pay the same taxes without a class or religious distinction. Any abuses during the collection of the taxes will be punished severely"(from *Telegraphos tou Vosporou*).
65. *He Hemera*, no. 43 (June 29/July 11, 1856).
66. *He Hemera*, no. 54 (September 14/26, 1856).

The regular army looks awful ... new recruits are badly dressed and badly armed, so much so that the Ottomans [that is, Muslims] here laugh hearti-ly at them.[67]

A correspondent from Dryinoupolis of Epirus described the terrible situation of the Epirot Christians caused by gangs of Albanians fleeing from the province of Delvino because of this new measure of conscription. He also mentioned that the Muslims in Albania were furious with the Hatt-ı Hümayun, for which they blamed the Christians:

How is it possible for the Christians to live among these beasts, against whom the Turkish government is powerless?[68]

It took three years and much persuasion to make the Albanians accept conscrip-tion. A letter from Shkodër dated August 1857 informs us that a sultanic *firman* had arrived there postponing disarmament and conscription until further orders were received:

The people were greatly pleased by it and some villagers who were resisting these measures gave up their fight and so order was restored to all Albania.[69]

This report proved optimistic. In October 1857 the Ottoman Greek press reported that

the Ghegs are rebelling against the pashas of Skopje and Prishtina. The revolutionaries are mostly Muslims.[70]

and a few weeks later:

the province of Mirdit, inhabited by Catholics, mostly armed men, does not agree with paying the new [conscription] tax and is even more unwill-ing to lay their guns down.[71]

After months of hesitation the government finally decided to crush the revolt and make an example of it. So:

they sent the pasha of Scodra [Shkodër] against this very important land of Albania. The subjugation of the Mirdit revolt will be an example to all the Epirots, especially those who call themselves Melissarit and live as shepherds or as thieves.[72]

67. Ibid.
68. *He Hemera*, no. 31 (April 6/18, 1856).
69. *He Hemera*, no. 103 (August 23/September 4, 1857).
70. *He Hemera*, no. 108 (September 27/October 8, 1857).
71. *He Hemera*, no. 110 (October11/23, 1857).
72. *He Hemera*, no. 112 (October 25/November 6, 1857).

But by November the revolt was still going on and the only positive outcome was that "some say that the Government discovered the thread of the conspiracy which had spread all over Albania" and eventually "the Albanians were given their salaries and were told to join the army."[73] Not all of them did.

Undertaking the conscription of the Arabs in Damascus, as the reader was informed, was a far more ingenious affair, masterminded by the general governor of Damascus, Izzet Pasha. His system was somewhat different to the ones used in other parts of the empire. Instead of "recruiting the youth by drawing lots, as was the custom in the rest of the Empire," he put young men in prison for the slightest misdemeanor and then conscripted them immediately into the army. "By now [August 1857] 400 new recruits have been collected, and the amount our province must give to the Ottoman army is 2,500."[74] This measure by the pasha was indeed ingenious, not only because it produced the necessary number of recruits from among an extremely unwilling population, but also because he succeeded in making the town "extremely quiet since all the young men were running away." There was one unforeseen problem, however:

> The peasants, who were providing the town with its food, fearing that they would be drafted into the army, rarely venture into our town anymore and as a result the people of Damascus are on the brink of starvation![75]

While conscription provoked mainly negative reactions both from the Muslim and the non-Muslim subjects of the empire, the acceptance of non-Muslims in the military academy (1857) was well received. Their number was extremely limited and the selection of candidates was made at the highest level:

> The Sultan called the Patriarchs of the various millets and the Chief Rabbi and asked them to choose ten young men to be trained as engineers in the Military Academy and as [officers] in the army and the navy.[76]

These officers were to lead an Ottoman army which

> in peacetime was to number 105,500, namely, 72,355 infantry, 18,000 cavalry, and 15,145 gunners. This did not include the irregulars.[77]

The number of non-Muslim students was far larger in the military medical school and we know that from among the Bulgarians alone, (part of the Rum milleti)

73. *He Hemera*, no. 62 (November 9/21, 1856).
74. *He Hemera*, no. 107 (September 20/October 2, 1857).
75. Ibid.
76. *He Hemera*, no. 73 (January 25/February 6, 1857).
77. From *Le Messager de l'Armée*; in *He Hemera*, no. 51 (August 24/September 5, 1856).

fifteen students were accepted.[78] It is not clear if this was the result of tough negotiations between the patriarch and the sultan or because there were not enough
recruits from the Muslim millet. The Greek press reported that

> the fifteen Bulgarians, who were admitted to the Military Medical school,
> insisted on being registered as Bulgarians [that is, on the basis of their
> ethnic identity] and not as Rum [their religious identity].[79]

This report is a clear indication that by the 1850s the process of developing a
Bulgarian national consciousness had reached the stage where many educated
Bulgarians identified more strongly with their ethnic identity than with their religious one and, equally, had begun to distance themselves from the Greek culture
and language dominant within the Rum milleti. While in the 1820s Bulgarians
still identified themselves with the Greek nation or aspired to belong to the Greek
culture and many had fought in the Greek Revolution for the establishment of a
Greek state,[80] by the 1850s a Bulgarian national identity distinct from the Greek
and the Rum was sufficiently developed. The struggle to impose the Bulgarian
language in Bulgarian churches and church schools eventually resulted in most
Bulgarians breaking away from the ecumenical patriarchate. This development
was directly linked in the Greek press, as we shall see later, with the reform of the
Ecumenical Patriarchate of Constantinople.

Judicial Reforms

The reader of the Ottoman Greek press was often made aware of the Ottoman
government's attempts to promote equality between Muslims and non-Muslims,
which was promised in the Hatt-ı Hümayun, at the highest levels of government
as well as in important institutions such as the Grand Council of Justice, being
a further development of the Ministry of Judicial Pleas, which had been created
between 1836 and 1838 by Mahmud II. According to articles 34 and 35 of the
Hatt-ı Hümayun, all religions had the right to appoint annually elected representatives, who would be called by the grand vizier in cases concerning the entire
Ottoman population:

> The representatives of each nation in the Ottoman Empire have been
> received by the Sultan and appointed.[81]

---

78. *He Hemera*, no. 51 (August 24/September 5, 1856).
79. *He Hemera*, no. 316 (November 15/27, 1856).
80. See for example Todorov 1982.
81. *He Hemera*, no. 40 (June 8/20, 1856).

Their names were also printed in the Ottoman Greek press: S. Vogorides for the Greeks (Rum milleti); Boghos Dadian, director of imperial TNT factories) for the Armenians; Mirhan Duz, director of the Ottoman mint for the Latin Armenians; and Hattan (son of a banker) for the Jews.[82]

Some historical studies indicate that in the eighteenth and early nineteenth century a small number of Orthodox Christians sought justice in Ottoman courts instead of their own millet courts when it came to inheritance disputes. There is some speculation as to why they chose to do so. One explanation given is that it offered a faster and absolutely final outcome.[83] It could also be argued that Islamic law, being different to Roman law, could be more beneficial in some cases of inheritance disputes than the latter. In all other legal cases, however, the inequality of justice awarded by Ottoman courts in cases of mixed claimants (Muslims and non-Muslims) seems to have been the cause of much resentment among non-Muslims, as it emerges from the Ottoman Greek press.

After the promulgation of the Hatt-ı Hümayun, which stressed equality of all Ottoman subjects before the law, the subordinate millets were observing closely the legal cases where Muslims were accused of wrongdoing against Christians. The Ottoman Greek press often received letters of complaint about Muslims who although found guilty were not punished by the Ottoman courts. A case that caught the popular imagination was the case of a Bulgarian girl called Nedelia. She was abducted by a Turkish/Muslim pasha, called Salih, who, when he had no more use for her, had her killed. The case of the daughter of Varna (a town in Bulgaria), as it became known, was front-page news from April until October 1856. This case attracted interest not least because it was eventually referred to the newly founded Grand Council of Justice, where all four millets had the right to appoint representatives. It was an interesting coincidence that the Orthodox Christian/Rum appointee was Stephanake Vogorides, who was himself a Bulgarian. The case of the murdered girl reached the Grand Council of Justice in June, after considerable pressure put on the government by the Patriarchate of Constantinople. The Orthodox Christian leadership intervened after the ordinary Ottoman courts had found Salih Pasha innocent and it became clear that the Ottoman judges were not ready to award equal treatment both to the Orthodox Christian Bulgarian parents of the murdered girl and the Ottoman pasha. Finally, in October, the trial ended. The Ottoman Greek press reported that the aide-de-camp of Salih Pasha, who had murdered the girl by strangulation, was condemned to death and four of his employees, who attended the murder, were sentenced to from six months to five years in prison. Although the person who had ordered the death of the girl, Salih Pasha, had already escaped with only a reprimand from the Turkish judge

82. *He Hemera*, no. 37 (May 18/30, 1856).
83. See, for example, Göçek 2005; cited in Greene 2005, 47–69.

before the case reached the Grand Council of Justice, the outcome of the trial was encouraging for the non-Muslim population of the empire because it seemed that in this higher level of appeal in the courts, at least in this case, Muslims and non-Muslims were treated equally.

The Reform of the Orthodox Church.

By far the most important political reform in the Ottoman Empire, as far as the Rum milleti was concerned, was the reform of the Orthodox Patriarchate of Constantinople. It was a reform that touched on some very complex issues with far-reaching domestic and international implications. When it was eventually concluded it not only changed the political situation of the Orthodox Christians of the empire, but also became a one-way road towards the loss of the empire's Balkan provinces. In order to tell the story of this reform as it unfolded in the Ottoman Greek press it would be useful to start by looking briefly at the various groups who either directly or indirectly would be affected by the outcome. The first group, whose life would be considerably altered by this reform, was the Rum milleti, and specially its major political players, some of whom were also directly or indirectly involved with the Ottoman Greek press.

Due to the privileges granted by Mehmed the Conqueror in 1453 to the Eastern Roman patriarch of Constantinople with a *berat* (a formal granting of a privilege by the sultan), the Orthodox community enjoyed both religious and civil privileges under the authority of the ecumenical patriarch. The patriarch of Constantinople was recognized not only as the head of the Greek community but later on and as the Ottoman conquests advanced also of all the other Orthodox Christian subjects of the empire, irrespective of ethnicity. By virtue of that *berat* the patriarch was responsible to the sultan and the Sublime Porte. He was in fact an Ottoman official, the *millet başı* (*ethnarches*), the leader of the Rum milleti, answerable to the head of the state, the sultan.[84] For, although he was selected by the synod, his appointment had to be confirmed by the sultan as supreme ruler of the state in conformity with Byzantine tradition. But any similarity with Byzantine tradition ceased there. For unlike the Ottoman point of view, which conceived of the church as a department of the state, the Byzantine conception differed fundamentally and conceived of the church as one of the two essential entities of a polity, these being the priesthood (*ierosyne*) and the imperial authority (*vasileia*). This conception, which was formulated in the sixth century and was re-affirmed in the ninth, followed Christ's clear distinction between Caesar and

---

84. Stavrides 1991, 13; Bayezid II's *berat* of April 9/18, 1483 to Patriarch Symeon I, in Zacha-riadou 1996, 174. In general, see Runciman 1968, 171–73.

God.[85] The patriarch, in the Ottoman context, was regarded as an appointee of the sultan and considered as an official with specific secular duties in addition to his religious ones, including the administration of justice, the issuing of passports, the provision of education and welfare, and the collection of revenues payable to the Ottoman treasury.[86]

At the time of the conquest the Orthodox Christian church had received certain assurances and privileges regarding its flock, which were re-affirmed each time a new patriarch came to the throne. Nonetheless, the amalgamation of political power with its religious duties was seen by the church as a sacrifice of its nature and mission made in order to help preserve the quality of life of its vanquished flock. Forced to serve both God and Caesar, the church had gradually grown intransigent in its traditional position within the state and resisted any innovation that could conceivably alter its established authority over its flock and its relationship with the Ottoman state.

For its part the Ottoman government was eager to reform the leading institution of the Orthodox church because it had proved to be a major challenge to the government's absolute authority and potentially to the security of the Ottoman state. Firstly, the church exercised a high degree of spiritual and political control over the affairs of arguably the most dynamic social group in the Ottoman population. Secondly, the Patriarchate of Constantinople had close relations with Russia, the principal enemy of the Ottoman Empire. Russia was a great Orthodox power, which took a deep interest in the affairs of the Orthodox community of the Ottoman Empire and the patriarchate. Thirdly, since the latter part of the eighteenth century there was a mounting dissatisfaction among some Orthodox Christians with the leadership of the Orthodox Church. Their criticism represented a threat to the Ottoman government because popular dissatisfaction against the church, while not being a matter over which the Ottoman government could exercise control, made it fear that it might provoke disturbances in the provinces among the various Orthodox Christian ethnic groups. This in turn could lead to foreign intervention and, possibly, further loss of Ottoman territory.

Before 1839, when Orthodox Christians were dissatisfied, they could only complain to their highest authority, the patriarchate. If the patriarch did not satisfy them, they had no other legal recourse, since they could not complain to the gov-

---

85. Justinian I, Novella 6: "The greatest blessings of mankind are the gifts of God, which have been granted to us by the mercy of Providence – the priesthood and the imperial authority. The priesthood ministers the things divine, the imperial authority is set over and shows diligence in things human; but both proceed from one and the same source, and both adorn the life of man ..." Schoell and Kroll 1928, 35–36. Introduction to Chapter 8, Novella 6: "As the constitution consists, of many parts and members, the greatest and most necessary parts are the Emperor and the Patriarch ..." Zepos and Zepos 1931, 242.

86. See Bayezid II's *berat* of April 9/18, 1483 to Patriarch Symeon I, in Zachariadou 1996, 157–60.

ernment about "religious matters," which were solely the concern of the patriarch-ate. In the Hatt-ı Şerif of Gülhane, however, the Ottoman government provided dissatisfied Christians with a legitimate reason for complaining to the government about matters hitherto regarded as "religious." "Religious" matters encompassed a very wide range of activities, such as appointing bishops, tax collecting, marriage, divorce, education, issuing passports, and several of these "religious" categories now fell within the remit of the government as facets of "life, honor and property." Because the Hatt included a clause that stated that the sultan promised to safeguard the life, honor, and property of all his subjects, after 1839 dissatisfied Christians could, at least in theory, resort to the Ottoman government about such matters and the Ottoman government was provided with a legitimate way of bringing to the attention of the patriarchate Orthodox expressions of dissatisfaction against the church, and, more importantly, a legitimate excuse to interfere in the affairs of the patriarchate, despite the privileges it enjoyed.

The efforts of the Sublime Porte to break up the absolute power of the pa-triarchate were greatly assisted by the outcome of the Crimean War. Russia, the great Orthodox power, with her particular interest in maintaining the integrity of the Orthodox Church in the Ottoman Empire, had been defeated in 1856 by the Ottoman armies in collaboration with a Catholic and a Protestant power (France and Britain). None of them had any interest in maintaining either the established position of the Orthodox Church in the Ottoman Empire or indeed preserving the Ottoman Orthodox population in one block with a special relationship with Russia. What all three Crimean victors would have preferred, but for different and in fact conflicting reasons, would be a patriarchate with diminished powers and an Orthodox population possibly fragmented into small national Orthodox churches. Some Greeks argued later that article 2 of the Hatt-ı Hümayun, which on the one hand confirmed the privileges given to the Orthodox by Mehmed II but on the other demanded the creation of special councils which would reform the millets according to current social and political thinking, was a result of the insistence of Napoleon III, who thought that

> the only way to secure the existence of the Ottoman Empire is to diminish the influence, prestige and power of the Patriarchate...[87]

For the Ottoman government a divided and therefore weaker Orthodox Chris-tian population could be more easily controlled, while at the same time Russian influence and its potential dangers would diminish. Interestingly, although the imperial edict of 1856 (the Hatt-ı Hümayun) aimed ostensibly to create equality among all citizens of the state, it contradicted itself by confirming the existence of the millet system as the basic organizational principle of the Ottoman Empire. It is possibly this contradiction that, after the euphoria died down, persuaded

87. Gedeon 1939, 169–70.

the Ottoman Greeks – as demonstrated in the Ottoman Greek press – that the reforms would not eventually take off. In any case, the maintenance of the millet system meant that the millet leaderships had to be changed accordingly so that they would serve Ottoman interests better.

The Orthodox Christian population was divided about the consequences of reforming the Patriarchate of Constantinople. Some felt that these reforms were destroying the existing status quo ante without offering a credible alternative and had the potential of eventually destroying the multi-ethnic Ottoman state. In 1856 in an article that articulated very clearly the despair of many Greeks at what they saw as a short-sighted and potentially self-destructing policy, the Ottoman correspondent of the Athens newspaper *Aion*, writing in *Vyzantis*, warned the Ottoman government that, in fact, it had been deceived by its Crimean "allies" and that it was destroying its natural ally, the Orthodox Church:

> It is very sad for one to remember the past and compare it with the Gov-
> ernment's present attitude, which consists of building up a deceitful policy
> against the [Orthodox] Nation. I cannot understand what the Porte thinks
> it is achieving by acting this way. Once it divides the [Orthodox] Nation I
> can assure [the Porte] that part of it will most certainly seek the protection
> of foreign powers against the Porte's government. They [foreign powers]
> will then actively intervene and who knows where things might lead [war,
> autonomy, independence?]. The Porte must not forget that reforms do not
> happen overnight and that in order to build on ruins one must first clear
> the place of all the rubble and then think of rebuilding. Otherwise, one
> merely piles rubble upon rubble and instead of a strong building with firm
> foundations, one will create a tower of Babel, which will have inherent in
> it the seed of its *ultimate destruction*. Its own state interests should move
> the Porte to remain with the Old [order] and not ask for reforms in mat-
> ters that it cannot understand [what they are and where they might lead]
> and about which it has no right to intervene.[88]

The author of this article might be alluding in particular to one side issue that had begun to occupy the national and international political scene: the rising nationalism of the Bulgarian-speaking Orthodox Christians. They had been for some time trying to assert their national voice by attempting to break away from the supra-national rule of the patriarchate and create their own national church. Bulgarian-speaking Orthodox Christians had been complaining for a long time to the Patriarchate of Constantinople about the Greek language being used exclusively both in education and liturgy in areas where Bulgarian speakers were in the majority, and demanded that it should be replaced by their own language. They also wanted

---

88. Reprinted in *He Hemera*, no. 88 (May 10/22, 1857).

ethnic Bulgarians and not Greeks to fill the senior clerical positions. For decades such demands from the Bulgarian-speaking Orthodox were for various reasons largely unfulfilled. In 1856, encouraged by the promises of the Hatt-ı Hümayun, some Bulgarian intellectuals, claiming that they were expressing the wishes of 6,400,000 of their fellow Bulgarians, sent a petition consisting of nine articles to the sultan, in which, among other things, they demanded the use of the Bulgarian language in churches and schools. They also demanded that "the Bulgarian nation should have the right to elect one of its co-nationals as the highest church leader," thus directly challenging the authority of the Patriarchate of Constantinople over the Bulgarian-speaking Orthodox. The petition demanded virtual autonomy from the Ottoman government as well:

> The [Bulgarian] nation should have the right to elect its own Bulgarian governor, who could appoint indigenous people to all public positions.... [T]he official language must be Bulgarian and not Ottoman.... [W]e should have our own armed police to keep the peace,... and a judiciary that would accept anyone from any nationality as a witness. [In the event of war] Bulgarian contingents should be organized separately ... with their own officers, who should be Bulgarian and the language of command should be Bulgarian.[89]

This petition, one of the first public demonstrations in the Ottoman press of rising political nationalist feelings among the Bulgarians, initially appeared to be directed against the Ottoman Greek patriarchate. The Ottoman government ostensibly assisted the Bulgarians in their struggle against the patriarchate by insisting on the reform of the latter. Some Orthodox Greek speakers – as we saw earlier – warned that this was only a short-term solution, which in the long term would damage the Ottoman Empire. Russia assessed the situation similarly. It concluded that the patriarchate could not maintain its unifying power over the Balkan Christians intact after the combined attack on its established position by the Ottoman government, Britain, and France, and readjusted its foreign policy in order to have maximum long-term benefit. The effective breakup of the Rum milleti in 1862 created a Slavic bloc that fell quickly into the patronage of Russia, which had meanwhile dropped its outdated pan-Orthodox policy to embrace pan-Slavism. In 1878, at the Treaty of San Stefano, the Russians created the Bulgarian national state.

Reforming the Orthodox Church in the Ottoman Empire was not a novelty brought about by the Ottoman government but an internal ongoing issue since the late sixteenth century. Greek intellectuals and clergymen, like Patriarch Kyrillos Lukaris (1572–1638), had identified and attempted to rectify several problems festering in the church as a result of its simultaneous assumption of both religious

---

89. *He Hemera*, no. 43 (June 28/July 11, 1856).

and secular duties. Such a position is incompatible with Eastern Christian theology and although in extremis it had always been a short-term option it was thought that, unless a constant balancing act was performed, in the long term it would inevitably lead to degeneration and corruption. In the nineteenth century, before the Ottoman government took the initiative and forced the patriarchate to reform, several attempts had been made already by people among the clergy and laymen to reform the church from within.

By the end of the eighteenth century, the system of electing the higher clergy (which included paying a sum of money to the church and the Ottoman government) was being abused by some candidates who, although lacking in social standing and education, had managed to enter the election process by producing large sums of money. At the same time the patriarchate relaxed its careful screening of suitable candidates for these positions because of its increasing financial deficit, due partly to a mismanagement of the patriarchal funds but mostly to the enormous regular and ad hoc taxes that were collected by the Ottoman government, and which became harsher and more difficult to pay during the time of the Greek Revolution. For example, in 1825:

> Mehmed, the Pasha of Thessaly, imposed a tax of fifty thousand *piastres* on the holy [Mount Athos] monasteries. Having already exhausted their coffers [from the previous year's taxes], the monasteries had to raise a loan (of 18,342 *piastres*) from the church, priests, and people of the Thessaloniki diocese through the good offices of Bishop Neophytos of Kampania. A year later the creditors demanded that the monasteries repay the loan. As they were not able to, they turned to the patriarch for help and protection. On 2 April 1826 the patriarch wrote to Bishop Theodosios of Polyane, the vicar of Metropolitan Mattheos, and the *prokritoi* of the Thessaloniki diocese, asking that they should extend the debt repayment period of the Mount Athos monasteries and should not cause anxiety to either Bishop Neophytos or the monasteries, since it was not that the monasteries were refusing to pay, it was simply that at that particular time they did not have a penny to their name.[90]

The patriarchate's increasing financial difficulties resulted in virtually "auctioning" the positions of metropolitans and bishops, and in some cases the new appointee turned out to be an ambitious priest who had borrowed vast sums of money in order to purchase such a socially desired position.[91] Upon reaching their dioceses,

90. Sokolov 2013, 285–86.

91. The custom of purchasing a government position was very similar to the Austrian system, where the emperor conferred on certain court officials the right to appoint their subordinates. The Austrian lord chamberlain, for example, could appoint new chancellors, each of whom [in the eighteenth century] had to pay him 200 ducats for the honor. (There were in consequence a great many chancellors). See, for example, Cassels 1966, 19, 20.

these religious entrepreneurs tried to recoup both their money and to make more for the patriarchal debt. Since the metropolitans and bishops had the right to collect taxes (*dosimata*), they set about imposing on their flocks as much tax as they felt would bring them a good return.[92]

Absenteeism of high clergy from their provinces was another cause for dissatisfaction. Some metropolitans visited their provinces only a few times a year, usually at the time of the collection of the taxes, and spent the rest of the time in Constantinople, where life was much more pleasurable for rich single men. The Ottoman Greek press mentioned some cases where the people of various provinces were petitioning the patriarch for the return of their bishop to his see:

> After repeated petitions by the people of Samokov to the Great Church [in 1849] it was agreed that the Metropolitan should return to his province. And as we mentioned in our previous number, he already left for his province with the blessings of both the Patriarch and the Holy Synod.[93]

This information probably refers to Metropolitan Mattheos, a member of the well-known Phanariot family of the Aristarches, who, because of his eccentricities, was rather disliked by most of his Bulgarian parishioners, who gave him the attribute Deli-Matei (Mad Matthew). He lived in palatial accommodation in Constantinople and tried to retain Samokov for as long as he could because of its large revenue.[94]

By the late eighteenth century, officials within the Ottoman government had found that deposing a patriarch was a good source of income deriving both from effecting his deposition – a secret payment by interested parties – and when the new patriarch was enthroned, the customary *bahşiş* (gratuity). In this the Ottoman officials had secured, either through blackmail or by manipulating the greed of some among the geronts (the electoral body of the patriarchate and financial administrators of the Orthodox Church), their collaboration in toppling the patriarch, expecting to make money from the election of his successor. The patriarchal election and dismissal were in fact events that had acquired great political, financial, and diplomatic importance, involving various groups of interested parties, such as Ottoman grand viziers, ministers, ambassadors, and important personalities within the Rum milleti.

---

92. A letter from the bishop of Lykostomion and Platamon (near Larissa) to his superior the metropolitan of Thessaloniki, dated May 29, 1789, illustrates the situation. The letter writer, a certain Bishop Dionyssios, wrote to his metropolitan – who has just been appointed – regarding the large sums of money he had demanded of him; "It is so charming of you my lord to ask me to give you so much and keep so little for myself. But then, I suppose, there is good reason for it [the Metropolitan had to pay back what he owed and make up some debt return] so I will not ask you to reduce the amount you have demanded of me." In Oikonomou 1962, page 2 of the introduction.

93. *Ephemeris tes Smyrnes*, no. 27, October 14, 1849.

94. The information was given to me by Dr. Leslie Collins, S.S.E.E.S., University of London.

In the period 1843–1848 there were a series of attempts to reform the structure of the patriarchate by a national assembly that consisted of clergy and – after a lot of power politics maneuvering – the most important lay citizens of Constantinople. In April 1847 a mixed national assembly was called. Although the reason for it was ostensibly the punishment of embezzling priests and the sorting out of the national debt, one must not overlook the ambition of some powerful lay members of the Orthodox nation, such as Stephanos Vogorides, Nikolaos Aristarches, and Ioannis Psycharis, to become ex-officio participants in the workings of the holy synod, thus legitimizing their involvement in the affairs of the millet. The end product of this assembly's workings was a code of regulations consisting of fifteen chapters dealing with the reform of a host of things, including the election of bishops, the membership of the holy synod, the institution of the geronts, the Common Fund, etc. Due to the reaction of the geronts, the regulations failed to be endorsed and all those who masterminded them, including the patriarch Anthimos VI, fell from power. At the same time (1848) both Aristarches and Vogorides suffered severe setbacks due to the democratic insurgencies that were spreading in the Danubian principalities. Aristarches was dismissed from the position of *kapı kâhya* (representative of the Porte) by the revolutionary government of Walachia and Vogorides lost power in Moldavia as a result of the difficulties of his son-in-law, Michael Sturdza.[95] Because of the close connection of the crisis in the principalities with the French, this was reflected also in the patriarchal group antagonisms with the increased influence of a faction.[96] By the end of the Crimean War France had assumed the position of support for the union of the principalities and was supported in this position by Russia and Austria. This position was a result of France's attempt to diminish the British influence in the Ottoman Empire, which was also manifested by France's support for the francophile reformers Fuad Pasha and Âli Pasha.

The geronts and the clergy in general were usually allied with another group in the Ottoman Greek society: the guilds. The members of guilds (Turkish *esnafs*; Greek *syntechnie*s) were part of the traditional socio-political structure together with the old Phanariot class, which after the Greek Revolution had become almost extinct. They represented the commercial interests of the old professions and usually sided with the church, especially against the new "bourgeoisie," whose interests were not always compatible with the interests of the guilds. According to British ambassador Stratford Canning, the guilds were the only social organizations related to commerce and trade that the Ottoman government created and recognized and therefore their opinion should be taken seriously, especially if it had to be measured against the self-interest of the various prominent members of the bourgeoisie who were involved in the affairs of the patriarchate.[97]

95. See Sturdza 1983, and Hitchins 1996.
96. There were also prominent groups with Anglophile and Russophile leanings.
97. F.O.78/1087, no. 711, Lord Stratford Canning to the Earl of Clarendon, September 17, 1855; in Stamatopoulos 2003, 54.

By the end of the Crimean War the ultimate protector and natural ally of the Ottoman Orthodox had been defeated and one could easily distinguish two emerging rival groups vying for power in the Orthodox Church. The first one was attached to the French Embassy and consisted of such people as Nikolaos Aristarches, Ioannis Psychares, Manuel Logothetis, Âli Pasha, and Fuad Pasha, and their friends, and the second one was attached to the British Embassy and included Stephanos Vogorides, Michael Sturdza, Alekos Mousouros, Alexandros Photiades, Stephanos Karatheodores, and Reşid Pasha, and their friends.

The origins of those two groups can be traced back to the beginnings of the Crimean War. As was its customary procedure before a war, the Sublime Porte issued a *firman* drafted by S. Vogorides and supported by British Ambassador Stratford Canning[98] in which all the ancient privileges given to the Orthodox patriarchate were re-confirmed, including the land and income rights of churches and monasteries. Although this was standard practice before a war to secure the co-operation of the non-Muslim populations by issuing various assurances, this *firman* can be seen as a precursor to the more far-reaching changes that were to be imposed on non-Muslims in the event that the war would be won by the Ottomans and their Western European allies.

The *firman* was handed to the new patriarch Anthimos VI, who had meanwhile succeeded Germanos IV, who died suddenly in 1852. Anthimos VI had been patriarch once before, from 1845–1848. During this first period, as mentioned earlier, he had presided over the issuing of a new code on patriarchal regulations. This work had been shelved thanks to the reaction of the geronts, but later on it became the basis of the reform of the Orthodox Church at the national council that was created after the promulgation of the Hatt-ı Hümayun.

Although it was generally assumed to be an accomplishment of S. Vogorides and his son-in-law A. Photiades, Anthimos's second accession to the patriarchal throne has recently been attributed entirely to the British ambassador, Lord Stratford Canning.[99]

The second period of Anthimos VI on the patriarchal throne (1853–1855) was fraught by several problems that can be summarized under two general headings: a series of confrontations with the geronts, and being caught in the crossfire between the Anglophile and Francophile groups in Constantinople. These problems, eventually, combined to make his hold on the patriarchal throne untenable and despite both the majority in the holy synod and the guilds supporting him, Anthimos VI was accused by the geronts of corruption and embezzlement and was again deposed. The Francophile Fuad Pasha effected his deposition.

The British ambassador considered the deposition of Anthimos a personal

98. Lord Stratford Canning to the Earl of Clarendon, June 24 and October 31, 1853. See F.O. 424/11, doc. no. 290 in Stamatopoulos 2003, 394.

99. Stamatopoulos 2003, 53.

failure[100] and tried to make Fuad Pasha recall his decision. Such direct intervention by a foreign power was ill received, even by the Anglophile faction. Stephanos Vogorides wrote to Constantinos Mousouros (Ottoman ambassador to Vienna) that such actions by the British Embassy weakened not only its own credibility but also the credibility and influence of the "Anglophiles" in the Orthodox community:

> Because I am very sensible of the British influence, which I consider a salvation for the Ottoman Empire and I am most saddened by its weakening, I am forced to use my own influence and that of my friends in the Church and elsewhere to support his lordship.[101]

The Francophile camp, on the other hand, was jubilant at Canning's diplomatic blunder. Fuad Pasha's strident comment, that "the foreigners have no right to interfere in our internal affairs,"[102] besides being a victory cry for internal consumption, covertly implied the Porte's burning ambition to interfere in the affairs of the patriarchate. Fuad Pasha admitted as much to Vogorides after the election of the next patriarch, which was very much a Francophile affair with the open support of the Porte. Despite being invited to give his opinion on the election of the next patriarch, Vogorides abstained on the pretext of ill health. In a private meeting, Fuad intimated to Vogorides rather sheepishly that

> because until now the Patriarchs belonged either to the one or the other party of the Christians, this time we must elect a Patriarch that belongs to the Porte.[103]

Writing to Mousouros about the whole business of the redefining of the patriarchal privileges, Vogorides commented:

> in short, the Privileges of the Patriarch are restricted or removed arbitrarily without previously been considered by the Nation and without the knowledge of the allied powers to whom a written promise was given about the maintenance of the privileges.... Patriarchs were always made by ministers who were bribed ... using the Christians as instruments of their corruption. But, today, Fuad Pasha has completely unmasked himself and openly declares that "from now on WE shall make the Patriarch." In other words, the way remains the same but harder and more shameless than before.[104]

The Greek press, reporting the deposition of Anthimos, singled out the British in-

100. AGMFA/1856, ααк Г' δ (19,1) doc. no. 101, Ambassador A. G. Kountouriotes to minister of foreign affairs A. R. Rangavis, October 26, 1856 in Stamatopoulos 2003, 60.

101. Archive of Konstantinos Mousouros, file 23, doc. no. 23 in Stamatopoulos 2003.

102. Archive of Konstantinos Mousouros, file 23, doc. no. 61 in Stamatopoulos 2003.

103. Archive of Konstantine Mousouros, file 23, doc no. 70; in Stamatopoulos 2003, 60.

104. Ibid.

terference on his behalf. Anthimos was described as intelligent and uncompromising but also as greedy – possibly a reference to his failure to carry out his predecessor's encyclical about the "national' debt."[105] In the same issue the papers reported the election of the new patriarch, Kyrillos VII, "about whom we know nothing as yet," a covert indication of disapproval matched with Vogorides' personal views about him: "a man unknown and gullible, whose greatest quality was that he has been a teacher for the children of [bankers] Zarifis and Zafeiropoulos."[106]

Another report, circulated in the press soon after in Constantinople, countered such views:

> The character of the new Patriarch, his natural calm, his great education, his impartiality and the expert leadership which he displayed for twenty-four years while he was Bishop in Aimos and Amaseia we are convinced will justify his election and the hopes of the nation. Although his tenure starts in difficult times, we think that it will be remembered as one of the most praiseworthy.[107]

Other reports were not as positive. For example this quote is from *Indépendance Belge*, reprinted in *He Hemera*:[108]

> [I]n truth we cannot say anything better about him [Patriarch Kyrillos] than we said about his predecessor [Anthimos]. Neither do we think that under his leadership the terrible embezzlements that burden the Greek community will cease. You must understand that he too owes his election to intrigue and plotting, and therefore he will fall the same way too. This is the way it is always done. The election is affected through money. Large sums are paid to the electors in order to attract their votes and the elected Patriarch uses every means to get his money, mostly borrowed with heavy interest, back. The best way to recoup his money is to appoint Bishops and Metropolitans all over the Empire purely for money. You understand that when these people go to their dioceses, they fleece their flock too to replenish their pockets.

Following this reprint, the Greek editor (Skylisses) pointed out that

> one could say much to counter this loquacity, malevolence, and ignorance of the [Catholic?] writer, which so vastly distorts the truth. If one wished to do so, however, one should visit the source of the problems, which we will do in due course.

105. *He Hemera*, no. 4 (September 30/October 12, 1855).
106. Archive of Konstantine Mousouros, file 23, doc. no. 70; in Stamatopoulos 2003, 60.
107. *He Hemera*, no. 5 (October 7/19, 1855).
108. *He Hemera*, no. 6 (October 14/26, 1855).

What Skylisses alluded to as the source of the problems was the role played by the various interested parties, foreign powers, and the Ottoman government, which was instrumental in the whole transaction.

The Reform of the Patriarchate in the Pages of the Ottoman Greek Press

The Ottoman Greek press took a great interest in the reorganization of the patriarchate and the creation of a salaried clergy, which began in 1856 and ended in 1862, and offers us a unique opportunity to follow this relatively little-known chapter of Ottoman history.[109] The reform of the patriarchate was carefully reported and commented on by both the editors[110] and a diverse readership. Although one can, today, re-create the story of the patriarchal reform using many other supporting documents currently available, the narrative below is made up solely from what was publicly available to the average Orthodox Christian who lived in the Ottoman Empire.[111] The coverage of the reform by the Ottoman Greek press offers for the first time an insight to how the Orthodox Christians at that time viewed the reform of the patriarchate and related issues.

The government order for the creation of a national assembly[112] that would

---

109. The patriarchal reform is of great interest to Bulgarian historians as the Bulgarian nation considers that its struggle against the patriarchate in order to achieve a national clergy and introduce the Bulgarian language in the schools and in the liturgy was the first step towards its national independence. Prominent Bulgarian works are: Burmov 1902, and Nikov 1929; and a host of articles, such as Drinov 1971), 137; Ivanov 1912, 158; Collins 1985; etc. M. Gedeon, archivist of the Greek patriarchate, has also written extensively about it in several books, including Gedeon 1908; Gedeon 1932; Gedeon 1939; Gedeon 1919–1920; Kyriakides 1892; Aristarchis 1876; and recently the excellent Stamatopoulos 2003, which includes an impressive listing of documents and private letters of personalities who were instrumental in the changes that were effected in the political, social, and economic life of the Orthodox Christians in the Ottoman Empire in the nineteenth century. There are also several books on the history of the Orthodox Church and the Church of Greece that mention the reforms of 1856. Finally, in 2013 the book of Russian author Ivan Sokolov appeared in an English translation *The Church of Constantinople in the Nineteenth Century* (first published in Russian in Moscow in 1904). Sokolov uses a lot of archival material and many secondary sources of the period to describe the reform, and provides supporting information for the reforms as presented in the Ottoman Greek press.

110. As mentioned earlier, *He Hemera* exists in almost complete runs and often in addition to its own correspondent reprints from all other Ottoman and several foreign newspapers. For this reason it is used in this study more often than any other.

111. Several works were published during the period of the reform (1856–1862) both by Greek and Bulgarian-speaking Orthodox. These are mostly of an emotional nature, attacking or defending the Bulgarian demands for a national clergy and a Bulgarian education. For example: Minçoğlu 1860; Tsoukalas 1859; Gerov 1852; etc.

112. Until the nineteenth century the national or mixed assembly was an unelected body appointed by the patriarchate and the Phanariot class consisting of specific clergy and lay representatives, assembled when the need arose to consider a specific matter and propose solutions.

organize a national council[113] to discuss the creation of a salaried clergy and a different system for electing the patriarch and the higher clergy (as announced in the Hatt-ı Hümayun) arrived at the patriarchate only two weeks after the order to read the decree in the churches.[114] It was a time when the patriarchate had to deal with a host of other problems, most of which were covered by the press. There were, for example, articles and reports on the dialogue between the Orthodox patriarchate and the Anglican Church (started in 1852) and other Christian sects. There were also reports on attacks against the Orthodox Christians in the Middle East, usually by the Maronites and the Druze of the Lebanon. Missionary activity concentrating on converting Orthodox Christians to the Catholic and Protestant faiths is also frequently mentioned already from the 1830s. Here I include an example from a slightly earlier period that highlights not only the attempts to curb missionary activity but also the power of British ambassadors to dethrone patriarchs in the nineteenth century. Patriarch Gregory VI (1835–40), like his predecessor, Gregory V, became known for his fervent care for the purity and inviolability of church teachings and canons, but miscalculated the protection offered by the states of Britain and France to their missionaries, or indeed the influence they exerted on the Porte, which eventually brought about his downfall.

> He zealously turned against the Western missionaries who spread the nets of their propaganda all over the East. He condemned the missionary activity of Lutherans, Calvinists, and Anglicans, exposed their delusions, and protested against the spreading of the Modern Greek translation of the Bible by the Bible Society. He reproached the bishops of the Ionian Islands for carelessness in fulfilment of their duties, and the local civil council for the new law in the spirit of Protestantism contradicting the Orthodox canons on marriage. The Ionian Islands were under the protectorate of England. The British ambassador in Constantinople, Stratford de Redcliffe, was displeased by the Patriarch's interference in the business of the Ionian republic because it was directed against his secret policy of annexing the islands for Britain, for which purpose the local population had to be torn away from the Orthodox faith and church. Treating Patriarch Gregory as a very dangerous enemy, Redcliffe went into battle against him. He relied

113. The national council or national mixed council was an elected body of clergy and lay representatives. The latter were elected by votes in each province from among all the Orthodox people of the Ottoman Empire for a specific purpose (in this case creating the new regulations that would govern the Rum milleti). Although these bodies were elected purely from inside the Orthodox Millet, the Ottoman Government had to approve their creation and usually this was a mere formality. The national councils were actually legislative bodies, but in the case of the national council we are examining here, its product, because the council was created at the command of the sultan and had as its purpose to change the existing sultanic law governing the election of the patriarch and the higher clergy dating back to1453, had to have the approval of the Ottoman government.

114. *He Hemera*, no. 50 (August 17/29, 1856).

upon the growing influence of British Eastern policy and the declining Russian influence in Turkey. Redcliffe openly asked the Porte for Gregory's deposition and demanded a trial of the Orthodox patriarch.[115]

The trial, whose transcript exists and is quoted verbatim by Sokolov,[116] found no guilt on the part of the patriarch but nevertheless the young Sultan Abdülmecid accused the patriarch of a political crime, and said that he deserved to be severely reprimanded for his mistreatment of Britain. The patriarch had no other recourse but to resign. The success of the British ambassador, Lord Redcliffe, in effecting the trial and dismissal of Patriarch Gregory VI in 1840 was still fresh in the patriarchal memory when the order to reform arrived at the patriarchate in 1856. From this and other more recent incidents, the patriarchate knew that it could neither rely on Britain nor on France for help.

Another issue exercising the patriarchate was the return to Orthodox Christianity by a number of Orthodox Christians whose families had converted to Islam some centuries before, or even more recently, to avoid persecution and taxation. In 1843 the Porte abolished the law under which Christian converts to Islam had to be executed if they returned to Christianity (until then anyone accused of apostasy from Islam had to be put to death). European outcry and diplomatic pressure forced the Porte to abolish this law but had to keep it secret until the following year, 1844, for fear of disturbances from the Muslim population.[117] Discussions about whether or not to adopt the Latin calendar, which the pope was trying at that time to impose on those Christians in the Ottoman Empire affiliated with the Catholic Church, are also reported. Some of the articles cover issues relating to the all-important power struggle between the Anglophile and Francophile factions as, for example, in several articles and reports on the union of the Rumanian principalities, where this rivalry was evident and where the French diplomatic victory became decisive for Ottoman internal politics as well. The union of the principalities was covered extensively by the Greek press for an additional reason: it was inextricably related to the control of the monasterial funds in these two provinces – an important issue for the patriarchate and in the struggle for its control. Another extensively covered item was the death of Reşid Pasha, the champion of the Anglophile group, which was also directly related to the reform of the patriarchate.

Most of the Orthodox reformers expected, as reflected in the Ottoman Greek press, that these new reforms, among other things, should go some way towards rectifying the current social and financial ills in the Orthodox community. They hoped that the reforms would assist in strengthening the relationship between the various Orthodox nations and stop the Catholic and Protestant sects from

---

115. Sokolov 2013, 341–42.
116. Sokolov 2013, 342–49.
117. Rosen 1860, part II:80–81; cited in Sokolov 2013, 341.

gaining any converts from among discontented Orthodox Christians. The Greek press began publishing articles, calculated, as we have seen earlier, to attack the financial mismanagement of the church, thereby adding to the pressure already exerted on the patriarchate by the government order to reform.

The Greek patriarchate knew that there was a strong group among the Orthodox who wanted more political power and their support for the status quo ante of the patriarchate was not to be taken for granted. They were also aware of the rising nationalism among the Bulgarians, which had been contained thus far by the supra-nationalist nature of religion.

So, when the order to reform finally arrived at the patriarchate, the patriarch had a multitude of internal and external problems to face and could neither count on the support of other Christian powers nor on the entirety of his own flock.

The patriarch's first reaction was to see this order as an opportunity to sort out the most immediate problem of the geronts. He made use of the fear, which had been generated in order to persuade the synod that the worst offenders among the geronts should be summoned to trial and the rest should leave for their provinces.[118] The patriarch hoped that in this way he would achieve some degree of concord among those Orthodox Christians who were complaining about absenteeism of bishops from their provinces and mismanagement in the running of the "nation's" (Rum miletti) finances.[119] Five bishops who were still loitering about in Constantinople were ordered to leave at once for their provinces (Iconion [Konya], Prespes [in the province of Macedonia], Bosnia, Crete, and Samokov). One of them, however, the bishop of Bosnia, was deposed just before his departure because of general complaints in his province,[120] while the rest left for their provinces in an uncharacteristic hurry. It took almost a year for the synod to decide who the scapegoats would be, but eventually, in March 1857, the patriarchate announced their names to the government. To everyone's surprise, one week later the Sublime Porte asked the patriarch in writing if these provincial bishops and one of the geronts, against whom so many complaints had been made, should be present at the national assembly, which was to organize the national council.[121] This was followed a few weeks later by an order from the grand vizier to the patriarch to make the necessary arrangements for the creation of a salaried clergy,[122] in accordance with article seven of the Hatt-ı Hümayun. Finally, an imperial decree arrived ordering the creation of the national assembly that would reorganize the church.

---

118. *He Hemera*, no. 53 (September 17/29, 1856).

119. Nation (*ethnos*). When capitalized it means the Orthodox Christians; lowercase designates a nation in a political sense (for example, *Boulgariko ethnos*).

120. *He Hemera*, no. 53 (September 7/19, 1856).

121. *He Hemera*, no. 83 (April 5/17, 1857).

122. *He Hemera*, nos. 85, 86, 87, 88, 90.

The inaugural meeting of the assembly took place on November 7, 1857.[123] The reform of the patriarchate had begun at a time when Reşid Pasha was too ill to intervene in any substantive way and this meant that the more moderate Anglophile reformers were significantly weakened. Reşid died soon afterwards and the Francophile faction in the government appeared to gain control. This impression was strengthened less than two months later, when the semi-official *Journal de Constantinople* published an article[124] – reprinted in the Ottoman Greek press – which argued that the sufferings of the non-Muslim peoples of the empire did not derive, as Europe thought, from the mistakes of the Turkish government. It was true that this government had committed some mistakes, but the source of the Christians' gravest problems was the extreme power of the higher Orthodox clergy, which combined religious with political powers. This article, echoing the views of Napoleon III, gave a clear message to its readers that the government, now under French influence, had decided to strip the church of most of its privileges. There was an immediate reply in the Greek press written by the Ottoman correspondent of the Greek newspaper *Aion* (see above), who was a Greek citizen and therefore immune from prosecution, stating that the proposed reform of the Orthodox church was a ploy to take away from it all its rights and privileges. He openly warned the government that it had fallen into the trap of its Crimean allies and that if it pursued this policy the Ottoman Empire would in effect be left without its Balkan provinces. Some other Greeks held different views. The reformist editor of *He Hemera* commented that a salaried clergy was an excellent concept, because of the simony of some of the clergy.[125]

At the same time as these articles were appearing in the Ottoman Greek press, the *buyuruldu* (imperial decree) regarding the creation of the national assembly arrived at the patriarchate. The patriarch, however, could not form an assembly, as requested, from those present because the grand vizier had to be informed in advance about its members and he wanted to have the right to approve them.[126] Eventually the names of the people chosen to become members of the national assembly were duly sent to the Sublime Porte. They were: (Prince of Samos) S. Vogorides (Ottoman Bulgarian), I. Logothetis (Ottoman Greek), I. Psychares (Ottoman Greek), St. Karatheodore (Ottoman Greek), K. Karatheodore (Ottoman Greek), V. Krikotsos (Ottoman Greek), Tz.. Constantinides (Ottoman Greek), Th. H. Photis, (Ottoman Greek) C. Adosides (Ottoman Greek), and A. J. Photiades (Ottoman Greek). The candidates were all well-known figures drawn either from the Ottoman civil service or banking, commerce, and medicine. Reşid Pasha removed three names from the list, those of G. Konstantinides, K. Adosides, and A.

123. *He Hemera*, nos 98, 99, 116.
124. Reprinted in *He Hemera*, no. 86 (April 19/May 1, 1857).
125. *He Hemera*, no. 88 (May 10/22, 1857).
126. *He Hemera*, no. 86 (April 19/May 1, 1857).

J. Photiades. [127] According to *He Hemera*, these people were then forced to resign so that their good names would not be compromised, but were instead promised positions on the national council.[128] In order to achieve the necessary number for the assembly, seven clergymen and twelve laymen,[129] intense negotiations began lasting well into August, when the final list was drawn up and approved. The members of the assembly were to be:

> *Clergy*: the geronts of Ephesos, Kyzikos, Herakleion, Nicomedia, Halcedon, Derkon, and Didimoteichon (the latter was their chairman);

> *Laymen*: S. Vogorides, N. Aristarchis, I. Psycharis, P. Mousouros, A. J. Photiades, I. Paleologos, S. Karatheodore, Sarantis Archigenis, Th. Photiou, V. Krikotsos, Tz.. Constantinides.[130]

In the final list the Greek reader observed the inclusion of the names of two of the three people whom the grand vizier had removed two months earlier. This revealed considerable behind-the-scenes bargaining. At the same time, the patriarch sent an encyclical to twenty of the most important provinces, ordering them to send their representatives to Constantinople to take part in the meetings of the assembly.

It was not until November that the national assembly was able to begin functioning. The meetings were to be held in secret but the patriarch undertook the responsibility of forwarding the minutes of the meetings to the relevant ministries. The *firman* of the Sublime Porte calling for the creation of an extraordinary council in the patriarchate in order to discuss alterations to the existing system for electing the patriarch and the high clergy and the creation of a salaried clergy was read out during the inaugural meeting.[131] This *firman* confirmed the worst fears of the conservative elements in the Rum milleti, who had already foreseen disaster since the signing of the Treaty of Paris. In its first paragraph the new *firman* announced to the non-Muslim millets of the empire that the privileges and immunities they had acquired from Mehmed II and his successors should be "improved" and brought up to date as "the present age of enlightenment demanded." For this reason, the sultan ordered that "extraordinary councils should be created in all non-Muslim millets in order to improve their situation, according to the agenda set by the sultan and under the supervision of the Sublime Porte." It was the first time in almost 400 years that the Ottoman government had interfered in such a direct way in the affairs of the non-Muslim millets. Moreover, this *firman* was in contravention of article 2 of the Hatt-ı Hümayun, which re-confirmed all the

127. *He Hemera*, no. 88 (May 10/22, 1857).
128. *He Hemera*, no. 90 (May 24/June 5, 1857).
129. *He Hemera*, no. 98 (July 19/31, 1857).
130. *He Hemera*, no. 99 (July 26/August 7, 1857).
131. *He Hemera*, no. 116 (November 22/December 4, 1857).

privileges and immunities given to the Orthodox Christians since the fall of Constantinople. The *firman* proceeded to give precise instructions about the election of the patriarchs, bishops, and the chief rabbi (*hahambaşı*), and to declare that these positions would be for life. Secondly, it abolished the voluntary donations to the clergy and replaced them with monthly salaries. The millet's internal affairs were to be managed by a mixed council composed of clergymen and laymen. In order to effect these changes an extraordinary council had to be created in the patriarchates of the Greeks (Rum), Armenians, and Catholics, and by the *hahambaşı* of the Jews. Regarding the Greek patriarchate, the extraordinary mixed council had to be composed of seven bishops elected from among the most senior and morally above reproach. Moreover, twenty laymen had to be elected, ten from among the most important members of the community, and ten from the most important guilds, as was the custom for the election of the patriarch. The Sublime Porte would then choose five from each group. The notables of each province would elect a landowner of good standing, resident in that province for the past ten years, and send him to the provincial capital. Here the resident notables would also elect three representatives. All of these would then assemble to elect one from their number to represent their province in Constantinople. In all the discussions of the patriarchate, except those of a purely religious nature, a representative of the Sublime Porte had to be present. The *firman*, which was printed in its entirety in the Greek press, presented the Greek reader with the new reality: government intervention would become a permanent fixture in the affairs of the millet.

Although the meetings of the assembly were held in secret, it was leaked to the Greek press that in one of them, one of the members, the sultan's doctor, and a member of the moderate reformers, K. Karatheodore, proposed to the assembly that it should ask the government to waive its demand to approve ten from the proposed twenty members that would form the national council and dismiss the rest. The assembly endorsed this proposal and sent it to the Sublime Porte.[132] Two weeks later, it was reported that "the minister of foreign affairs had dismissed the petition of the assembly of the Rum milleti (translated in Greek as *Romaïkon ethnos*)." It was also reported that the assembly respectfully reapplied with the same petition[133] but that it was dismissed for a second time.[134] Finally, on January 15, 1858, the national assembly produced a list of twenty names.[135] From these, the Porte would choose ten. The candidates for the national council, put forward by the assembly were: Stephanake Bey (Vogorides, prince of Samos), Archon Logothetis (Prince Lawmaker) N. Aristarchis, I. Psycharis, P. Mousouros, A. Photiades, K. Adosides, L. Lachovares, I. Paleologos, S. Karatheodore, K. Karatheodore, V.

132. *He Hemera*, no. 117 (November 29/December 11, 1857).
133. *He Hemera*, no. 119, (December 13/25, 1857).
134. *He Hemera*, no. 117 (November 29/December 11, 1857).
135. *He Hemera*, no. 122 (January 3/15, 1858).

Krikotsos, D. Apostolides, G. Kartales, Th. H. Photiou, G. Photiades, E. Kyriakou, Z. Konstantinides, P. Sgouros, V. Zographos, and G. Alaseirles.

As these names arrived at the ministry of foreign affairs the Greeks were informed through their press that the great grand vizier, Reşid Pasha, mastermind of the Ottoman reforms, had died. This was a great blow to the Anglophile group and the moderate modernizers, who feared that his whole reform program would be misused. According to the Greek press, his death

> came at a time when he had begun to persuade even his enemies of the correctness of his actions and he was able to ask for concessions from all parties and to present painful truths even to the Sultan.[136]

For the Greek press the main concern was that the death of Reşid was

> not the death of a man but the death of a whole system. Reşid alone managed to win over the critics, restrain inordinate ambitions, and calm enmities. Moreover, his great belief in his work managed to convince both the Sultan and the people, who gave him an undertaking to connect the interests of Turkey with those of Europe and introduce such reforms in the Empire as were deemed necessary by the progress of the times.[137]

The patriarchal assembly felt that under the circumstances it was better to wait until the new power center would form within the government. But while lay and clergy involved in the imposed reform of the Orthodox Church were waiting to see what Reşid's successor would make of the reform program, the Greek press of Constantinople and Smyrna began to air the grievances of the Bulgarian Orthodox Christians against the patriarchate.

The Bulgarian grudges against the "cultural imperialism" of the Patriarchate of Constantinople had their roots deep in the history of this nation. The Bulgarians had their own national church, established in the tenth century when the Greeks of the Eastern Roman Empire converted them to Christianity. The Bulgarian church was taken over by the Patriarchate of Constantinople in the fifteenth century, after the Ottomans conquered Bulgaria.[138] The Bulgarians never forgot the way in which they passed into the jurisdiction of the Patriarchate of Constantinople. Nor did they ever readily accept the imposition of the Greek language in their schools and churches or, still worse, the often excessive taxation by the church's mostly Greek-speaking high priests, who were appointed as their bishops. In the

136. *He Hemera*, no. 120 (December 19/31, 1857), and no. 122 (January 3/15, 1858).

137. Ibid.

138. The Bulgarian patriarch who had led the opposition to the Turks in the three-month siege of Trnovo (1393), together with his higher clergy, were imprisoned by the Ottomans. The Patriarchate of Constantinople took over the Bulgarian church afterwards, arguing that it had to save the Bulgarian Orthodox Church from destruction.

nineteenth century they began their struggle for national self-determination, which eventually not only gave them their own independent church but also created the preconditions for an independent Bulgaria. As the attempts to reform the Orthodox Church gained momentum in Constantinople and the antagonism between the pro-French and pro-British factions intensified, with the Russians apparently joining the French on the issue of the Danubian principalities, the Bulgarians were encouraged to intensify their demands for religious and eventually national independence. Russia's pan-Orthodox policy had stifled such demands for several decades, but the shift in Russia's foreign policy interests from pan-Orthodoxy to pan-Slavism, after the Crimean War, gave the Bulgarians the green light to pursue their own political agenda.

Many articles on what became "the Bulgarian question" were reprinted in the Trieste Greek paper *He Hemera*. All Ottoman Greek-speakers who had access to a Greek newspaper were reading reports about Bulgarian resentments, which the reporters traced back five years earlier. According to these reports, Bulgarian-speaking peoples in some places in the provinces of Thrace, Macedonia, and Bulgaria had been trying to introduce their language into church services, which until then had been held in Greek, the official language of the church. When the patriarchate refused to relent, they began attacking local Greek-speakers, whose sole offence, as was stressed in the articles, was their language, which, for historical reasons, was the same as the one in which the gospels were written. Moreover, the Bulgarians were reported as having been prompted by the local representatives of Russia to adopt this stance towards the patriarchate and their Greek Orthodox brethren. These reports were followed by others claiming that in reality the Bulgarians wanted political independence and that Russia was supporting the creation of an independent Bulgaria. The publication of a petition from some Bulgarians demanding linguistic, political, and religious autonomy within the Ottoman Empire was given great prominence in the Greek press. The patriarchate appeared to attempt to calm matters and some local bishops began to accede to Bulgarian demands when the overwhelming majority in the area was Bulgarian.[139]

One of these reports, regarding the province of Adrianople, which was first published in *Vyzantis* of Constantinople and then reprinted in *He Hemera* of Trieste,[140] stressed that

> for a very long time Greeks and the few Bulgarian-speaking peoples of
> the capital of the province [Adrianople] lived in complete harmony. The
> Greeks were inseparable from the Bulgarians and they all obeyed the laws
> of the Great Church. In their churches the liturgy was performed in the

139. See, for example, *He Hemera*, no. 161 (October 3/15, 1858).
140. *He Hemera* no. 127 (February 7/19, 1858).

traditional Greek language and no one ever asked for this tradition to be broken and for Slavonic to be heard in the churches.

This harmony was interrupted, according to the report, at the beginning of the Crimean War, when the Bulgarians started demanding that the language of the liturgy should be Slavonic, and began quarrelling with the Greeks. "We will not examine here whether this quarrel might have a just cause or not," wrote the editor of *Vyzantis*; what was important for him was that during the Crimean War "two thirds of the churches outside Adrianople city held the liturgy in Slavonic" and that in 1856 "there was an attempt even in the capital, Adrianople, to impose such a thing." Apparently there was a great dispute between the Bulgarians and the Greeks there for two years and it was only when the Great Church intervened and "ordered the metropolitan of Adrianople to avoid such innovations and to try to reconcile the two sides" that things cooled down. The reconciliation was, however, brief because

> the so-called Bulgarian element did not cease trying, and gradually … some Slavonic exclamations were introduced in all the churches and mass was reduced to a multilingual mess.

But worse, according to the writer, was yet to come. In 1857 the Russian agent (probably meaning consul), a certain Mr. Stupen, asked the Great Church for a Slavonic liturgy every Friday in a church that belonged to the monastery of the Holy Sepulchre in Jerusalem. The Great Church granted his demand but the local metropolitan extended the use of Slavonic to all the liturgies held in that church. Moreover, it seems that the metropolitan secretly gave his permission for the liturgy to be held in Slavonic in another church, called Kereshane. That church, however, had a large Greek congregation, which bridled at this change. "We are not advocates of exclusivity," argued the editor of *Vyzantis*:

> [T]he peoples have their traditions and their respected customs and when these get trampled on, they get upset. Their actions must not be judged severely. On the one side [the Greeks] learned of the secret permission to change the language of the liturgy and they felt that their ancient tradition and rights had been violated and they got upset about it. On the other side, those who had effected the change [the Bulgarians] declared that they were prepared to die for it.

Things came to a head and it was decided to close the church in order to avoid clashes between the quick tempered on both sides. It seems that it was the wife of the Russian agent, Mrs. Stupen, who started the trouble when upon arrival at the church for mass she found it closed.

Having suffered the heavy cold of the journey unnecessarily, she demanded the keys of the church from the metropolitan. He agreed to re-open the church if everybody agreed that the liturgy would be recited alternately in Greek and in Bulgarian under the supervision of the archdeacon and two notables of each side. This arrangement was a sort of temporary compromise until the Great Church would come to a permanent decision.

The liturgy started and everything was going well until

> the psalt who was going to sing in Slavonic, not knowing, apparently, the timing of his interjection, started singing prematurely, so that the Archdeacon had to intervene, telling him to stop and wait his turn. This simple event had a mixed reception. The Bulgarians rose as if they were waiting for it and started cursing at the Greeks and the deacon, who was thrown out of the Church.

The episode ended after everybody was removed from the church:

> But no one wanted in the slightest to offend [the Bulgarians] and no one retaliated [to their curses], which proves that the one side [the Greeks] were not interested in a quarrel, which could have had a very serious outcome.

The worst thing for the Greeks and the editor of *Vyzantis* was that next day

> Mr. Stupen gathered the Bulgarians to decide what to do … while this was, in fact, entirely a matter for the local religious and state authorities.… the presence of Mr. Stupen in an affair that was none of his business was considered a scandal.

The meeting ended when it was decided to inform the Great Church.

The following week *He Hemera* had a front-page report about a "revolt in the Slavonic provinces of Turkey,"[141] followed on the fourth page by a report on the patriarch's success in reconciling the Greeks and Bulgarians in Adrianople. Other reports warned of the increasing demands of the Bulgarians for independence, supported by the Russians.[142]

In March of the same year (1858), the Greek press took a respite from the Bulgarian issues in order to inform its readers that the metropolitan of Salonica, Kallinikos, who had been elected and appointed by the holy synod as the new patriarch of Jerusalem, had refused the position. Eventually, a reluctant Kallinikos accepted the patriarchal throne. His initial refusal to accept the position, followed by his subsequent enthronement, prompted articles about the real underlying

141. *He Hemera*, no. 128 (February 14/28, 1858).
142. For example, *He Hemera*, no. 161 (October 3/15, 1858).

issue, the reform of the patriarchate. In response an official letter of caution was circulated by the government, which was published in the Greek press. In this letter, the government complained that:

> some newspapers of our capital are entering into futile discussions regard-
> ing the affairs of the Patriarchate of the Romans [Rum] and its clergy and
> are condemning acts on which they have no competence.

The government warned that it held the dignity of the clergy of the various millets in high regard and it considered it its duty to protect them from any insult.
It went even further in anticipation of more commentary on the reform of the
patriarchate and warned:

> the above-mentioned newspapers must abstain from insulting remarks
> directed at religious matters and from derogatory comments every time
> the Patriarchate makes an announcement.[143]

This *firman* coincided with the government's closure of the Constantinopolitan
paper *Vyzantis*. The warnings and the closure led to a period of relative silence
regarding the affairs of the patriarchate. Secret meetings had resumed with the
object of finding the lay and clerical members who would take part in and nego-
tiate an agenda for the national council agreeable to all and accommodating the
government's orders. But, finally, *Vyzantis* resumed publication at the end of August
1858, and immediately resumed its reporting on the reform of the patriarchate.
This signalled the end of a period of enforced silence on this subject as far as the
Greek press was concerned, and at the end of August *He Hemera*'s correspondent
in Constantinople wrote a long article on the proceedings of the national assembly,
in which he stressed that

> there is no doubt that the most important preoccupation of the Assembly
> will be the creation of a salaried clergy, something which the ex-Prince of
> Samos, Mr. Stephanos Vogorides, has already been trying to create for the
> past eighteen years.

The article confirmed that the seven geronts, considered by many to be a great
obstacle to the modernization of the patriarchate, were

> exempted from this Council by the Sublime Porte, which, in addition,
> ordered the Patriarch to remove seven other Metropolitans.[144]

In September 1858, as the patriarchal assembly was nearing the completion of
its preliminary operations regarding the organization of the national council, *He*

143. *He Hemera*, no. 133 (March 21/April 2, 1858).
144. *He Hemera*, no. 155 (August 22/September 3, 1858).

Hemera reprinted from the German-language *Trieste Zeitung* a long letter written from the Dardanelles regarding "the ecclesiastical question in Bulgaria."[145] According to this letter, the Patriarchate of Constantinople had received displeasing news from Bulgaria:

> The burning desire of the Bulgarians to see a national clergy established among them and governing alone their ecclesiastical affairs is today more alive than ever before; some people say that the Bulgarians are finding warm support in some places. The Bulgarians, whose population is up to three million souls, are united to the Great Church by the bonds of faith, but following their national memory they do not want to be subject to a clergy not speaking their father's tongue.

The letter-writer tried further to explain why "Bulgarians" were attacking "Greeks":

> There are forces, which are trying to develop an antipathy between the Greeks and the Bulgarians ... so that they will be able to undermine the influence that the Patriarchate exerts on all the Orthodox Slavs of the Ottoman Empire ...

In the writer's opinion, this was partly the fault of the synod in Constantinople, which:

> through their possession of all the Archbishoprics and the running of many rich monasteries, secured for the Greeks a superior position amongst the Slavs of Turkey, which is neither proportional to their number nor pleasing to the Slavs.

The letter-writer continued by suggesting that the privileges given to the synod in Constantinople by the Ottoman government to lead the Slavic Orthodox churches must be used purely

> for the management of Church affairs and not as a means of stifling the national character of the non-Greek Orthodox nations in the Empire.

The letter continued with an analysis of Russia's role among the Orthodox of the empire:

> Since the treaty of Küçük Kaynarca, the Eastern Christians realized that the right of protecting the Orthodox Church became in the hands of Russia a double-edged sword, which could be used against both friend and foe, depending on the circumstances.

145. *He Hemera*, no. 157 (September 5/17, 1858).

According to this analysis, Russian policy was not to render support to her religious kinsmen, but

> to incite the Slavs against the Greeks when it is in her interest to do so, and to promise the latter all her protection and influence if they do not oppose her Eastern policy.

Russia's policy seems to have been divide and rule:

> A developed Hellenism [Greek culture and language] will never please Russia, whose Eastern policy consists mainly of maintaining the existing differences among the Orthodox nations, sometimes by sowing the seed of division, by supporting their hopes and expectations based on their historical memory, and at other times by claiming that Russia has a common goal with these nations.

The letter ended by suggesting that the Orthodox Church did not have the right to allow the Bulgarians to have a national clergy, which was a political request, and would initiate a strong political movement among the various Orthodox nations of the empire. What should be done and could be done, however, was for

> the higher and lower Greek clergy to take a far greater interest in the real needs of the Bulgarians in education and local government.

The article informed Greek readers about several issues that were unfolding among the Bulgarians and their more general repercussions: the Bulgarians desired their own national clergy, which would break up the unity of the Orthodox millet. Russia was named as being behind this political demand that could not be satisfied by the church. Nevertheless, the writer pointed out that the church should make a far greater effort to look after the needs of the Bulgarian Orthodox. The article, in short, made two clear points. The first was that the patriarchate had to reform in such a way as to satisfy the needs of the non-Greek-speaking Orthodox in education and local government. The second was that if it reformed itself in this way it might avert the break-up of the Orthodox nation – a political move that would only benefit Russia.

The political dimension of the Bulgarian demands for a national clergy was stressed in an article in the *Newspaper of Temeshvar* (in Austria-Hungary) a few weeks later, reprinted in *He Hemera*,[146] which reported that

> foreign incitement no doubt plays its part in the unrest of the Slavs.... The Bulgarians having become increasingly bolder in demanding their political

---

146. *He Hemera*, no. 162, (October 10/22, 1858).

emancipation.... The local governor of Trnovo met with the general governor of Vidin and upon returning [to Trnovo] asked the Muslims to have
their guns ready and to carry them when they go out of their houses.

In its next number, *He Hemera*[147] reprinted a report from the Italian *Osservatore Triestino*, which related how

[t]he Patriarchate of the Phanar, moved by a spirit of extreme bigotry and
injustice, refused to enlist in the catalogue of the state Medical School all
those candidates who were Bulgarian.

The editor of *He Hemera* devoted almost half a page to refute this "Catholic"
accusation, arguing that "such a spirit cannot exist in the Eastern Orthodox
Church." He added that when in Western Europe (the Catholic and Protestant
lands), Jews and others were persecuted and burned at the stake, the Orthodox
Church always followed a tolerant and loving attitude. In fact, we know that fifteen
Bulgarian students had already been admitted to the medical school in 1856. Their
registration became news[148] when they insisted on being registered at the school
as Bulgarians rather than as Rum.[149]

Eventually, in September 1858, *Vyzantis* printed the names of the final ten
people approved by the Sublime Porte to sit in the national council. Among them
one encounters the members of both the Anglophile and Francophile groups.
They were, "Prince S. Vogorides, Archon Great Logothetis N. Aristarchis, the
gentlemen I. Psychares, C. Adosides, K. and S. Karatheodorides [another form
for Karatheodore], V. Krikotsos, E. Kyriakou, Tz. Constantinides, Ch. Victoros.[150]
The church now had the names of all the lay and clerical members who would
participate in the deliberations of the national council. There was no excuse for
delaying things further.

In October 1858 the national council finally began its deliberations. The
patriarch opened the proceedings with a speech, which stressed the importance
and seriousness of the occasion:

[This occasion is i]mportant because the Sultan is showing his fatherly
interest in our Church and, while continuing to safeguard our privileges,
demands that we reorganize [our Church] so that we will function better.
Serious, because if we fail in this task, we are going to lose the respect of
our own people and bring upon us the wrath of the Sultan.[151]

147. *He Hemera*, no. 163 (October 17/29, 1858).
148. *He Hemera*, no. 22 (February 3/15, 1856).
149. The "Bulgarian question" occupied the Greek press especially after the end of the reform
of the church.
150. *He Hemera*, no. 156 (August 29/September 10, 1858).
151. *He Hemera*, no. 163 (October 17/29, 1858).

It was agreed that the national council was to meet once a week, and that the meetings were to be held in secret. What the patriarch failed to spell out was, however, reported in the Greek press. The report from Constantinople to *He Hemera* summed it up thus:

> Today the Council started its proceedings, on which depends the fate and future of our [religious] Nation and our Church.

Although the meetings were held in camera, Ottoman Greek journalists competed with each other to discover the subjects under discussion in the council and even the speeches of the participants. *Amaltheia* and *Vyzantis* did their best to provide their news-hungry readership with as much information as possible. *He Hemera* faithfully reprinted everything and added reports by its own correspondents. It seems that both the third and the fourth meetings were devoted to the election of the patriarch and to whether he was to be elected only by the synod or by a mixed council of laymen and clergymen:

> In the vote that followed the laymen won because they were supported
> by the Metropolitans of Adrianople, Kyrillos; of Amaseia, Sofronios; and
> of Didymoteichon, Meletios. Thus, it was agreed that the Synod would
> propose three candidates and then both the Synod and the laymen would
> vote for the prospective candidate to become Patriarch.[152]

Amaltheia of Smyrna was the first newspaper, in its issue of November 17/19, to succeed in publishing at length the proceedings of one of the meetings of the council – the fifth. It is possible that details of the meeting were leaked to the editor by the representative of Smyrna to the national assembly, Yağcoğlu (a Greek usage of Yağcıoğlu), who argued in favor of the provincial representatives and their active involvement at the proceedings. The meeting began with a reading of the minutes of the previous meeting and the registration of the speeches by Messrs. Karatheodore and Yağcoğlu. Then the discussion for the election of the patriarch continued. Yağcoğlu, who represented Smyrna, demanded to know exactly which members would form the committee that would elect the patriarch.

> Then Mr. Karatheodore read out a plan for the election of the Patriarch,
> which in short is this: When the Ecumenical throne becomes vacant one
> of the oldest members of the Synod should be appointed as regent and he,
> together with the Synod, should inform the Metropolitans about the event
> in an encyclical and ask them to submit in writing within a given period
> of time their opinion about who they considered suitable to become a
> Patriarch. As soon as the replies arrive a general meeting should be called

152. *He Hemera*, no. 167 (November 14/26, 1858).

from the following: the members of the Synod (candidates to be discussed later), all the Bishops and Archbishops residing in Constantinople, two professors of the Theological school and the Megale tou Genous Schole, two honorary Bishops [presiding over provincial churches], three leading parish priests [*economos, protosyngelos,* and *archimandrites*], and a priest from among the epitropes of Mount Athos. Lay members should be chosen from among the notables of Constantinople, the representatives of the Principalities, two from the most eminent merchants of our nation, five from the leading craftsmen of the guilds and those military and political men who work for the government.[153]

Mr. Karatheodore was interrupted by Mr. Yağcoğlou, who observed that at such a general meeting not only the notables from Constantinople but also representatives from all other areas of the state should participate.

[He] demanded that it should be agreed that in such cases the representatives of all the provinces should be invited – in fact they could appoint someone from among their most respectable compatriots, merchants, or others residing in Constantinople and he should then be given a relevant document of appointment.

His proposal was accepted and Mr. Karatheodore took the stand again and continued by proposing the election of three candidates from among those put forward by the provincial metropolitans and bishops and the synod. Then from those three, the whole mixed assembly should elect the patriarch:

This plan was immediately accepted by the lay members and they asked that it be approved, but the clerical members of the Assembly, although not rejecting the proposal completely, as they did before, argued that because this reform was to be permanent, they should not rush a decision to endorse it. Instead, it would be better to postpone the decision for a week in order to think the matter through. Otherwise, they risked being misunderstood by the whole Nation and condemned by future generations for changing the ancient custom and traditions of the Church.[154]

They also asked for a copy of the proposals so that they could study them for a week. Then they proposed the creation of a mixed sub-committee in order to discuss the matter of mixed participation and church custom, and promised to return the following Friday with a definite answer. The sub-committee was agreed and seven clergymen, the two Karatheodore brothers, and Mr. Ioannis Yağcoğlu were appointed to it. They met the following Monday at the house of the metropolitan of Salonica in order to deliberate.

153. *He Hemera*, no. 168 (November 21/December 3, 1858).
154. Ibid.

The next subject for debate in the national council was the necessary qualifications required of candidates for the ecumenical throne:

> It was agreed that the candidate should have the following qualifications:
> a) He must be a subject of the Sublime Porte; b) he must be over forty
> years of age; c) he must be a high priest who has governed a province for
> at least six or seven years, so that he would have experience in govern-
> ment; d) he must be well educated; e) he must possess both religious and
> secular knowledge and an excellent knowledge of the laws of the Church,
> so that he can give the correct opinion on any given occasion; f) he must
> know two foreign languages: Turkish and French or Latin; g) he must
> have a healthy body and a sound mind, and be moral, virtuous, calm, and
> collected, pious....[155]

The council was adjourned until the following week. *He Hemera*'s correspondent reported that on the following Friday the mixed committee presented its findings but members of the council disputed them and the discussion was postponed for a further week.[156]

Amaltheia again managed to get the full story behind yet another setback in the work of the national council. In a report from Constantinople, written on November 10 and reprinted in *He Hemera*,[157] *Amaltheia* presented a short account of a critical meeting of the council, one which could potentially destroy the work of the previous six weeks. In the same number *Amaltheia* corrected its previous report, by pointing out that the number of the lay members of the mixed committee (previously reported as three) were in fact four, and added the name of Mr. Djanos. According to *Amaltheia*'s account of the fifth meeting, the secretary of the council read out the minutes of the previous meeting, then the patriarch asked the president of the mixed sub-committee to present their findings to the council and the metropolitan of Arta read the report. According to *Amaltheia*, the report did not receive unanimous approval from the members of the council. Two notables from Constantinople disagreed with the report of the sub-committee, and moreover condemned all the decisions taken already in the council (as illegal), because they were taken in their absence:

> So they started to challenge [the decisions] and there was a danger that six
> weeks' work and five meetings were going to be undone despite the fact
> that all the members present had agreed on everything, except for three
> Bishops, who had not signed the protocol about the election of the Patri-
> arch. After four and a half hours of exchanges, no agreement was reached,
> although according to the rules of the Council, this matter should have

155. *He Hemera*, no. 169 (November 28/December 10, 1858).
156. Ibid.
157. Ibid.

been resolved by a majority vote. The discussion became heated, and in order to avoid quarrels and scandal, one member of the committee proposed the following: "Gentlemen, we did what we were ordered to do. After careful consideration we have produced a written report, which we read out in front of everyone; you are bringing your objections verbally. Since *verba volent* why don't you put your observations and objections in writing and after they are read out at our next meeting we can decide by majority vote." Everybody agreed to this and they dispersed.

The sixth meeting of the council saw the end of the public career of Prince Stephanake Vogorides, when he submitted his resignation due to old age and illness. At the same meeting an imperial decree was read out ordering the replacement of archon postelnikos C. Photiades, the brother of Vogorides' son-in-law Alexandros, who can be considered as part of the Anglophile group, which after the death of Reşid Pasha, the resignation of Vogorides, and the replacement of Konstantine Photiades, had lost some of its most important members.

In the same number of *He Hemera* the editor included a report from the newspaper *Vyzantis*, which he had received the day before his own newspaper went to press. *Vyzantis* reported on the seventh meeting of the national council and printed what was agreed regarding the procedure of the election of the patriarch:

> When the Patriarchal throne falls vacant the resident Synod will elect the regent of the Patriarchate, who will then within sixty-one days, invite the provincial Bishops to the Capital for their recommendation regarding their preferred candidate; alternatively, they could send their vote in writing to one of the Bishops in Constantinople. After that the governor of the Patriarchate will invite a General Council of the Nation and in its presence the secretary of the Patriarchate with two of its members, a cleric and a layman, will collect and count the ballots. At the same time the votes of the resident Bishops of Constantinople should be collected. The three Bishops with the most votes would then be considered as candidates for the Patriarchal throne. They will then have to be interviewed by the Synod as to whether they have the necessary qualifications. After that the General Council will vote in a secret ballot to elect the Patriarch. The General Assembly, which will elect the Patriarch, will consist of the twelve Bishops of the Synod, all other Bishops residing in the Capital and those from the provinces, the Grand Lawmaker [*Megas Logothetes*], those clergymen of the Capital who are graduates of Theology, the four [lay] representatives of the principalities of Moldavia, Wallachia, Serbia, and Samos, the political leaders, two representatives from the army with the rank of Colonel [*Miralay*], two representatives from the Sciences, ten

representatives from the commercial club, ten representatives from among the best leading craftsmen of the most important guilds, and twenty-eight representatives from the great provinces of Rumeli and Anatolia and the various islands. The assembly will also take into account the views of those from the smaller provinces; those twenty-eight representatives of the provinces should be selected from among the merchants or other people of good standing residing in the capital who should be authorized with the relevant documents. Thus elected, and after the election is approved by the Sublime Porte, the Patriarch should be enthroned with the appropriate ceremony.[158]

In the same number of *He Hemera*, in addition to the reports about the national council from *Amaltheia* and *Vyzantis*, there was a report from *He Hemera*'s own correspondent in Constantinople (dated October 21/November 3, 1858). He was reporting on an important issue, which had become the cause célèbre of the Bulgarian Orthodox Christians, namely the lack of Bulgarian high clergy in the Bulgarian-speaking provinces of the Ottoman Empire. The report mentioned the enthronement of the new bishop in the province of Durresh, who was

> Mr. Auxentios, of Bulgarian origin. So, you see that despite so much mud-slinging by her enemies the Great Church is in fact appointing Bulgarian bishops.

By the end of November, the matter of the election of the patriarch was decided. Then a report from *Amaltheia* (correspondence from Constantinople November 26/December 8, 1858) discussed the organization of the elections for the metropolitans and bishops, which was decided at the eighth meeting of the council:

> When a throne becomes vacant, the Synod should propose three candidates and the one who receives most votes in the ensuing secret ballot should become the successor to that throne. He should have the following qualifications: He must be over thirty years of age, be a subject of the Porte, be of sound mind and of healthy body, be a graduate of the Theological school with the Degree of Doctor of Theology; in general, all candidates for the office must be graduates and must have served five years under a provincial Bishop or in the Patriarchate so that they acquire experience in ecclesiastical matters. At the same time, they should be able to preach the word of God in the churches. After five years they would be accepted as candidates. For these positions other candidates with Doctorates from other schools should be considered but their Diplomas should first be examined. When the death of a Metropolitan is announced, the

158. *He Hemera*, no. 169 (November 28/December 10, 1858).

Synod cannot choose and appoint his successor before taking the advice of the local notables and the priesthood of the province. The Metropolitans and Bishops cannot be relocated except for political or important religious reasons or for abusing their position, and even in those circumstances they can be relocated only once, so their position is for life. The provinces should send an adequate number of students to the Theological school so that they can be prepared for the position of high clergy. When a bishop is accused of some wrongdoing, the Great Church will send an Exarch to his province to listen to both sides; if there are sufficient grounds, the Exarch could then send the accused bishop to the capital with two representatives of the province in order to be tried in the appropriate court; for simple violations, the appropriate court will be the Holy Synod; misdemeanors and larger crimes will be tried by a mixed permanent committee of laymen and clergy. Those bishops who are found innocent will return to their provinces with proof of their innocence, and will receive financial compensation. Those who are found guilty of minor crimes will be suspended, and will spend their punishment time in a monastery and then be transferred to another province. Those who are found guilty of considerable crimes will be defrocked and imprisoned. The appointed Metropolitans can only spend sixty days in total in Constantinople and during that time they should present themselves to the Holy Synod and listen to the debates. Moreover, the successful candidates should be competent, not only in Ottoman, but also in the language of the area to which they will be sent. The bishops are appointed by the appropriate Metropolitan and they should also be Doctors of Theology.[159]

The national council then deliberated about the election of priests and holy deacons:

At the twelfth meeting of the National Council the question of the election of the high-ranking clergy was finally resolved. They would be elected in the same manner as the bishops. They should be "Ottoman subjects or else acquire Ottoman citizenship. They should have a degree from the Theological school of Chalke. If they held a Doctorate from another school, they should have to pass a qualifying examination by a committee from the Theological School at Chalke, which will then award them the Degree of that school. Besides Ottoman, all high clergy should be familiar with the language of the place to which they would be sent; for example, if they were sent to Bulgaria they should speak Bulgarian, etc. They should be over thirty years of age and have the necessary qualifications."[160]

Moreover, it was proposed that when a metropolitan died, if the people of the

159. *He Hemera*, no. 170 (December 5/17, 1858).
160. *He Hemera*, no. 174 (January 2/14, 1859).

province proposed someone with all the necessary qualifications, the synod should consider him seriously as a candidate:

> This was agreed by the majority of the healthy [meaning here thinking in an adaptive way] section of the members of the Council.[161]

The process for the election of a patriarch seems to have caused a rift in the council, as clerical members did not wish lay members to have a say on the matter, citing tradition:

> Clerical members insisted that the lay members should not take part in the election of the Patriarch as he is a Church and spiritual leader and not a political one, and therefore [by insisting] the laymen disregarded the ecclesiastical and apostolic regulations....[162]

Lay members argued for the de facto position of the patriarch in the Ottoman reality. In the end a compromise was reached:

> [Clerical members] succeeded in amending the previous proposal regarding the election of the Patriarch and in limiting the involvement of laymen to the election of the three candidates for the Patriarchal throne, but the final decision was left to the Synod, who alone would elect the new Patriarch in a secret ballot.[163]

The next matter for discussion was the composition of the synod and how often its members should rotate. A committee to discuss the matter was elected from seven clerics and seven lay members.[164]

A letter from a subscriber to *He Hemera*, writing from Constantinople on January 9/21, 1859,[165] informed Greek readers about the way the question of membership of the synod was resolved:

> ... [T]he Synod will consist of twelve members from among the high clergy invited in rotation from all the provinces. Every year half of those people will return to their provinces and a fresh group should be invited and then, in a year's time, the older group should retire and a new one should be invited, etc. The first Synod after the law is passed will consist of two members from the old Geronts, four from among those who took part in the National Council and the rest in order of precedence from

161. Ibid.
162. Ibid.
163. Ibid.
164. Ibid. The lay members were Logothetis N. Aristarchis, Messrs. A. Photiades, V. Krikotsos, K. Karatheodore, T. Konstantinides, L. Yağcoğlou, and E. Nikolaides.
165. Ibid.

the provinces ... thus the so-called Geronts will not possess the right to permanent seats in the Synod any more, which means that they will not be able to spend their life in the capital and influence the affairs of the Church with the ultimate aim of benefiting themselves.

The next matter in the agenda concerned the duties of the synod and the mixed council, about which there was no information in the press.

Having arranged the election of the high clergy of the Rum milleti, the council turned its attention to the next matter under consideration, the creation of a salaried clergy. *Amaltheia* printed a report from its correspondent in Constantinople, which informed its Greek Orthodox readership that in effect the council could not abide by the order of the Sublime Porte because "the creation of a salaried clergy goes against the Apostolic and Ecclesiastical laws." This was the opinion of a sub-committee composed of clergymen, convened by the council to consider the question of a salaried clergy. After a long discussion, the council was persuaded that paying a salary was not proper and decided to send a four-member committee to the Sublime Porte to announce their decision that:

> although the Hatt-ı Hümayun and the Imperial Decree that ordered the creation of the National Council mentioned the establishment of the regular pay of a salary to the Patriarch and the high clergy, the Council, after careful deliberation, found that paying a salary goes against religious and ecclesiastical custom and therefore asks respectfully that its unanimous decision be considered [by the Porte].[166]

The committee consisted of Messrs. Karatheodore, Adosides, Krikotsos, and Yağcoğlou, who met with the minister (of foreign affairs).

Amaltheia's correspondent was unable to discover what was said at the meeting with the minister. But *Vyzantis* did. According to its report, reprinted in *He Hemera*,

> The Minister of Foreign Affairs, Fuad Pasha, gave the following answer to the committee of the National Council of the Greeks: "The purpose of the government is to stop the financial abuse which occasionally occurred by some Metropolitans, without, however, breaking the rules of the Church. The Government desires that the higher clergy should continue to receive their suppliance fee, regulated properly, but wishes that their arbitrary income should be abolished because it is both against your religion and the laws of the government. Because the Metropolitans have a triple office – they are representatives of the Government, governors of the Orthodox people, and leaders of the Christian peoples of the province they are

---

166. *He Hemera*, no. 187 (April 3/15, 1859).

appointed to – they have to live with all the dignity [required by their position] and the Government does not want them to pay for their expenses from their private income; because the Government is going to abolish the [church's] revenue [derived from local taxation], this should be replaced by a contribution per family on the part of the Christians of the provinces, in order that the priest should have a decent living. Since you inform me that the Metropolitans complained that the salary goes against the laws of the Church, you can call this contribution either grant or assistance or revenue or any other name you approve of. In short, the Government's wish is that the financial abuse should stop, the revenue should be regulated properly, that the laws of the Church should not be broken, the dignity of the clergy should be maintained, and, most of all, that the Christian people should be happy. On these things the National Council should deliberate and take the appropriate measures."[167]

While the council deliberated the minister's five points mentioned above, the geronts continued with their ever-negative attitude towards any proposed reform in the church and their usual scheming and behind-the-scenes activity to disrupt its work. By the summer of 1859, the patriarch and the modernizing elements in the council decided that it was time the geronts went back to their provinces. They succeeded in persuading the minister of foreign affairs to come to the same conclusion, as his assistance was of paramount importance. The Greek press printed the translation of the *firman* sent to the patriarch on 18 Zilkade 1273 (July 6/18,1859),[168] which called for the immediate return of the metropolitans of Chalkedon, Nikomedia, Ephesos, Kyzikos, Herakleia, and Derkon, to their provinces because:

> … as His Holiness knows well no law or any affair can demand the continuous presence of those metropolitans here [in Constantinople]. As a result of their presence here, their provinces are abandoned, which should under no account be tolerated, because the present members of the Council are adequate for the deliberations regarding the new regulations. For this reason the Government has issued a Decree, which orders the said Metropolitans to return to their provinces. We leave it to the care of Your Holiness to announce to those Metropolitans this decision and execute the Imperial Decree as soon as possible.

The patriarch did not lose any time.

---

167. *He Hemera*, no. 187 (3/15, 1859).
168. See, for example, a reprint from *Vyzantis* in *He Hemera*, no. 204 (July 31/August 12, 1859).

He immediately removed from them the four parts of the National seal, which was then given, after a ballot, to the Metropolitans of Arta, Amaseia, Adrianoupolis, and Dimitrias. The Metropolitan of Arta was appointed Treasurer, in place of the Metropolitan of Ephesos. The Geront Metropolitans of Herakleia, Nikomedia, and Ephesos had left already for their provinces, and the rest were preparing to depart. Before they departed, they handed the Patriarch a written protest alleging disregard for Church rules and established practices and declaring that they did not recognize any act of the National Council. They asked for and received from His Holiness a certified copy of their written protest, and then they departed.[169]

The departure of the reactionary figures of the geronts, as if by magic, seems to have removed the reservations of even the most conservative elements of the committee regarding the creation of a salaried clergy. According to a letter from Constantinople,

> the salary of the Patriarch will be 50,000 *kuruş*[170] per calendar month; that of the first grade high clerics [archbishops and metropolitans] 10,000 *kuruş* per calendar month and that of the second grade ones [bishops] 6,000 *kuruş* per calendar month.[171]

The national council continued its deliberations with the aim of finding the necessary monies to pay the salaries of the patriarch and the higher clergy. It was proposed that the income of the monasteries should be used for this purpose. The council established a special committee whose purpose would be to register the exact income of the monasteries. The newspaper *Vyzantis* commented that

> it was an excellent idea to use the monasterial income because it was vast and in the past it was used for unknown purposes.

This comment was seconded by the editor of *He Hemera*.[172]

While still in session, the national council was confronted by the reforming church's first challenge. According to the Ottoman Greek press, the agents of the Catholic Church in the Ottoman Empire had already been trying for some years to take advantage of the mounting dissatisfaction that Orthodox Christians felt towards their ecclesiastical leadership. Great publicity was given by *Vyzantis* to proselytism in the bishopric of Polyane in the province of Macedonia, which:

---

169. *He Hemera*, no. 204 (July 31/August 12, 1859).

170. According to currency exchange prices quoted in *He Hemera*, no. 53 (September 7/19, 1856) one British pound was equivalent to 125 *kuruş*, one Austrian florin equivalent to 60 *kuruş* and 20 *francs* equivalent to 100 *kuruş*.

171. *He Hemera*, no. 207 (August 21/September 2, 1859).

172. *He Hemera*, no. 211 (September 18/30, 1859).

has greatly occupied the Great Church, including the Metropolitan of Salonica [in whose province proselytizing was taking place] and the other important synodic Bishops.[173]

The newspaper reassured its readers that the problem was solved and that

> those few apostates, moved not from personal convictions but rather from obstinacy, were going to return to the religion of their fathers because the Great Church ... has decided to change the Bishop of Polyane [who was quite instrumental in alienating his parishioners] and has chosen in his place Archimandrite Parthenios, who was promoted last Thursday to Bishop and is shortly going to his new province.

The newspaper described the actions of "those few who for vain reasons resorted to the disgusting act of apostasy" as desperate and lamentable, while at the same time it praised the swift action of the holy synod in replacing the unwanted bishop with a new one.

Apostasy appeared in other places, including Crete. There, according to the Greek press, the Catholic priest:

> Father Joseph, was touring the poorest provinces promising French passports to anyone who would sign with their mark (being illiterate) on an application form. Totally by accident it became known to those people that they were in fact signing a declaration to become members of the Catholic Church. Infuriated, the notables of the people of the provinces of Selino and Kissamos sent an open letter to Father Joseph, stating that they had been under the impression that they were registering themselves for a French passport and the protection offered by glorious France and her Emperor to enslaved peoples, without violating their conscience. [Instead,][174] "we found ourselves signing letters for a change of religion which you brought from Smyrna [the headquarters of proselytism in the empire], deceiving us in this way and suggesting that the faith of the Catholics is the same as the true Orthodox faith."

What Father Joseph in fact was trying to achieve was to make those people recognize the pope as head of their church but keep the Orthodox faith, as is clear from reading the published application form. Notwithstanding, the efforts of the Catholic sect to attract Orthodox Christians failed, with only a few exceptions, notably among the Bulgarians in 1860, who used the conversion or threat of conversion to force concessions from the Great Church. The case of the Bulgarian apostasy took on epic proportions in the Greek press.

While still in session the council had the opportunity to make sure that the

173. *He Hemera*, no. 219 (November 13/25, 1859).
174. *He Hemera*, no. 240 (April 8/20, 1860).

holy synod took provincial complaints against various bishops seriously, such as "the ones of Prussa, Kassandra, Larissa, Imvros, and other places because of oppressive behavior against their flock. They suggested that the necessary measures should be taken so that what had happened in Prussa and in Polyane where proselytism had increased greatly"[175] would not recur.

At the same time, serious talks were taking place between the patriarchs of the Armenians (whose church also suffered at the hands of Catholic proselytism) and of the Orthodox Church towards a possible union of the two churches, which have few dogmatic differences. By 1859, the Greek press was growing uneasy about the possibility of a fragmentation of the Orthodox in the empire, which it felt would weaken their position, so it supported these moves towards union wholeheartedly, and encouraged the Greek patriarch to accept it. The press further advised him not to be as donnish as:

> a few years ago, when, unfortunately, because of the excessive religious zeal of our own side, which displayed great obstinacy over unimportant minutiae, our Church did not recognize the baptism of the Armenians.[176]

For the Greek press such a union would strengthen

> the two most numerous and advanced nations, both intellectually and materially, in the Empire and improve their already good relations for mutual benefit.[177]

Eventually, in February 1860, *Vyzantis* printed an article in which it announced that the national council had finally finished its work and the minutes, which "arranged our National affairs have been signed and submitted to the Government for approval and sanctioning."[178]

But then, it announced the bad news: not everyone had signed the minutes. The bishops of Demetrias and Selyvria had refused to sign and announced that they didn't recognize the decisions of the council:

> After many discussions and quarrels they left the meeting, and immediately afterwards the Bishop of Adrianople followed, though he returned after a while and handed His All Holiness the Patriarch, who was the president of the Council, a signed letter by him and the Bishops of Demetriada and Selyvria and three of the other Bishops who found themselves outside the Council.

175. *He Hemera*, no. 215 (October 16/28, 1859).
176. *He Hemera*, no. 221 (November 20/December 2, 1859).
177. Ibid.
178. *He Hemera*, no. 233 (February 19/March 2, 1860).

In their letter they alleged that

> the minutes of the Council went against the ecclesiastical canons and cop-
> ied their letter to the Sublime Porte requesting that the Ottoman Govern-
> ment form a committee consisting of previous and current Patriarchs and
> the most prominent of the Bishops in order to review the decisions taken
> [by the council].

The laymen had all signed the minutes and a mixed committee of clergymen and
laymen was appointed to present the finalized agreement to the Sublime Porte.

In its next number, on February 10/22, *Vyzantis* announced that the mixed
committee, presided over by the patriarch of Alexandria, handed the agreed document to the minister of foreign affairs:

> His Beatitude the Patriarch of Alexandria, recited a suitable speech on be-
> half of the National Council, stressing that the National Council, realizing
> the urgency of the matter and wanting to execute faithfully the order of
> the Imperial Government, as soon as it ended its deliberations appeared
> before him in order to notify him of the arrangement for the affairs of the
> Nation.[179]

The patriarch of Alexandria had to account for the fact that the minutes were not
signed unanimously as ordered. He attributed it to malicious plotting by individuals who "as your Excellency knows, are trying to obstruct such a holy work" and
implored the minister on behalf of the national council to

> hasten the inspection and approval of the new regulations of the National
> Council and order their immediate enforcement in order to reassure the
> Nation, which is very anxious about a settlement of its national affairs.

The minister, answering His Beatitude, said that

> the Imperial government desires the well-being and the good settlement
> of the affairs of the Greek [Orthodox] Nation and promised to hasten the
> new regulations to the Ministerial council so that the ministers can exam-
> ine them and issue their order of approval.

It seemed, for a moment, as if the modernizers had won the day. Everything that
the Orthodox Christians had been complaining about had been rectified. The
reform program was ready despite the concerted efforts of some conservative
elements to delay or stop the proceedings. The higher clergy were put under the
scrutiny of the laymen, the standards for their election were improved, and their

---

179. *He Hemera*, no. 233 (February 19/March 2, 1860).

salaries were set in order to ensure that there would be no further embezzlement or oppression of the Orthodox flock.

But congratulations were not yet in order. The conservative elements of the council, namely the geronts and some other senior bishops, had succeeded in delaying the ratification of the reforms by the Porte, which acceded to their demand for an inquiry into the legality of the proposed reforms. The modernizing elements, most of the clergy, and the laymen, who were bitter about the delay and angry with the conservatives and the Porte for spoiling the work of years and the chance to reform the ailing institution of the church, tried to retaliate through the press. From February 1860, letters appeared in the Ottoman Greek press calling for the dismissal of several conservative bishops, and especially the three who had provoked the problems by not signing the draft reform program. They were referred to pejoratively as revolutionaries, conspirators, or even criminals.[180] To such letters were added open allegations that "two-thirds of the National debt was owed to senior members of the Holy synod" and that this was "a matter which will continue to provoke much discussion and will move people to join the Catholic Church."[181]

These public attacks, coupled with reactions against the patriarch by the geronts, resulted in the patriarch's resignation in May 1860. Patriarch Kyrillos, himself a conservative, but one who, in hindsight, played a very positive role in establishing the reforms in the church by minimizing the opposition of the geronts, was caught in the crossfire between the two factions. Speaking to the synod, summoned in an extraordinary meeting, Patriarch Kyrillos said that he had decided to resign

> because the affairs of our Church have reached a very sad state and it is the duty of the One [the head of the Nation] to perish for the benefit of our Nation.

Then he revealed that certain quarters had circulated "the rumor that I am plotting to get rid of or exile some among the high clergy."[182]

This rumor had resulted in several of the bishops who were hitherto neutral turning against him, thus making his position untenable. He then told them that he was tendering his resignation to the Sublime Porte directly (and not to the holy synod first as was customary) because it was the Porte that had appointed him.

This was an unprecedented move for a patriarch. The manner of his resignation was intended to be a major statement to Orthodox Christians that things would never to be the same for the nation of the Rum. This, his final act as leader of his nation, conveyed to the Orthodox that the autonomous status of the patriarchate within the Ottoman Empire – as it had developed with the various privileges given

180. *Vyzantis*, no. 346 (March 3, 1860).
181. *Vyzantis*, no. 350 (March 31, 1860).
182. *He Hemera*, no. 246 (May 20/June 1, 1860).

to the patriarch since the time of the conquest – had ended. It had now become completely subordinate to the Ottoman government. Moreover, his deliberate snub of the synod was in effect an unspoken comment against some of the members of the church's highest governing body for alienating, through their continuous mismanagement of the church's affairs, a part of the nation that had eventually sided with the Ottoman government in order to destroy the autonomy of the Orthodox Church within the Ottoman state. His action was perceived as casting serious doubt on the holy synod's continuing authority over the affairs of the Orthodox Church and Orthodox Christians in the Ottoman Empire. But it can also be seen as a tactical move that forced the Porte's hand by finally approving their draft reforms. The Porte would now have to approve the draft as soon as possible in order for a new patriarch to be elected.

Such an insult against the synod's authority by its departing leader could not be left unanswered. In replying to the patriarchal speech, one of the members of the holy synod pointed out to him that

> there is a grave error in your irrelevance to tender your resignation [direct-
> ly] to the Porte. A Patriarch receives his appointment by the divine grace
> of the Holy Spirit ... and his actions should be governed by the Holy rules
> and regulations.... [H]e should therefore tender his resignation first and
> foremost to his Holy peers. Notwithstanding, since he is also recognized
> by the state as a political leader, he should inform the state of the reasons
> for his resignation.[183]

Thus, the synod retaliated by openly accusing the patriarch of acting unlawfully and against the interests of the church. But the patriarch shrugged off the accusation by telling the synod to "add this one as a finishing touch to all the other illegal acts [that had occurred in the past]."[184]

The resignation of Kyrillos threw the Orthodox Church into turmoil, not least because the draft reforms regarding the election of the patriarch had not yet been approved by the Porte, which had, as we mentioned above, yielded to the geronts and had requested clarification and modifications to the draft. Indeed, the Porte bided its time in approving the draft reforms. Each month there was another excuse for the delay reported in the Greek press: in March there was the illness of the foreign minister;[185] in May the dismissal of the grand vizier[186] and the new grand vizier's tour of the Balkans. That month "the machinery [of the patriarchate] stopped."[187] No appointments were made, and geronts who had

183. Ibid.
184. Ibid.
185. *Vyzantis*, no. 350 (March 31, 1860).
186. *Vyzantis*, no. 368 (August 6, 1860).
187. *Vyzantis*, no. 372 (September 13, 1860).

been sent to their provinces returned to the capital, while the trials of accused bishops were postponed. Then, the government demanded further clarifications to the draft, an act generally thought in the press to be the work of the scheming geronts. By June 1860 the reformers of what now resembled a headless corpse began to wonder whether they had not made a terrible mistake in tampering with the 1,500-year-old institution of the Orthodox Church. The press began to carry articles asking the question whether the order prevailing before 1856 was not superior to the new one, because, at least

> under the Geronts, despite all the quarrels, whenever an issue concerning a general question arose, everyone worked together and considered how best to solve the problem.[188]

At the beginning of July, the national council agreed in desperation to the Porte's alteration to their draft regarding the election of the patriarch, an alteration, which added insult to injury for the embattled reformers of the church. According to this alteration:

> the Minister of Foreign Affairs should [also] approve the list of the three finalists for the Patriarchal office. The Council added that after approval by the Minister the successful candidate should be recognized as Patriarch immediately and enthroned without the necessity for a further approval by the Porte, as was the custom until then.[189]

The latter was an attempt by the council to sweeten the bitter pill of the new reality that someone else was now the head of the church. The Porte played along:

> Fuad Pasha [Minister of Foreign affairs] reassured the Committee [which had submitted the altered draft] that he would now act to secure the decree of acceptance of the Patriarch's resignation so that the Synod could appoint a regent and elect his successor.[190]

But it wasn't until July 17 that the limbo of Kyrillos's situation was finally settled. That day,

> three Bishops and some representatives [of the council] were summoned by the Porte and given the Decree [of acceptance of Kyrillos' resignation] together with another approving the Council's regulations for the election of the new Patriarch.[191]

Two days later the synod and the representatives of the nation gathered in the

188. Ibid.
189. Ibid.
190. Ibid.
191. Ibid.

patriarchate and elected, by secret ballot, the metropolitan of Nicaea as regent, and this they announced to the government. Then the mixed council began deliberating about the election of the new patriarch. The Greek press was filled with advice:

> Let us hope that the clergy residing in Constantinople and the notables
> of the Nation, realizing the seriousness of the situation, will conduct
> themselves in this election with all necessary sincerity. We shudder when
> we consider the great dangers of the times in which the new Patriarch will
> be asked to lead us and we believe that it will be difficult to find a man
> willing to carry such responsibility. In fact, it will be interesting to see who
> is going to display such self-denial for the sake of the crew of the Great
> Church of Christ.[192]

The writer's curiosity was not satisfied until the following October when, contrary to the new regulations that demanded that the patriarch should be elected within a month of the throne being vacated, the new patriarch was finally chosen.

In fact, the election of the new patriarch was not only contrary to the new regulations, but also a feat close to a miracle. In late July conservative members of the synod, trying to render the draft reforms null and void,

> sent to the provincial Bishops letters urging them not to send in their
> votes [for the election of the new patriarch] but to claim that they did not
> know the content of the works of the Council [that according to the new
> regulations was assembled solely for the purpose of electing the patriarch
> (see above, pages 128–129)]. Their purpose is to cause more confusion in
> the Church's situation so as to succeed in their secret ambitions.

The deadline for the election of the new patriarch came and went. Insufficient votes were submitted. Moreover, the geronts, who were on holiday at the time, refused to return to the capital for the election. Eventually, in September, the council succeeded in persuading the Porte to issue:

> an order for the return of the Geronts of the Synod but only the five that
> are mentioned in the Imperial *berat* of the Patriarch; they are [the geronts]
> of Herakleia, Kyzicos, Nikomedeia, Nicaea, and Chalcedon. The other
> three, who were also the least vocal, [the geronts] of Kaisaria, Ephesos, and
> Derkon, are left out.

The correspondent writing from Constantinople to *He Hemera* of Trieste was pessimistic about the outcome of the church reforms:

> The present confusion over our national and ecclesiastical matters follows
> the general disorder [in the country]; we have neither a presence of mind,

192. *He Hemera*, no. 255 (July 22/August 3, 1860).

nor a healthy conscience at the moment to be able to propose anything virtuous, secure, and permanent. May God be merciful to His people. We neither have a Patriarch nor are we likely to find a suitable one.[193]

At the end of September, the same correspondent wrote that

[O]ur ecclesiastical matters go from bad to worse because the arrival of the Geronts caused quarrels, disagreement, and divisions, again. The Geronts composed a letter to the Porte, which was also signed by the other Bishops (except three, as they say) demanding either the revision of the reformed regulation regarding the election of the Patriarch, because of its great and important deficiencies, or that the election takes place using the old system. Meanwhile another two Geronts were allowed to come to Constantinople by order of the Porte; the one of Ephesos and the one of Derkoi.[194]

At the beginning of October, the Porte answered the petition of the geronts with a letter addressed to the patriarchal regent. In it, it was stressed that because of the twin nature of the patriarch as a religious and also as a political leader:

considered by the Porte as its Minister of the Government, the Porte had reserved the right to remove from the list of candidates, when necessary, one, two, or at most three names.[195]

At the same time, the Porte sent a second document to the patriarchal regent, in which it requested the speeding up of the election process for the new patriarch in accordance with the new regulations.

It would seem that the reactionary forces in the patriarchate had lost the battle for dominance but in fact the election of the new patriarch gave a confusing signal to the Greek reader. The new patriarch, Ioakeim of Kyzicos, was a geront. Ioakeim was only the third choice of the mixed assembly, having received thirty-seven votes in comparison with ex-Patriarch Anthimos of Ephesos, who received forty-seven, and the patriarch of Alexandria, Kallinikos, who received forty-nine. In the last and secret ballot of the synod, however, the geront of Kyzicos received nineteen out of the twenty-four votes and thus became the new patriarch.[196]

In Sum

The election of the patriarch under the new regulations signalled for the Orthodox Christians of the Ottoman Empire the end of an era that had begun in 1453. The weekly reporting of the reform of the patriarchate, the parallel reporting of

193. *He Hemera*, no. 261 (September 2/14, 1860).
194. *He Hemera*, no. 263 (September 16/28, 1860).
195. *He Hemera*, no. 264 (September 23/October 5, 1860).
196. *He Hemera*, no. 267 (October 14/26, 1860).

rising Bulgarian nationalism, the reporting of other major political reforms, and their reception by Christians and Muslims, gave the reader of the Ottoman Greek press adequate information about the changing political circumstances facing the Rum milleti. The influence of foreign powers on the Ottoman government and their attempt to use the reforms to promote their own state interests within the Ottoman Empire is also discussed in the press. Ottoman Greek readers had enough information to form an opinion about the complexity of the various issues arising from the reform program and their short- and long-term implications, which led some parties involved to push for reform and others to resist.

Regarding the reform of the Patriarchate of Constantinople, the Ottoman Greek press identified three main domestic players: the Ottoman government, those among the Rum milleti who had a Greek national consciousness, and those who had developed a Bulgarian national consciousness. According to its editors, for the Ottoman government the reform of the governing institution of the Rum milleti was a matter of centralizing its control over the country. The attempts of the Ottoman government at reforming the patriarchate, especially under the Francophile group, which gained power after the death of Reşid, were commented on widely in the Ottoman Greek press. Some Greek journalists went so far as to argue that by diminishing the powers of the supra-national patriarchate, the Ottomans almost inevitably risked encouraging national self-determination movements.

For the Ottoman Greeks themselves the reform of the patriarchate was a far more complex issue, with both positive and negative aspects, and there was not a unified response to it. According to the Ottoman Greek press, some Ottoman Greeks were apprehensive that the removal of political and judicial privileges from the patriarchate and its further incorporation into the Ottoman government would impoverish and endanger the quality of life of the Christians. Although there were, throughout the reforming process, expressions of hope for the introduction of a Western European-style, secular government in the Ottoman Empire, Ottoman Greeks, some immediately, some within the next few years, spoke out, as shown earlier, about their doubts that such an outcome were possible "because the Turks are and insist on remaining backward." Regarding the reform of the Orthodox Church, none of the Orthodox quoted in the press publicly doubted the need for improvements in the financial management of the "national fund," or the need for the better education of their children, or, indeed, the return to the Christian principle of a church confined to moral leadership. The Ottoman Greek press articulated the Ottoman Greek fear that the removal of the patriarchate's political powers could abandon Christians to the mercy of a state where "everybody is equal before a law that doesn't exist"[197] and a culture that considered the Christian as inferior to the Muslim. Reports of massive violence perpetrated against Christians

197. *He Hemera*, no. 316 (September 22/October 4, 1861).

by their Muslim compatriots on learning of the government's promise of equality between Muslims and non-Muslims fueled those fears further.

Reports, comments, and articles in the Ottoman Greek press show that despite the Greek Revolution (1821–1830) and the creation of a Greek state (1830), Ottoman Greeks from the 1830s to the 1860s had no plans to continue the revolt against or sever themselves from the Ottoman Empire. On the contrary they were critical of the revolutionary talk emanating both from the Greeks of Greece and the Bulgarians. For them this was their home and they were its original and oldest inhabitants. Their hitherto unhappy position in the Ottoman Empire was blamed on their unequal treatment – as Christians – by the Muslim establishment and their Muslim compatriots. The heralded equality under the Hatt-ı Hümayun promised them a chance to flourish within the framework of a multinational empire and they were eager to respond positively to the offer.

The Ottoman Greek press presents the Bulgarian members of the Rum milleti as perceiving the reform of the patriarchate solely in the context of their own struggle towards national self-determination. The Bulgarians' attempts to use the reform of the patriarchate and the new international status quo in order to break away from the Ottoman Empire and create their own national state was reported in depth in the Ottoman Greek press.

In sum, the three main political reforms that were covered in the Ottoman Greek press up to 1862 were all presented in a balanced way. The new laws were translated and published; the editors presented the government actions, and then newspapers reported the reaction both from the various quarters of the Rum milleti and from the other millets. Diplomatic efforts and foreign power policies pertaining to the reforms were also frequently reported. Occasionally, the press succeeded in exposing the political maneuvering that took place behind the scenes. Greek readers of the Ottoman Greek newspapers during this thirty-year period could form a clear picture of the political reforms effected in the Ottoman Empire and of their reception by their own and other millets.

Referring to the early industrial landscape of England, the British politician, Edward Bulwer-Lytton, commented that, "Every age may be called an age of transition ... but in our age the transition is visible."[198] Identical words could be employed to describe the Ottoman Empire in the same period. The Orthodox Christian population of the Ottoman Empire was indeed entirely aware of the transition in their own milieu and deeply concerned about their fate and that of the Ottoman Empire, and this was manifested clearly in their press. Despite their concerns, however, they took advantage of every opportunity arising from the process of Westernization that was taking place at the same time in the empire, as will be shown in the next chapter.

198. Bulwer-Lytton 1833, appendix C.

Chapter 5

Everyday Life in the Ottoman Empire through the Lens of Its Greek Newspapers

THE POLITICAL AND SOCIAL REFORMS introduced in the Ottoman Empire during the nineteenth century had a profound effect on its people. In the previous chapter we looked at the reporting of political reforms and their impact on the Ottoman population and in particular their reception by Muslims and Orthodox Christians as reported in the Ottoman Greek press. In this chapter we will examine the social and everyday life of a generation of Ottoman Greeks, seen through the lens of the Ottoman Greek press. Its diverse articles, reports, letters to the editor, and advertisements paint a colorful picture of how they lived, what they ate, how they entertained themselves, educated their children and earned a living. The content of the Ottoman Greek press forms a crucial primary source for understanding how they thought about a host of everyday issues and how they reacted to the various challenges they faced.

An initial overview of this generation through the lens of the Ottoman Greek press suggests that the Orthodox Christians were quick to assert their Tanzimat rights to be different but equal. The reforms of the Tanzimat were hailed in the press as freeing the Ottoman Greek people from a yoke of enforced backwardness imposed by their Muslim masters. The reforms were perceived as encouraging non-Muslim people to employ their talents and skills in many new ways and to assert themselves socially. Ottoman Greek journalists played their part in encouraging their co-nationals in the empire to use their newly-acquired freedoms to bring their social aspirations into line with those of Western Europeans. Their arguments were based on the assumption that the fundamental principles of both Western European societies and the Ottoman Greeks – a Greek classical heritage, Roman law, and Christian values – were identical.

The Ottoman Greek press argued that although historical reasons had forced the Ottoman Greeks and the other Europeans to follow different paths, towards the late eighteenth century, the classical revival and the ideals of the French Revolution brought Western European and Ottoman Greek societies closer together. It was natural then, it was suggested in the press, for the Ottoman Greeks, or Rum, to feel a strong kinship with the Europeans and strive to reclaim their place in that family of nations. The Tanzimat era was seen as closing the historical gap between the Greeks of the Ottoman Empire (previously the Eastern Roman Empire) and the Western Europeans, while at the same time offering beneficial opportunities for all inhabitants of the empire irrespective of their religion. Interestingly enough, after the first few years of the Tanzimat it seems that it was the commercial and business opportunities, rather than its political changes, that readers and writers seemed to consider most beneficial to their social well-being.

This chapter attempts to illuminate the social development of the Orthodox Christians in the Ottoman Empire in the Tanzimat era, especially the ordinary folk who normally slip through the net cast by the historian. Using the Ottoman Greek press as a source, we will examine the reception and impact of the introduction of Western-style social norms, the Orthodox Christians' perception of themselves, the other, their lives, and the progress of reforms in the Ottoman Empire. Articles, reports, announcements and advertisements unveil the prevalent ideas of both readers and editors of the Ottoman Greek newspapers and paint the image of Muslims and Christians as seen through the eyes of the readers and the editors of the Ottoman Greek press.

The Muslim Image

Although the Ottoman Greek press went to considerable lengths to encourage social and political reforms in line with Western Europe as the best way forward for the Ottoman Empire, at no time during the period under review did it question whether the European social and political values that were essentially of Greek/Christian origins were compatible with Turkish/Islamic values. Nor did it question whether illiterate people from all Ottoman cultures would be able to understand and adopt innovations that derived from those European values.

Moreover, it could be argued that at that time some "enlightened" upper-class Ottoman subjects from varying religious/ethnic backgrounds had more in common with each other than with the lower classes of their own ethnic/religious groups. The discussion of the internal problems within the Orthodox Church included in the previous chapter indicates that in that community too there were clear divisions between modernizers and conservatives, which were in some respects parallel to the divisions between reformist Muslims and the "backward Muslim masses."

Notwithstanding the above, the image of the Muslims as it emerges from the Ottoman Greek press was that they were governed by their willingness to support, or at least not obstruct, the reform of Ottoman society on a European blueprint.

Only two groups of Ottoman Muslims were considered by the Ottoman Greek press as "progressive" and received a consistently positive write-up in the Greek press: the first included the sultan and his chief ministers, the second Turkish writers and newspaper publishers. Both groups were perceived as agents of positive change as they also looked to Western Europe for the blueprint of a progressive Ottoman society.

The Ottoman Greek press had developed something akin to royal court reporting about the sultan and his family's movements. It took great care to stress the Ottoman leader's benevolent interest in all his subjects without discrimination. It was reported that the sultan, who was also the Muslim leader and caliph Abdül-mecid I, attended the society wedding of Prince Stephanake Vogorides's daughter, Domnitsa Kyra Mariora, to Ioannis Photiades in 1851, and that he joined in the subsequent banquet at the Vogorides house.[1] There were further reports of visits by the sultan to this and other Christian and Muslim homes,[2] as well as a description of his visit to the bereaved family of Reşit Paşa.[3] The Greek reader could not fail to notice the significant change in the attitudes of the Ottoman monarch, who appeared in the Greek press to be openly caring and compassionate. In addition, the press represented the sultan as a charitable individual interested in education by reporting his donations to schools, his presence at various openings of public buildings, which had been either inaugurated or restored,[4] and his attendance at the exams of the much-hailed new military school[5] where non-Muslims were accepted as students.

The Sultan's extensive tour of the Aegean islands in 1850, an area heavily and in most cases solely, populated by Orthodox Christians, was also highlighted in detail. This tour was regarded as further confirmation of the Sultan's interest in the wellbeing of non–Muslims, in this instance, the Ottoman Greeks. There were several reports titled, for example, "The Departure of the Sultan for his Aegean Tour,"[6] "The Tour of the Sultan,"[7] "The Arrival of the Sultan in Smyrna,"[8] "The Aegean Tour of the Sultan," and "The Speech of [British] Ambassador Canning on His [the sultan's] Return to Constantinople."[9]

The sultan and his mother were both portrayed as actively interested and directly involved in the important changes being effected in the empire. For example, the sultan was presented as personally supporting secular education and also establishing a medical academy.[10] His mother was reported as inaugurating new schools and presented as a patron of education.[11] The sultan was also portrayed

1. *Telegraphos tou Vosporou*, no. 418 (December 24, 1851).
2. *Mnemosyne*, no. 11 (May 18, 1835).
3. *Telegraphos tou Vosporou kai Vyzantis,* no. 146 (February 15, 1858).
4. *Amaltheia*, no. 403 (October 18, 1846).
5. *Amaltheia*, no. 402, (October 11, 1846).
6. *Ephemeris tes Smyrnes*, no. 59 (May 26, 1850).
7. *Ephemeris tes Smyrnes*, no. 65 (July 7, 1850).
8. *Ephemeris tes Smyrnes*, no. 62 (June 16, 1850).
9. *Telegraphos tou Vosporou*, no. 340 (June 24, 1850).
10. *Amaltheia*, no.394 (August 17, 1846).
11. *Ephemeris tes Smyrnes,* no.55 (April 28, 1850).

as a patron of Greek and even European types of art, and it was reported that he had commissioned the building of a theatre.[12] It was also reported that he actively supported new enterprises by, among other things, buying shares together with his family in the new Ottoman Steamship Company.[13]

The arrival of various dignitaries and heads of state in Constantinople, their reception by the sultan, accounts of their visits, and announcements of their departure were also reported in the Greek press. As an example, we could mention the extensive reporting of the visit of Serbian Prince Milosh Obrenovich to the sultan in 1835,[14] the visit of Prince Varvos Stirveis (Barbu Shtirbey) to Constantinople in 1850,[15] the arrival and reception of the princes of Moldavia and Wallachia by the sultan, the patriarch and the grand vizier,[16] and their departure from Constantinople.[17] There were also reports of the sultan's changes of residence according to the season.[18]

Finally, the Greek press reported on all foreign honors received by the sultan. This was probably meant to be read as a sign that Western European society approved of the sultan and his reforming activities. When, in 1856, the sultan received the Order of the Garter from Great Britain, the Greek press took great pains to present it as a clear signal of approval of his policies by a major Christian and democratic power.[19] There were also references in most newspaper issues to honors bestowed by the sultan on various dignitaries and to appointments of various individuals.

The other Muslim group that received a positive press were the Ottoman intellectuals, and especially Muslim colleagues of the Greek journalists who worked in the Ottoman newspapers. The Greek press supported Ottoman publications and encouraged its public to buy them. When Agâh Efendi and İbrahim Şinaşi began publication of *Tercüman-ı Ahval* in 1860, the Ottoman Greek press not only advertised it but also urged its readers to read it. The Ottoman Greek press also advertised some books written in Ottoman Turkish, as well as grammars and dictionaries of the Ottoman language, which it recommended to its readers to learn. Turkish books were also advertised in the Ottoman Greek press by Muslim "Turks." One example is the book *İnşâ-yı Cedid*, published in Smyrna,[20] which was advertised in the Greek press by its author, a professor of eastern languages in the School of Propaganda named Nassif Mallouf, a Lebanese Christian linguist. He advertised his and other educational books written in Ottoman Turkish. In

12. *Amaltheia*, no. 421 (February 14, 1847) .
13. *Ephemeris tes Smyrnes*, no. 88 (December 15, 1850).
14. *Mnemosyne*, no. 25 (September 5, 1835).
15. *Ephemeris tes Smyrnes*, no.61 (June 9, 1850).
16. *Ephemeris tes Smyrnes*, no. 14 (July 15, 1849).
17. *Ephemeris tes Smyrnes*, no. 17 (August 5, 1849).
18. *Elpis*, no. 2 (May 23, 1841).
19. *He Hemera*, no. 62 (November 9/21, 1856).
20. *Telegraphos tou Vosporou*, no. 456 (September 13, 1852).

addition to school textbooks Mr. Mallouf also published "a novel called *He Terpne Koilas* (The Pleasant Valley), written in Arabic and Turkish with a small Arab, Persian, and Turkish lexicon at the back."[21] In addition to advertisements from private authors there were others for Ottoman and Karamanlı books emanating from the printing press owned by Evangelinos Misaelides. Among other things he published the famous and long-running Karamanlı newspaper *Anatole*, and his was the major publishing house for Karamanlı and, to a lesser extent, Ottoman books at that time. A typical advertisement from *Anatole* emphasized the value of books in Ottoman Turkish, a language which the publisher of *Anatole* described as extremely important. The following advertisement of the publishers Misaelides and Phardes is interesting in that it presents the Ottoman language as a mixture of Arabic and Persian, and argues for the necessity for the Greeks of learning this language:

> Ottoman consists of Arabic, the mother of all Asiatic languages and Persian. This language is necessary for those of our co-nationals who inhabit neighboring Greece, because ignorance of it can affect their interests [in the Ottoman Empire] negatively…. Although there are grammars teaching adequately the Ottoman language, there is a great need for a dictionary, which persuaded us to write a [Ottoman] Turkish-Greek dictionary with Greek letters, starting with the Arabic and then the Persian words as they are used in [Ottoman] Turkish translated into Greek. In editing this dictionary, we based our work on the official Arabic and Persian dictionaries and we are advised by the wise intellectual Sakı Efendi, member of the newly created Ottoman Academy of Constantinople and many other intellectuals from our co-nationals, and on various books…. [W]e ask all Greeks to support us generously in order to finish this most ambitious work, which would be divided into three volumes of a big size and would contain 24,000 words and one thousand pages. The price of this dictionary will be 200 *kuruş*. For subscribers it will be reduced to 150, paid in three instalments, each of which should be paid upon receipt of a volume…. Subscriptions are received in the press of ANATOLE in Constantinople, in Pera in the bookshop of Chrysopoulos, in Galata in the bookshop of Lazarides, in Smyrna by the psalt Misael Misaelides in the church of Aghia Photeine, in Greece by Mr. Nicolaides-Philadelpheos in Athens, and in all of Anatolia by the correspondents of the newspaper *Anatole*.[22]

Although the Ottoman Greek journalists never debated the suitability of European-style reforms for a Muslim society, the Ottoman Greek press did record that the sultan and his government and Muslims who espoused "European ideas" were

21. *Ephemeris tes Smyrnes*, no. 34 (December 2, 1849).
22. *Telegraphos tou Vosporou*, no. 485 (March 21, 1855).

considered by the majority of Muslims to be betraying their own cultural heritage. For their resistance to the adoption of European values, the Muslim masses were generally labelled in the press as "backward and insisting on remaining backward."[23]

These "backward" Muslims were, generally speaking, divided by the press into two subgroups: lesser government officials and provincial governors on the one hand, and the general Muslim masses on the other. The former were presented as corrupt and obstacles to the modernization of the empire. While uncovering their corruption, the Ottoman Greek press gave simultaneous publicity to the various new *firmans* issued by the government as it attempted to remedy the situation. The *firman* "against luxury," issued in 1835, was one of them. According to the newspaper *Mnemosyne* the *firman* ordered that:

> No official would be allowed from now on to go to his office followed by a throng of servants carrying packets of tobacco and a *narghile* as if he was going to a banquet. The custom to offer coffee from the coffee pot in public offices would be abolished; the mass of employees who fill the ante-rooms of all the offices and live mostly from gratuities, which everyone wishing to reach an official is forced to give them, will not bother anyone anymore and they will not obstruct any meeting by blocking the doors to the offices; from the simplest manager to the highest officer everyone will have to behave with modesty and even the Grand Vizier would be forbidden from now on from having more than two or three servants and more than three coffee pots.

The editor of *Mnemosyne* commented that this wise measure would benefit the people in two ways:

> Firstly, it would constrain the extravagance and secondly, it will abolish bribery, so common among the Turks. When they finally clear the ministries of the entire unnecessary rabble of bribery and incompetence, the ministers will be paid by the state an adequate salary so that they will embezzle no more.[24]

The Muslim masses were also portrayed in the press as unenlightened and fanatical, "scarcely different from beasts in their ignorance."[25] The violent Muslim reaction against the Christian population that followed the announcement of the reform program and the general difficulties of the state in imposing the rule of law and guaranteeing the security of all its citizens has been covered in the previous chapter, but will occasionally be referred again in this chapter as it was a constant – albeit

23. *He Hemera*, no. 46 (July 20/August 1, 1856).
24. *Mnemosyne*, no. 4 (March 30, 1835).
25. *He Hemera*, no. 46 (July 20/August 1, 1856).

unwelcome – companion to the everyday life of the Ottoman Christians, as was reported in the Greek press up to 1862.

In addition to politically incited violence, the press reported in almost every issue crimes of theft, robbery, and piracy.[26] Crimes committed by Muslims against Christians and others and action taken by the authorities were usually followed through by the press until the subsequent punishment or acquittal of the purported Muslim culprits, and included headlines such as:

> The Drunkenness of Ottomans Is the Cause of Killing Christians[27]
>
> Turks Killing Christians[28]
>
> Muslim Attacks Christian and Is Punished for It[29]
>
> Tunisian Kills Greek Sailor in Constantinople[30]
>
> Murders, Robberies, and Street Beatings in Constantinople by Ottomans against Christians[31]
>
> Abdi Paşa Sent to Thessaly to Catch Thieves[32]
>
> The Cruel Treatment of a Rich Jew in Palestine[33]
>
> Halil Bey Arrested because He Beheaded a Criminal without a Trial[34]
>
> Gang Robbery in Turkish Provinces and Albanian Gang Robber[35]

Extensive coverage was given, as we saw in the previous chapter, to the abduction, rape, and eventual murder of a Bulgarian girl called Nedelia by an Ottoman officer, who was arrested, tried, and subsequently acquitted.[36]

Unrest, local revolts, and the treatment of people by local armies in the Ottoman Empire were also extensively covered. Indicative headlines are:

---

26. *Mnemosyne*, no. 7 (April 20, 1835); *Aster tes Anatoles*, no. 24 (March 28, 1842); *Elpis*, no. 4 (June 6, 1841) and no. 5 (June 13, 1841); *He Hemera*, no. 7 (October 21/November 2, 1856), no. 36 (May 11/23, 1856), no. 46 (July 20/August 1, 1856); *Ephemeris tes Smyrnes*, no. 65 (July 7, 1850), no. 92 (November 12, 1851), no. 93 (January 19, 1851) etc.

27. *Elpis*, no. 4 (June 6, 1841).

28. *He Hemera*, no. 30 (March 30/April 11, 1856).

29. *Elpis*, no. 3 (May 30, 1841).

30. *He Hemera*, no. 39 (June 1/13, 1856); no. 48 (August 3/15, 1856).

31. *He Hemera*, no. 40 (June 8/20, 1856).

32. *He Hemera*, no. 7 (October 21/November 2, 1855).

33. *Ephemeris tes Smyrnes*, no. 22 (September 9, 1849).

34. *Ephemeris tes Smyrnes*, no. 32 (November 18, 1849).

35. *He Hemera*, no. 38 (May 25/June 6, 1856).

36. *Telegraphos tou Vosporou*, no. 653 (July 7, 1856). *He Hemera*, no. 30 (March 30/April 11, 1856); no. 35 (May 4/16, 1856); no. 36 (May 11/23, 1856); no. 38 (May 23/June 6, 1856); no. 55 (September 21/October 3, 1856).

Revolt in Crete[37]

Unrest in Bulgaria[38]

Unrest in Rumeli, Macedonia, Epirus, Thessaly, Syria, and Bosnia[39]

Revolt against the Ottomans in Ayara of Trabzon[40]

Revolt by the Sherif of Mecca[41]

Troubles in Barbary[42]

Unrest in Iconio of Karamania[43]

Unrest in Naplussa [Nablus] in Palestine[44]

The Atrocities of the Egyptian Army in Beirut

Albanian Muslim Gangs Attack the Christians[45]

Revolt against Prince Daniel[46]

War reporting was also extensive and diverse. One could read, for example, about the dynastic wars in Persia,[47] or a week-by-week account of the Crimean War, including the treaty, with every article explained, and a commentary.[48]

A mixed image of uncertainty over life and property but with a glimmer of hope for the future thanks to an enlightened sultan was the backdrop against which the daily life and social development of the Orthodox Christians of the empire unfolded in the Ottoman Greek press.

The Orthodox Christian Image

It would be wrong to assume that kinship would influence the Greek press to paint the Orthodox Christians with a singularly sympathetic hand. At first glance, their image in the Greek press was, to say the least, mixed. On the right of the picture was the conservative establishment of the Ottoman Greeks, which according to

37. *Elpis*, no. 3 (May 30, 1841); no. 4 (June 6, 1841); no. 5 (June 13, 1841); no. 6 (June 20, 1841).

38. *Elpis*, no. 6 (June 20, 1841).

39. *He Hemera*, no. 38 (May 25/June 6, 1856).

40. *He Hemera*, no. 44 (July 6/18, 1856).

41. *He Hemera*, no. 46 (July 20/August 1, 1856).

42. *Mnemosyne*, no. 23 (August 10, 1835).

43. *He Hemera*, no. 31 (April 6/18, 1856).

44. *He Hemera*, no. 35 (May 4/16, 1856).

45. *He Hemera*, no. 48, (August 3/15, 1856).

46. Ibid.

47. *Mnemosyne*, no. 23 (August 10, 1835).

48. See for example *He Hemera*, nos. 1 (September 4/21, 1855) through 68 (December 21, 1856/January 2, 1857).

the outspoken young publisher of *Elpis*, Petros Klados, was averse to the idea of popularizing knowledge and preferred to keep people "blind, in order to suck their blood and grab the fruit of their pains and sweat with greater ease."[49] On the left were those who opposed all ties with the past. Editors were often critical of those who jumped into these new, unchartered waters of change with a naive enthusiasm, without considering what lay beneath the surface or indeed if they were deep enough. The press was equally critical of the Bulgarian-speaking Orthodox, who were castigated for their nationalistic aspirations, and citizens from the kingdom of Greece were sanctioned for similar reasons. The picture was blurred further by the portrayal of common criminals of Christian origin. There was full coverage of the interrogation and trial of famous pirates and highwaymen, such as Theodoros Karayannis[50] and Tsamis Karatassos.[51] These negative examples of Orthodox Christians were banished to the edges of the picture while at its center the Greek press painted with exquisite craftsmanship the ideal models of contemporary Greek men and women, those who were imbued by the shining moral principles of ancient Greece and Orthodox Christianity.

Although Western Europe appeared at the time to be basking under a "Hellenic" sun, Greek writers did not portray Western societies as ideal settings to be copied wholesale by the Greek-speaking Christians of the Ottoman Empire. While embracing the positive elements of the classical revival, for example in social democratization, economic progress, general prosperity, social and educational advancement, and improvements in health in those societies, readers were cautioned about the negative potentials of Westernization. These included the skin deep "progress" advocated and aspired to by a new class of people in the empire, who although economically affluent had limited social or cultural backgrounds and education. If the Muslims were generally regarded as "backward" because they rejected social change according to European principles, some Ottoman Greeks were considered by the press to be equally "backward" because they wanted to change too much and too fast. French literature was read avidly in the nineteenth century both in the original and in translation, Italian opera was performed regularly in Smyrna, and French fashions were replacing the traditional dress of the Greek bourgeoisie. These changes notwithstanding, the newspapers cautioned that importing Western European social ways uncritically was not necessarily beneficial. There was significant criticism in the press as early as 1835 of the Western lifestyle. Critics argued that advocates of merely mimicking European manners and dress and speaking among themselves in French had chosen the superficial and ignored the values of their own glorious historical, political, and intellectual past, which

49. *Elpis*, no. 4 (June 6, 1841).
50. *Ephemeris tes Smyrnes*, no. 54 (April 21, 1850) and no. 55, (April 28, 1855).
51. *Amaltheia*, no. 392 (August 3, 1846).

was shared with Western Europe. They were accused of encouraging their young to "spend three hours dressing with great care and attention in front of a mirror, dancing all the new dances with great accuracy and skill, playing cards, drinking, fraternizing with loose women,"[52] rather than insisting on their children being provided with a good education in the classics, the Greek language, and in moral judgement. Some writers went as far as castigating affluent people who employed private teachers rather than sending their children to school, thus failing to support a national education for all.

The diet of French popular fiction that was served up in the literary supplements of the Ottoman Greek press illustrates this point well. The choice of Eugène Sue, for example, is not insignificant. Arguably the most avidly read author of the 1840s and 1850s, Sue advocated a moral middle class, a family-oriented society of hard-working, honorable men and chaste, loving women. At the same time, his books painted a harrowing picture of the ills of an industrialized, post-revolutionary society. The ambitious, atheist, and blasé generation that was emerging in France in the 1840s was imbued with disillusionment and pessimism. The aristocratic pretensions of the nouveau riches were also to some degree relevant to the emerging commercial classes of the Ottoman Empire.

The moral lessons of Sue's novels were largely espoused by the editors of the Ottoman Greek press, as is clear from many of its editorials, and they were especially attractive to the female readership.[53] They were also to some degree espoused by the growing Greek intelligentsia, the teachers, writers, and poets of Smyrna, Constantinople and other, smaller Ottoman cities. But despite the concerted efforts of its editors to restrain the newly affluent from their gourmandizing taste for the superficial, the reports of the Ottoman Greek press and especially the Smyrna press reveal that they made no great inroads among the smart crowd of early nineteenth-century Ottoman Greeks.

Ephemeris tes Smyrnes was at the cutting edge of fashionable news and provides crucial information on these new social trendsetters. As we are informed, they had to be well dressed, well groomed, educated, and live in grand houses, surrounded by beautiful things, speak French, and dance well. Women were additionally expected to play the piano.

Ephemeris tes Smyrnes hosted articles on the latest clothes fashions for women,[54] with information on new Parisian dresses[55] and illustrated fashions for the ladies of

---

52. *Mnemosyne*, no. 28 (September 13, 1835).

53. Information from the Ottoman Greek press suggests that literate females were by no means scarce among the Greeks living in cities, and that their number was growing fast with the great push for education in the nineteenth century.

54. *Ephemeris tes Smyrnes*, no. 1 (April 15, 1849).

55. *Ephemeris tes Smyrnes*, no. 36 (December 16, 1849).

Smyrna,[56] with advice on "how to dress and comb your hair."[57] In addition, apart from its weekly literary supplement, it carried two monthly supplements devoted to fashionable society: one supplement included music scores of the most popular songs and the other provided instructions on how to make the latest French clothes. For the more impatient, ready-to-wear clothes, underwear, and white linen goods were also advertised in the press:

> SHOP OF IOUSTINOS MARENGOS – GREAT PERA AVENUE, NO. 250, OPPOSITE POSTA STREET. Mr Ioustinos Marengos, ex-partner in the well-known *ANGLIKON* [English] shop in Stavrodrom-ion, is pleased to announce to the honorable public that he has opened his own shop for the sale of cloth and all white goods [table linen, bedding, towels, and underwear] and all kinds of fashionable garments at very reasonable prices.[58]

The wealth of the Orthodox Christians in the big Ottoman cities was so vast that they could support an expensive life style in every way. For the trendier set the acquisition of the desired appearance was catered to by an army of stylists: personal maids, hairdressers, pharmacists offering cosmetic aids, and a variety of tutors for music, dance, manners, and languages, mostly French. Personal advertisements from people offering to cater to these special needs formed a large category in the Greek press. Apart from people of Greek origin, foreigners who had arrived in the Ottoman Empire in the hope of a better future advertised their services in the Greek press. A few examples of what was on offer follow below:

> Mr. Athanassios Demetriades, former teacher of Greek in the School of Valinos, has rented two large rooms appropriate for teaching, and gives private lessons opposite the school for a small fee. He teaches Greek, all encyclical lessons, Ottoman, and French.[59]

> Mrs. Maria Anna Pellis, an Italian lady, who has recently arrived in our city from Milan, is an expert in various types of embroidery. Those ladies who are interested in educating their children in the important principles of upbringing, such as high-quality women's dressmaking, embroidering for ball-gowns, etc., may come to our office and inquire. Mrs. Anna would also consider a position as a lady's maid. Moreover, Mr. Pellis, husband of the above-mentioned lady, is a teacher of Italian, French, and German,

56. *Ephemeris tes Smyrnes*, no. 40 (January 13, 1850).
57. *Ephemeris tes Smyrnes*, no. 46 (February 24, 1850).
58. *Ephemeris tes Smyrnes*, no. 56 (May 5, 1850).
59. *Ephemeris tes Smyrnes*, no. 59 (May 26, 1850).

and is one of those Italian refugees worthy of sympathy. He was previously one of Garibaldi's officers.[60]

※

Baron Friels, a venerable, old, erudite gentleman desires to give lessons in drawing and painting in your own home. Those interested should come to our office.[61]

Finally, pharmacists advertised their cosmetics and other beauty aids to members of both sexes, as it seems that men of the bourgeoisie were as keen of being seen as fashionable as women:

Liquid for an easy tint of your hair and beard, prepared by Antonios Sepout, Pharmacist-Chemist.[62]

There were also advertisements for nail polishes and facial creams, among which Oil of Olay was as prominent in Smyrna in 1857 as it is today in England.[63]

Nice houses, style, and elegance were only some of the many components that formed the standard against which social status was measured among Ottoman Greek city dwellers. Another was the possession of unusual objets d'art, foreign jewelry, and furs. A foreign origin, as so often, attached to the owner the labels of affluence, distinction and style as domestic goods were considered within easy reach of everyone, inferior in taste and banal. Travelling merchants carrying such goods multiplied quickly as demand rose vertically by the middle of the nineteenth century. Itinerant merchants would arrive in Constantinople or Smyrna, book themselves into a hotel, and then advertise their exciting novelties in the press, like this one:

In Halide Han no. 43, a merchant has brought from St. Petersburg and Moscow silverware that one cannot find in Constantinople, such as tobacco boxes, large and small goblets, bracelets inlaid with enamel for the ladies and other such goods, top quality cloth for clerical dresses, furs from Siberia and Bokhara, etc. The same man can show you a most technologi-cal [*sic*] thing, fit for a European Royal study. Those who are interested in buying the above-mentioned goods at excellent prices could also ask to see a most wonderful and precious emerald weighing 320 karats.[64]

It was a natural development for those who took such pains over their appearance and possessions to desire to be immortalized with their fashionable hair, clothes,

60. *Telegraphos tou Vosporou*, no. 470 (December 28, 1852).
61. *Ephemeris tes Smyrnes*, no. 71 (August 18, 1850).
62. *Telegraphos tou Vosporou kai Vyzantis*, no. 436 (January, 25, 1861).
63. *Telegraphos tou Vosporou kai Vyzantis*, no. 91, (July 24, 1857).
64. *Telegraphos tou Vosporou*, no. 373 (February 10, 1851).

and jewelry. Instead of portrait painting, which does not feature in the press of the time, photography became the preferred medium for the Ottoman Greeks. Photographic shops advertised extensively, and besides taking photographs the photographers would also give lessons in photography and sell photographs and lithographs. They also advertised their special services for Muslim women:

> In our photographic shop, near the Russian Embassy we make colored pictures. The Ottoman [Muslim] women can go to private rooms, where they will be attended by European ladies, who will take the desired photo-graphs. These ladies undertake to go to the various harems as well.[65]

Prompted by such advertisements one could assume that the information con-tained in the Greek press was somehow expected by the advertiser to find its way apart from the Greek-speaking clientele both to the private boudoirs of Muslim ladies and to the harem. These expectations seem to have been based on common knowledge about a social reality regarding inter-communal relations in the Ot-toman Empire. Indeed, as will be shown later, there are several other instances in the Greek press of such inter-communal expectations by advertisers, which need to be researched further.

Living in a society with a high crime rate and elevated levels of violence and general insecurity of life, as reported in the Greek press, did little to suppress the outgoing, fun-loving character of the Orthodox Christians and especially those who called themselves Romans (*Rum* in Turkish and *Romioi* in Greek) or Greeks (Hellenes) in the press. Whether residing in villages and provincial towns or in the big cities of the empire, entertainment, we are informed, was abundant. As well as religious festivals (*giortes* and *panigiria*) of all kinds,[66] either celebrating the birthday of the patron saint of the village,[67] or fire-jumping and shooting at the festival of St. John the Prodrome,[68] the Easter celebrations and the Good Friday parade in Constantinople,[69] the celebrations of the first of May,[70] marriages, christenings, and personal onomastic celebrations (the Saint's feast day, whose name is given to a person upon baptism). All were widely celebrated, whether in the small vil-lages or in the capital itself. Although occasionally faced with local antipathy and sometimes with downright hostility from the local Muslim population, religious festivities had been celebrated without interruption since the fall of the Eastern Roman Empire to the Ottoman Turks in 1453. Over the centuries, Christian

65. *Telegraphos tou Vosporou kai Vyzantis,* no.99 (September 11, 1857).

66. For example, the fiesta of Uzunova. *Ephemeris tes Smyrnes,* no. 25 (September 30, 1849) and no. 26 (October 7, 1849).

67. For example the fiesta of Aghios Therapon, in *Ephemeris tes Smyrnes*, no. 60 (June 2, 1850) .

68. *Ephemeris tes Smyrnes*, no. 6 (May 20, 1849).

69. *Mnemosyne*, no. 9 (May 4, 1835).

70. Ibid.

ritual and traditional celebrations had become intertwined with local Muslim reactions to them, and although the Christians considered the latter as disrespectful
and demeaning, both sides continued their dual existence unabated. Following
the promulgation of the Tanzimat and the new social expectations it generated,
letters began to find their way into the in-trays of the editors of the Greek press
complaining about these local "anti-customs" devised by the Muslim villagers to
diminish and annoy their Christian neighbors. Two examples of such letters are
translated and included below. The first was written in Kydoniae [Turkish Ayvalık]
on April 28/May 9 and published in *He Hemera* of Trieste on June 15/27, 1856.
According to the writer, who signed himself *one of your readers*, "... in Attalia
[Turkish Antalya] of Pamphylia [Turkish Pamfilia], [it is an old custom] when the
Christians came out of Christmas Mass the Ottomans [Turks or Muslims] would
force them to clean their stables." The same writer also related that in Elmalı of
Pamphylia "the Ottomans are burning old straw mats in the square during Easter, saying: 'like this smells the Easter of the Christians.'"[71] The latter account is
supported by another letter from Elmalı itself dated July 7/19, signed "also one
of your readers" and printed in *He Hemera* of Trieste on July 20/August 1, 1856.
According to the indignant account of this writer:

> [O]n Easter Sunday a throng of [Muslim] children and young men invade
> the Christian houses with cries and shouts and grab the straw mats with
> which the people usually cover their floors, often beating up the owner of
> the house. They then gather the mats in the squares. During Easter they
> set fire to them and shout publicly: "In such a way smells the Easter of the
> Christians," which they don't call in Turkish Bayram but Vetnan [proba-
> bly a local dialect word for *boktan*], which means excreta. Last year they
> went so far as to light a fire outside the Armenian Church while the priest
> was still chanting mass.... You might, perhaps, wonder what the Gover-
> nor says about it. The Governor, called İdrisoğlu Salih Ağa, to whom we
> complained about this unholy performance, laughing in the customary
> naive way of the Turks, replied "It doesn't matter, I will warn them (*zarar
> yok te[m]bih edelim*)." Together with lighting pyres the Turks have also the
> custom of attaching nettle leaves to their saris with a needle and walking
> around until the evening of Easter day saying the following curse: "May
> the needle be nailed into the eyes of the unbelievers and may the nettle
> leaves be forever their bed." Wearing such ridiculous things, indicative of
> their religious hatred [against non-Muslims], inspired from childhood, not
> only do they wander around the streets but they have the impudence to
> greet the Christians with whom they are acquainted.[72]

71. *He Hemera*, no. 41 (June 15/27, 1856).
72. *He Hemera*, no. 46 (July 20/August 1, 1856).

It is clear from various articles that the Christian population of the Ottoman Empire believed at first that the Hatt-ı Hümayun would stop Muslims behaving in such a manner towards the other millets. They gradually realized, however, that government orders, unless followed by strong military presence, were powerless because "no one [among the Muslims] cares."[73]

Despite the occasional Muslim mischief, Christian celebrations continued and in addition to festivities of a religious or traditional nature the nineteenth century saw a rise in secular entertainment. Such opportunities arose mostly in the big cities of Smyrna and Constantinople, where social clubs, concerts, theatre, opera, and an array of cafés and restaurants offered a vast choice and variety of amusements. The activities of the various clubs were frequently the subject of reports and advertisements. The clubs of Smyrna[74] were especially famous for their intellectual debates and their lavish balls, where all the new dances from France were taught and performed.[75] Other club entertainments included poetry readings and musical performances. The poets themselves often performed readings of their work. Judging from the advertisements, they were mostly of Greek, French, or Italian origin and included several internationally renowned figures, such as Lamartine. The latter was vastly popular in the empire, as reflected in the sultan's decision to gift him a plot of land to establish residency there.[76] Poetry readings were advertised in the press of Constantinople and Smyrna, such as the following: "Next Tuesday, the poet Regaldi [Giuseppe Regaldi (1809–1883)] will read his poems in the Circolo Levantino."[77]

The clubs also held concerts:

> Next Tuesday, March 12, the pianist Mr. Pereli will give a concert at the Circolo Levantino Club. The entrance fee is 10 *kuruş*. The concert starts at half-past eight.[78]

It seems from the above and other advertisements that the clubs and especially that of the Circolo Levantino, had stages or areas large enough for a complete orchestra, several of which were resident in Smyrna:

> Next Tuesday, March 2, around 9 o'clock in the evening at the Circolo Levantino, there will be a musical performance by Mr. Leopold Ferus. He is a German, living in our city, who has been honored in various theatres of

73. *He Hemera*, no. 40 (June 8/20, 1856).
74. See for example: *Ephemeris tes Smyrnes*, no. 23 (September 16, 1849) and *Aster tes Anatoles*, no. 6 (November 21, 1841) and no. 14 (January 16, 1842).
75. *Aster tes Anatoles*, no. 37 (July 3, 1842).
76. *Ephemeris tes Smyrnes*, no. 63 (June 23, 1850).
77. *Ephemeris tes Smyrnes*, no. 65 (July, 7, 1850).
78. *Aster tes Anatoles*, no. 21 (March 7, 1842).

Europe. He will sing some of the best-known songs in Europe, assisted by the resident [in Smyrna] Italian orchestra. The program is to be performed in the Club and later at other such places, where people who wish to enjoy such pleasure can go. Entrance fee 15 *kuruş*.[79]

The price for concerts and poetry readings was usually the same. In the 1840s, for example: "Entrance fee [was] 10, 15, and 30 *kuruş*."[80]

Constantinople's clubs were equally active in offering theatrical and musical evenings, but at slightly cheaper prices:

> Mr. Max Bohren, cellist, lead musician at the court of the King of Würt-temberg, recently honored with the Order of the Cross of the Savior, and a knight of various orders, has the honor to inform the public that, with the collaboration of the Prima Donna Morinkelli, and the Master of Ottoman Music, Mr. Bartoloumis, he will perform a great symphony for voices and instruments. This will take place next Tuesday around 8–8:30 in the evening in the Pera Club, and will be performed only once, as he will be departing for Germany immediately afterwards. Tickets are available at the booksellers, Kohler Bros., and Sibf., in the patisseries of Mr. Rotas and Mr. Balthazar in the Great Street of Pera, by Mr. Kinzelbach, no. 1 Bakh Pazar in Galata, and in the Pera Club. Entrance fee 5 *kuruş*.[81]

People also enjoyed the theatre and the opera. Smyrna possessed the first pur-pose-built theatre in the Ottoman Empire, called Euterpe after the muse of music and lyric poetry, built in 1841.[82] But long before its appearance opera and plays had been performed in the empire. Valuable information about the operation of the Smyrna theatre is gained by its advertisements in the press:

> Mr. Kamillieris, Director of the theatre of our city, announces to the pub-lic that the theatre will open at seven o'clock and the performances will start at eight.

It seems that the theatre operated with tickets as well as by subscription, and some people would have to stand for a performance:

> Those of our subscribers who come to the theatre before the beginning of the performance and cannot find a place to stand can, if they wish, have their bill of subscription returned and leave. Those who stand for one act and then wish to leave will lose their bill.[83]

79. *Ephemeris tes Smyrnes*, no. 46 (February 24, 1850).
80. *Amaltheia*, no. 379 (May 17, 1846).
81. *Telegraphos tou Vosporou kai Vyzantis*, no. 96 (August 28, 1857).
82. *Aster tes Anatoles*, no. 2 (October 24, 1841).
83. *Aster tes Anatoles*, no. 18 (February 14, 1842).

A typical announcement for a forthcoming attraction would contain about three lines, informing the public of the day, name, and genre of the play.

> Next Wednesday the play *Tasso Quarto* [*Torquato Tasso* by Goethe?] opens. The play is a tragi-comedy and it will greatly please the Smyrnian public.[84]

Contemporary Greek playwrights wrote a number of the plays performed and there were also performances of ancient Greek tragedies and comedies. Foreign plays were translated and performed in Greek but occasionally there were performances in French, Italian, and German by foreign acting groups on tour:

> By the end of the month [September 1850] the Vaudeville Theatre Company of Mr. Danglemont arrives from Constantinople and will stay in our city all winter. We have not had such entertainment for a long time, and you, our youth, in particular, will learn many French phrases and a multitude of French manners.[85]

Operas were performed in the original language, usually Italian. The first advertisement for Bellini's *Norma* appeared in 1841.[86] Since it does not refer to that performance as a Smyrna premiere, one could assume that *Norma,* which was first performed at La Scala in Milan in 1831, had already been staged in Smyrna previously. Thus, it seems that Smyrnaean Greeks had the opportunity to enjoy some operas almost simultaneously with people in the cultural centers of Europe. Frequent advertisements for Greek operettas with erotic, bucolic, or political themes reveal that they were also popular at this time.

Apart from clubs and the theatre, live music could be enjoyed in certain coffee shops and patisseries:

> Mr. Kiouzes, owner of the coffee shop He Oraia Thea [The Beautiful View], has the honor of informing the respected public that the newly arrived Italian orchestra will play in the above-mentioned coffee shop in the evenings of Wednesday, Saturday, and Sunday. He hopes that the public will encourage him with its presence, just as much as he will try to please the public with his excellent service.[87]

During the summer months, another form of entertainment, sea bathing, began to capture the attention of the "modern" crowd of Smyrna.[88] Newspapers were quick to report on this new extravaganza, which was at the same time "recommended

---

84. *Aster tes Anatoles,* no. 21 (March 7, 1842).
85. *Ephemeris tes Smyrnes,* no. 74 (September 8, 1850).
86. *Aster tes Anatoles,* no. 5 (November 14, 1841).
87. *Ephemeris tes Smyrnes,* no. 55 (April 28, 1850).
88. *Ephemeris tes Smyrnes,* no. 62 (June 16, 1850).

by doctors as of great benefit to our health." Another form of fashionable entertainment in Smyrna[89] included various experiments by local and foreign scientists
performed in public.[90]

Smyrnaean ladies and gentlemen were keen to be regarded as trendsetters not
only in their own city but also in any milieu. Naturally, visits of society ladies from
other parts were significant and meticulously reported in the society columns.
We note among them a report of a visit of Athenian ladies to Smyrna,[91] an event
of particular importance as it was a matter of pride for the hosts not to be seen
as inferior in any way to – and even surpassing, if possible – the ladies from the
Greek capital.

Constantinople, being the capital of the Ottoman Empire was the other prominent exemplar for social mores. Society reports from Constantinople
were included in all Ottoman Greek newspapers.[92] The women of "Byzantium"
(Constantinople)[93] are portrayed as astonishingly emancipated even by European
standards. Defending them against an article from a German newspaper which
criticized them for impropriety because "they are often seen frequenting the palaces
of the grandees unaccompanied, the editor of *Ephemeris tes Smyrnes* argued that:

> Byzantine women [Greek women of Constantinople] are renowned for
> their intelligence, education, and commanding presence, equal to that
> of any man, and are perfectly capable of dealing with business affairs on
> their own without being accompanied by their husbands, something that
> should have been admired rather than criticized by the writer.

The British Embassy seems to have been a pole of attraction for Constantinopolitan high society, and there were accounts of its receptions and balls attended by,
among others, the sultan, the ecumenical patriarch, the Armenian patriarch, and
the chief rabbi.[94] Such was the high regard with which the embassy was held that
the patriarch was even reported to have attended one of the British ambassador's
fancy dress balls![95] This report, however, would not have caused as great a sensa-
tion as the unprecedented break with tradition by the patriarch when he granted
permission to the wife and daughter of Ambassador Stratford Canning to enter
the until then and since then[96] male-only monastical state of Mount Athos![97] Such

89. *Ephemeris tes Smyrnes*, no. 36 (December 16, 1849).
90. *Ephemeris tes Smyrnes*, no 35 (December 9, 1849).
91. *Ephemeris tes Smyrnes*, no. 5 (May 13, 1849).
92. *Ephemeris tes Smyrnes*, no. 15 (July 22, 1849).
93. *Ephemeris tes Smyrnes*, no. 79 (October 13, 1850).
94. *He Hemera*, no. 22 (February 3/15, 1856).
95. *He Hemera*, no. 23 (February 10/22, 1856).
96. Dalrymple (2005, 5) claims that in 1857 his great aunt, Virginia Somers, was the only
woman ever to have spent time in Mount Athos (two months in a tent along with her husband Lord
Somers-Cock, a conservative politician, and the Pre-Raphaelite artist Coutts Lindsay).
97. *He Hemera*, no. 88 (May 10/22, 1857).

singular acts reflected the respect with which the British Embassy was held and should not be regarded as a sign that tradition was giving way to new mores. On the contrary, the press reported that attempts by some churches to break with Byzantine tradition by introducing polyphonic music into the liturgy were quashed by the patriarch,[98] as indeed was the new practice of distributing fancy packaged sweets after weddings, baptisms, and funerals.[99] This was a blow to the social trendsetters among the Ottoman Greeks, who had found yet another way of displaying their newly acquired wealth by packaging the offerings in extravagant ways.

Although it is tempting to carry on describing the gaieties of life for the beau monde of the big cities, it would be unjust to focus only on the superficial features of this emerging, affluent, and fashionable class of people. When the press illuminates the more substantive side of the bankers, the merchants, and the new professionals a great number of them are seen to exhibit an ethos of hard work coupled with an ardent dedication to education and an admirable propensity for philanthropy.

Since the middle of the eighteenth century a growing number of Ottoman Orthodox began to perceive education as a means of improving their own individual and others' social position and there was an ever increasing drive towards universal education, especially among the Ottoman Greeks. Until the eighteenth century the Ottoman government did not interfere in the education of the Orthodox Christians of the empire, which was the sole responsibility of the patriarchate. When Selim III occupied the throne, the Phanariot Demetrios Mourouzis managed to persuade him that "the Greek schools and colleges should be authorized officially [with a *firman*] by the Turkish government."[100] In this way Mourouzis managed both to break the absolute authority of the patriarchate on education and at the same time create for himself, "by order of the sultan," the position of inspector general of schools and hospitals.

The educational system followed by the Orthodox Church was the one decided upon in the ecumenical synods of Constantinople (680) and Nicaea (787), and further developed by Emperor Leo VI (the Wise) (866–912) in his *Biblion Eparchikon* (Eparchic Book).[101] As far as the primary schools were concerned – which constituted the overwhelming majority of schools until the nineteenth century – education was firmly based on religion. It consisted of learning how to read and write, learning by heart and reciting various religious texts such as the Octoechos, the letters of St. John Damascene, the Letters and Acts of the Apostles and so forth, plus some mathematics. Wealthy individuals employed teachers for their children's education at home.

In the nineteenth century the new professional classes challenged the pa-

---

98. *Amaltheia*, no. 421 (February 21, 1847).
99. *Amaltheia*, no. 412 (December 20, 1846).
100. Chassiotes 1881, 33.
101. Evangelides 1936, LI. See also appendix II.

triarchate's provision of education as inadequate and even attacked the private tuition hitherto enjoyed by the old wealthy families and the Phanariots. This attitude found allies in the Ottoman Greek press. As we have seen in previous chapters, Greek editors, such as Kyriakos Labrylos Hadjinikolaou of *Mnemosyne*, had claimed as early as 1835 that those who employed private tutors and did not send their children to school so as to support the universal education of Ottoman Greek children committed a crime against the nation.

Education and its main tool, language, had by the late eighteenth century become the subject of an intense debate, principally between two general groups. The first included those who were preoccupied with developing a Greek national consciousness and identity, and improving the position of underprivileged social groups within this nation through education; the second group was made up of the conservative establishment (the church, old wealth families, Phanariots), who wanted to preserve the status quo. Greek "modernizers" perceived education as a means of reaching national homogeneity and developing all Ottoman Greeks from the status of subjects to that of citizens who would be able to think and participate in the government of the state. They also believed that through education one would improve one's social position, since many of the new professions required skilled employees. Although all the modernizers aimed at the same main objectives, they were divided as to the best way forward. Their main debates concerned two issues: the kind of education required and the tool which would provide it, the Greek language.

The system of education had continued from the Byzantine period through to the Ottoman period basically unaltered. By the nineteenth century, the thousand-year-old educational system was outdated and unable to meet current needs. In the beginning of the nineteenth century the movement for the popularization of education among the Ottoman Greeks imported into the empire the Bell-Lancaster "mutual instruction" method, which was suggested and introduced into Ottoman Greek education by Adamantios Koraes.[102] This system of primary education was devised by A. Bell, J. Lancaster, and J. P. Girard, and was widely used in the nineteenth century to provide the rudiments of education for underprivileged children in Europe and Africa. Secondary education was also overhauled at that time. It was divided into six grades. Its curriculum – unofficial until 1846 but generally accepted by all Greek schools in the empire – was based on a detailed study of the Greek language, a study of the classics, the speeches of the holy fathers, history, philosophy, theology, physics, and mathematics. A good knowledge of French – the lingua franca of the upper classes and of diplomacy – was required and many schools taught Ottoman Turkish. The patriarchate was suspicious of the new style of mass education for various reasons, not least because it originated in Catholic or Protestant countries, and could therefore include incorrect religious beliefs.

102. Evangelides 1936, XC.

As this type of education was beginning to gain momentum, a rumor begun to circulate that the church considered any teacher or school that taught sciences and philosophy as

> a tool of Satan, which on the pretext of enlightening the people taught atheism, freemasonry, and magic, thus undermining the foundations of the Father and – most of all – the obedience due to the authorities.[103]

Although there is no evidence to suggest that this became the official church view, there were instances when local bishops took it upon themselves to destroy such "tools of Satan." A notorious case was the Philologikon Gymnasion of Smyrna (est. 1809), which was forced to close down in 1810 by the church of Smyrna. The then metropolitan of the city, the ultra-conservative Gregorios V (several times patriarch, lastly patriarch of Constantinople [1819–1821], hanged by the Ottoman government) roused the people of Smyrna against the school and in favor of the independent but extremely conservative Evangelical School of Smyrna.[104] Gregorios was just one of several conservative bishops who employed everything in their power to prevent modern education from spreading among their flock. Some ultra-conservative bishops were also known to burn books – sometimes whole libraries – if they were suspicious of their contents. The Athens newspaper *Hellas* mentioned, for example, that the metropolitan of Ioannina, Ioannikios was accused of exactly such a deed in a report published on Wednesday, November 8, 1839. In his support his defenders argued that:

> he had burned only the books of the English Bible Society and from these only the ones containing teachings against the holy scriptures that are received from the translation of the Septuagint and the rest of the holy fathers of the Eastern Orthodox Church.

They added that the metropolitan of Ioannina was a tireless prosecutor of those people

> who under the pretext of teaching were trying to put into the innocent soul of youth the snake of atheism, impiety, and heresy.[105]

Some bishops were also eager to close down printing houses, and some newspapers were also prosecuted at times. A letter from Salonica to the newspaper *He Hemera* in February 1860 informs us that:

> Ten years ago, Kyriakos Darzelovites established here a bookshop with its own printing press. Some people from the Metropolis tried to present this

103. S. Oikonomou 1871, 1–7.
104. One of the teachers, Steph. Oikonomos, wrote about the events that led to the enforced closure of the Philologicon Gymnasion. See S. Oikonomos 1871. Also see Eliou 1983.
105. *He Hellas,* no. 20 (November 8, 1839).

venture as a bad thing [to the government] but the people here – the Jews too – insisted that it was a very good thing and so it managed to survive.[106]

By the 1830s the need for a different kind of education had overcome any remaining conservative opposition and among other things created the conditions for a profitable new business. Private schools mushroomed and advertisements for educational establishments were prominent in the Greek press in the period 1830–1862. In addition, the Greek press frequently reported on the foundation of new schools, such as the account of the building of St. Photeine School for girls in 1842,[107] the establishment in 1847 of a school for agriculture and a school for arts and crafts,[108] an account of the schools of Ioannina,[109] a report on the schools of Chios,[110] and the schools of Smyrna.[111]

There were also announcements by private, community and church schools of the beginning of the school year and calling on parents or prospective students to register:

> We inform the public that we have begun registrations in the newly built Djilambi School for Girls and all those who wish to register their daughters must do so promptly, because when fifty places are filled we will not admit anyone else.[112]

School examinations were also announced in the press. In Greek schools they were oral and took place in public. Attendance was open to all but priority was given to the students' relatives:

> The governors of the Greek School of Stavrodromion have decided that the annual examinations will take place between the 6th and 20th of July. On Sundays they will take place after the liturgy and on weekdays from 8 o'clock until noon every day. All grades will be examined in all the subjects taught ... starting from first-grade Greek. Entrance to these examinations is free for members of the public. Apart from their own teachers anyone can pose questions to the students. Questions should be relevant to the curriculum. If any question is not relevant to what a student has been taught, it will be withdrawn as inappropriate. After the examinations of the Greek Schools [emphasis on the classics] the examinations of the Allelodidactic Schools will take place [that is, in the afternoon]. They will start on the 4th of July and finish on Sunday the 20th. All parents and guardians

106. *He Hemera,* no. 230 (February 11/23, 1860).
107. *Aster tes Anatoles,* no. 27 (April 17, 1842).
108. *Amaltheia,* no. 423 (March 7, 1847).
109. *Amaltheia,* no. 358 (May 26, 1846).
110. *Amaltheia,* no. 425 (March 21, 1847).
111. *Amaltheia,* no. 396 (August 31, 1846).
112. *Mnemosyne,* no.24 (September 3, 1835).

are invited to attend the examinations in order to support the students and inform themselves of the progress of our children. Pera, 27th June 1852, the Ephors G. S. Kylitses, D. Mestheneus, N. Zantiotes, and A. Deros.[113]

After the examinations most schools published the names of those who excelled in them. It is interesting that some Turkish-speaking schools also advertised their examinations in the Greek press and there is an account as early as 1835 of the examinations of the newly-established Turkish high school[114] of Smyrna and of Ottoman schools in Constantinople.[115] It is not clear whether these were state-run schools, but Abdülmecid I and his mother were often present at the examinations after he became sultan in 1839.

Several schools from other parts of the world, mostly Greece and the Greek communities in Africa, Western Europe, and the Black Sea placed advertisements. So too did a few foreign schools, such as the English School of Malta,[116] but the majority were placed by schools in Athens and Piraeus.[117]

The most interesting group among the educational advertisements are the ones referring to the opening of new schools. These are fairly numerous and demonstrate the increasing need for secular education among the Greeks of the Ottoman Empire. Most private schools, such as the one below, advertised in the Smyrna press. These announcements also provide us with a fairly clear idea of the curriculum in the various schools, the types of student services available, and the cost of education to the parents:

THE ESTABLISHMENT OF MESSRS. ROUX AND NEOKLEUS announces that in their school, the Greek language will be the object of special attention and students will be divided into classes according to mental ability. They will be taught Mathematics, History, Mythology, Geography, Calligraphy, etc. The French language will be taught to all students. Other languages will be taught according to the parents' wishes. Students will be divided in four categories: a) Boarders: annual fees 110 *distilo*s, b) Day boarders: annual fees 74 *distilo*s. They will attend between 6 a.m. and 7:30 p.m., eating with the boarders and teachers, c) Non- boarders: annual fee 48 *distilo*s. They are to attend daily from 6 a.m. to noon and from 1:30 to 7:30 p.m., except on Thursday afternoons and Sundays. They will take part in all of the lessons and study period, d) Auditors: annual fee 24 *distilo*s. They will attend daily from 8 a.m. to noon and from 1:30 to 5 p.m., except on Thursday afternoons and Sundays. English, Italian, and any other language, as well as sketching, music, and dance will be taught

113. *Amaltheia,* no. 457 (October 23, 1847).
114. *Ephemeris tes Smyrnes,* no. 13 (July 8, 1849).
115. *Ephemeris tes Smyrnes,* no. 55 (April 28, 1850).
116. *Amaltheia,* no. 445 (July 31, 1847).
117. *Ephemeris tes Smyrnes,* no.16 (July 24, 1849).

by special arrangement with parents. School fees are payable each quarter in advance. Lessons begin next May. Smyrna April 25, 1849, Simon Roux, Elias Neokleus.[118]

The first half of the nineteenth century coincides with a great push for the education of women, which was warmly supported in editorials and numerous articles in the Smyrna newspapers. Several advertisements in the Greek press refer to the education of women, such as the following of 1849 by the allelodidactic group of schools in Smyrna:

> There is a large group of people, mostly women, who neither study in the Gymnasiums [High Schools] nor in their own courtyards [at home], nor are they ever going to open a serious book in their lives. This is the group we set out to reach and educate. We are the Allelodidactic Schools, the first step to a higher education.[119]

Self-styled teachers without the necessary qualifications occasionally answered the rising demand for schools. Particularly in the case of girls' schools the "moral values necessary to bring up a family" taught in the schools seemed in some cases to compensate for the absence of an academic curriculum. This is clear from some of the advertisements, such as the following for a girls' school in Constantinople:

> All education and culture start with a good home life. A mother and daughters, with great experience in the upbringing of children, absolutely guarantee a home run with honest zeal and motherly and sisterly care. Two young ladies have opened a school for girls. The school is at present behind the English Palace near the new fish-shops. The school appears crowded because of the many girls who attend both as daygirls and boarders. New premises are now being sought. The lessons taught are Reading, Calligraphy, Mathematics, Greek and French, synopsis of Greek History, Geography, Catechism, and various handicrafts. Parents who seek a good Christian upbringing for their daughters can trust us unreservedly. Fees should be paid monthly. Antiope and Calliope Koupa, Pera, Constantinople, October 11, 1852.[120]

Schools founded by people with inferior or no qualifications whatsoever caused concern both to the patriarchate and to old-established schools. It was therefore decided to create a formal set of regulations for primary, secondary, and tertiary education. The first official school regulations for Orthodox schools in the Ot-

---

118. *Ephemeris tes Smyrnes*, no. 25 (September 30, 1850).
119. *Ephemeris tes Smyrnes*, no. 17 (August 5, 1849).
120. *Telegraphos tou Vosporou*, no. 460 (October 11, 1852).

toman Empire were published in 1846, probably as a result of the government's *hatt* on education, issued in 1845, which made it easier for private individuals to open schools. These regulations were devised by the allelodidactic school of Aghia Kyriake in Kontoskali of Constantinople. Later, in 1853, the Balta Liman school in Constantinople made additions to them. Then in 1864 the patriarchate published the "Regulations for Allelodidactic and Secondary Schools" with an introduction by Patriarch Anthimos VI.[121]

Education had a significant impact on book publishing in the Ottoman Empire. Book advertisements featured largely from the beginning of the Greek press and the number of book-publishers, printers, and booksellers increased many times over within the thirty years covered in this study. These advertisements and the sections on literary criticism provide significant information about the authors, the readership, and related issues. One type of advertisement in the Ottoman Greek press was placed by authors asking people to subscribe for their forthcoming books (either novels, books of poetry, educational books, translations of foreign works into Greek, and so forth). When the books were ready, authors would advertise a second time to ask those who had subscribed to buy the book. To make subscriptions attractive to readers, their names were printed in the back of the book. This practice had the additional benefit of "gently" coercing readers who had pledged their financial support – but were reluctant to part with their money when the book appeared – to come forward. From this and similar information it emerges that such subscriptions were considered by many as investing an individual with the qualities of refinement and class superiority. Although it seems that many aspired to such an image by subscribing, others were either unwilling or unable to pay the price. Occasionally, frustrated authors resorted to printing open letters in the press exposing non-payers. As an example, *Aster tes Anatoles* printed a letter by a gentleman from Constantinople, signed *your subscriber* Φ, who exposed a certain George Zarachanis, teacher at the public school of Tsoumbali in the Phanar. According to Φ this man honored his signature "as much as the young scamps gathering outside St. Sophia."[122] The letter writer explained that the reason for exposing Zarachanis was that he did not want other people "to suffer what I had suffered." It seems that Zarachanis had a habit of subscribing to "every list that was presented to him by putting his honorable signature on it." Then, when the book was ready "he denied ever signing anything." Φ explained that he did not want "to harm the man but to reform him and to teach him not to supply his signature so frivolously," and finished his letter by promising to expose "more

121. See *Encyclopaedia Britannica*, 15th edition (1992), 7:47.
122. Young beggars frequenting the area outside St. Sophia.

such gentlemen as soon as I have to,"[123] As shown earlier, the Ottoman Greek press also suffered much from the same problem and it also resorted, in some cases, to similar measures.

Various printing houses and bookshops from the big cities of the Ottoman Empire and Greece were also advertising in the Ottoman Greek press. Books bought from Greece were obtained either by post or from agents of the printing house in the empire.

Besides selling books, booksellers and printers created lending libraries, where books could be borrowed for a small monthly fee. In this way they increased their readership with people who were not yet accustomed to buying books or could not afford them. More people could now read and write due to the popularization of education in the nineteenth century and these measures benefited poorer people and women, who were often financially dependent. A typical advertisement for a lending library would run as follows:

> The Smyrna book-seller and printer, Mr. K. N. Stamemis, informs the public that he has received from Europe the complete works of the following writers: Sue, Dumas, Paul de Kock, Balzac, and others. He has created in his bookshop, which is opposite Yol Vezesteni [Bedesteni], a Western library. The monthly subscription is 20 *kuruş*, 10 *kuruş* prepaid. The same book-seller/printer undertakes to find any book required at the same price as in the European catalogues. No order is accepted unless money is paid in advance.[124]

The types of books advertised in the Ottoman Greek press varied considerably. There were a large number of Greek classics printed with notes and translations. There were many novels and books of poetry; translations from French, Italian, English, Russian and, to a much lesser degree, German novels, poetry, and educational works. There were many religious and educational books, including grammars and books on syntax, for languages such as Greek and French.

The arts sections of the newspapers added to the popularization of and interest in education, books, and culture in general. They included literary and art news,[125] literary criticism of new books,[126] essays on various subjects,[127] poems and criticism,[128] reviews of theatrical and musical performances,[129] and also featured

123. *Aster tes Anatoles,* no. 4 (November 7, 1841).

124. *Telegraphos tou Vosporou,* no. 378 (March 27, 1851).

125. See for example, *Mnemosyne,* no. 2 (March 16, 1835), *Ephemeris tes Smyrnes* no. 1 (April 15, 1849) and no. 34 (December 2, 1849), *Aster tes Anatoles,* no. 19 (February 21, 1842), etc.

126. *Mnemosyne,* no. 16 (June 22, 1835).

127. *Ephemeris tes Smyrnes,* no. 3 (April 29, 1849).

128. *Ephemeris tes Smyrnes,* no. 13 (July 8, 1849).

129. *Ephemeris tes Smyrnes,* no. 42 (January 27, 1850).

several debates about the development of the Greek language (literary news and language),[130] a literary discussion between *Telegraphos tou Vosporou* and *Amaltheia* on the language question,[131] a critical approach to Koraes's Greek,[132] and an open letter to historian Constantine Paparregopoulos from I. I. Skylisses on the language question.[133] There were also reports on recent archaeological excavations, such as the one conducted by Charles Fell in Lycia,[134] an extensive report on the restoration of St. Sophia,[135] the issue of a coin by the imperial mint of Constantinople to commemorate the repairs of St. Sophia,[136] a report about the creation of the Academy of Science and Philosophy in Constantinople[137] and a poetry section which featured contemporary poets like Karasoutsas,[138] I. I. Skylisses,[139] and some anonymous poets publicly eulogizing well-known personalities.[140]

Newspapers and magazines were also advertised in the Ottoman Greek press and sometimes these notices are our only source of information concerning certain short-lived publications, which otherwise disappeared without trace. Between 1835 and 1862, at least fifty-five newspapers and magazines were advertised in the Ottoman Greek press.

One way for the Greeks to exhibit their substance was through charity (*philanthropia*). Philanthropy had always been expected of affluent Greeks since antiquity and was further emphasized as a social duty after the adoption of Christianity. Although during the Byzantine and Ottoman eras donations went almost entirely towards religious institutions, the introduction of the Tanzimat reforms coincided with a change in prevalent attitudes towards charity among the Ottoman Orthodox, as reported in the Ottoman Greek press. The majority of donations recorded there during our period were directed towards schools, the printing of school books (and in particular of grammars and history books), towards scholarships and salaries to teachers and the "nation" (usually meaning the Greek state with carte blanche to use as required for its needs). As an example, the donations appearing in a single issue of *He Hemera*,[141] on October 21, 1856 are included here:

130. *Ephemeris tes Smyrnes*, no. 64 (June 30, 1850).
131. *Ephemeris tes Smyrnes*, no. 90 (December 29, 1850). This was an on-going dispute – not resolved until 1976 – about whether the official language of Greece should be the vernacular (Demotic Greek) or a formal, archaic, and literary idiom (Katharevousa).
132. Ibid.
133. *Ephemeris tes Smyrnes*, no. 38 (December 30, 1849).
134. *He Hemera*, no. 20 (January 20/February 1, 1856).
135. *Ephemeris tes Smyrnes*, no. 16 (July24, 1849). The report referred to St. Sophia as a "church," though it had at that time been a mosque for nearly 400 years.
136. *Ephemeris tes Smyrnes*, no. 27 (October 14, 1842).
137. *Telegraphos tou Vosporou*, no. 394 (July 7, 1851).
138. *Ephemeris tes Smyrnes*, no. 2 (April 22, 1849).
139. *Ephemeris tes Smyrnes*, no. 67, (July 21, 1850).
140. *Ephemeris tes Smyrnes*, no. 4 (May 6, 1849).
141. *He Hemera*, no. 55 (September 21/October 3, 1856).

Mr. Ch. Charisiades from Epirus, who died in Vienna, left 2,000 *florin*s for the educational needs of Greece.

⁂

Landowner, Archon Kaminaris [Byzantine title, later awarded by the Patriarchate of Constantinople, a tradition which is continued even today] Alexios Zavale, donated to the Jannina High School a complete printing press from Leipzig.

⁂

Constantinopolitan Mr. Zariphis sent a deacon, graduate of the theological school of Chalke, to Germany to complete his education.

On November 16, *He Hemera* reported that:

M. Tositsas [a major merchant and banker in Alexandria of Egypt] died and left 1,000,000 golden *drachma*s to the nation'[142] Just before his death M. Tositsas had given "funds for the building of a [Orthodox] church and two [Greek] schools in Alexandria.[143]

Baron von Sinas [a merchant banker in Austria-Hungary] left funds

for the building of the Academy of Athens and the salaries of the academicians.[144]

Less wealthy Greeks from the Ottoman Empire and abroad gave money for Greek schools in Greece. For example, on April 6, 1856, a

Mr Sophianos from Odessa … 7,000 silver *ruble*s to Greek schools … and Constantine Trampanos from Zagoria [Epirus] … left 5,000 Austrian *florin*s, a house, etc., to the schools of Greece.[145]

Another, smaller category of donations, included those towards helping victims of natural disasters, fires, and so forth. These donations were usually publicized by letters from grateful recipients. In November 1849, for example, *Ephemeris tes Smyrnes* published the letter of

one of our readers in Constantinople to publicize the generous assistance of Antonios Alleon … to the victims of the fire in Tatavla [Constantinople].[146]

An even smaller category of donations was those to the church. These were almost

142. *He Hemera*, no. 63 (November 16/28, 1856).
143. *He Hemera*, no. 32 (April 13/25, 1856).
144. *He Hemera*, no. 48 (August 3/15, 1856).
145. *He Hemera*, no. 31 (April 6/18, 1856).
146. *Ephemeris tes Smyrnes*, no. 30 (November 4, 1849).

exclusively given by the clergy and were usually only partly for the church:

> The metropolitan of Smyrna Athanasios, who died recently left 80,000
> *kuruş* to be divided equally between the school of his native Mytilene
> and various churches, charitable and educational institutions of our town
> [Smyrna].[147]

One cannot be certain whether at that time donations to the church decreased in
real terms while donations to schools became the main concern of Greek philanthropists, or whether this picture was distorted by the Greek press, whose editors
were more interested in promoting education. Certainly, what emerges from the
published donations in the press is that schools and secular education were of
considerable concern to Orthodox Greek philanthropists at the beginning of the
nineteenth century. It is also worth noting that Greek people who lived outside
the Ottoman Empire preferred to donate their money towards schools in the
new, small and insecure Greek state rather than to the Orthodox Greek-speaking
peoples still living in the Ottoman Empire.

The new freedoms awarded to the Ottoman non-Muslim populations and their
increased affluence brought about an increase in travel. People began to travel within
the empire much more frequently both for business and pleasure. The increase in
travel to the Ottoman hinterland brought about significant changes in the industries
that catered to it. The Tanzimat generation of travelers was no longer content with
the basic accommodation provided by the traditional *kervansaray*, where guests
slept on the floor and where other services were scarce or non-existent. In response
to the demands of a more affluent clientele for improved living quarters, food,
and services, a new type of hotel made its debut in the Ottoman Empire. These
hotels had separate rooms with comfortable beds, room service, and restaurants
that provided five-course meals. We get some idea of what was provided from the
advertisements placed by some hotel owners in the press:

> HOTEL OF THE EAST [*Xenodocheio tes Anatoles*] The hotel is found
> in the Great Street of Stavrodromi, opposite the Janissary Barracks and
> is managed by Mr. Bekiaris. He announces to the public that his hotel
> is reasonably priced for everyone. The service is quick and clean in order
> that people will honor the hotel with their custom. The hotel also boasts a
> restaurant with an à la carte menu. Breakfast consists of two courses, [plus]
> dessert and two types of wine. Price 6 *kuruş*. Dinner consists of 5 courses,
> [plus] dessert, fruit, coffee, and two types of wine. Price 10 *kuruş*. There
> are rooms with beds in the hotel available by the day or by the month.
> Pera of Constantinople July 12/24, 1852. Andreas Bekiaris.[148]

147. *Ephemeris tes Smyrnes*, no. 90 (December 29, 1850).
148. *Telegraphos tou Vosporou*, no. 448 (July 19, 1852).

At the same time hotels began to crop up in spa towns and holiday resorts all over the empire. Where before people either had to rent a house or resort to the limited comforts of the *kervansaray*, now they had a choice of hotels with proper bedrooms, bathrooms, restaurants, and servants:

> Prussa [Turkish Bursa]. In the place of the mineral spa of Prussa [Bursa], I built a hotel so that those who come in need of the spa will have a nice room with all the necessaries, excellent food, good servants, and bathrooms. The only thing they will have to bring with them is their clothes. The manager, Vassilakis Kalligeris.[149]

Travelling for business or pleasure opened people's horizons and produced a desire for learning about the other. The rigidity of Ottoman social institutions in previous times, the mainly agrarian system of the economy, and the difficult and dangerous modes of transportation meant that both social and individual mobility were restricted. People often were quite ignorant of the customs and habits of other people even if they belonged to the same ethnic and cultural background and lived but a few hours away. The variety of nations, religions, customs and professions that had gradually accumulated in the Ottoman Empire over the centuries, created a rich and colorful tapestry which to most people living in the empire was largely invisible. The new freedom of movement brought with it, as is evident from the Ottoman Greek press, increased curiosity and possibilities of contact. The Ottoman Greek press responded by carrying several articles on geopolitical and demographic matters, as well as information concerning local folklore.

The geopolitical information included not only reports on natural disasters and fires, as we have seen, but also accounts of various cities, towns, and villages in the Ottoman Empire and the principalities, and articles describing various national groups. Examples of titles include:

> The Earthquakes of Smyrna[150]
>
> Earthquakes in the Ottoman Empire[151]
>
> Fire in Salonica[152]
>
> Fire in Beshiktash [Constantinople][153]
>
> Fire in Constantinople[154]

149. *Telegraphos tou Vosporou kai Vyzantis*, no. 165 (April 23, 1858).

150. *Ephemeris tes Smyrnes*, no. 50 (March 24, 1850), no. 51 (March 31, 1850), no. 52 (April 7, 1850), no. 53 (April 14, 1850).

151. *He Hemera*, no. 58 (October 11/24, 1856), no. 61 (November 1/14, 1856).

152. *He Hemera*, no.45 (July 13/25, 1856), no. 46 (July 20/August 1, 1856), no. 47 (July 27/August 8, 1856).

153. *Mnemosyne*, no. 9 (May 4, 1835).

154. *Telegraphos tou Vosporou*, no. 447 (July 12, 1852).

The Meletia Valley[155]

Vouzas[156]

Accounts of Varna and Einouda and Perikleista[157]

Thessalonike [158]

The Islands of Constantinople[159]

Sillyos and Akropedion[160]

Tarsos[161]

Korakision, Ephesos, Thermision[162]

The Danubian Principalities[163]

Valdjic and Soulinas[164]

Amisos and Oinoe[165]

Caesaria,

Galatz[166]

Vraila[167]

Scopia[168]

Armenia and the Armenians[169]

The Gypsies[170]

The demographic reports of the Greek press included articles on families changing their religion, the population of villages and towns, the numbers of casualties (from fires, epidemics, and natural disasters, usually divided according to nation), and information on passenger, letter, and parcel circulation within the Ottoman Empire as well as abroad. Examples include:

155. *Ephemeris tes Smyrnes,* no. 48 (March 10, 1850).
156. *Ephemeris tes Smyrnes,* no. 50 (March 24, 1850).
157. *Ephemeris tes Smyrnes,* no. 57 (May 12, 1850).
158. *Ephemeris tes Smyrnes,* no. 58 (May 19, 850).
159. *Ephemeris tes Smyrnes,* no. 27 (October 14, 1849).
160. *Ephemeris tes Smyrnes,* no. 59 (May 26, 1850).
161. *Ephemeris tes Smyrnes,* no. 61 (June 9, 1850).
162. *Ephemeris tes Smyrnes,* no. 62 (June 16, 1850).
163. *Ephemeris tes Smyrnes,* no. 63 (June 23, 1850).
164. *Ephemeris tes Smyrnes,* no. 71 (August 18, 1850).
165. *Ephemeris tes Smyrnes,* no. 75 (September 15, 1850).
166. *Ephemeris tes Smyrnes,* no. 77 (September 29, 1850).
167. *Ephemeris tes Smyrnes,* no. 78 (October 6, 1850).
168. *Ephemeris tes Smyrnes,* no. 84 (November 17, 1850).
169. *Mnemosyne,* no. 2 (March16, 1835), no. 15, (June 15, 1835), and no. 16 (June 22, 1835).
170. *Mnemosyne,* no 5 (April 6, 1835) and no. 6 (April 13, 1835).

Eighty Maronite Families in 1849 Became Orthodox[171]

The Number of Dead People in Constantinople from the Cholera Epidemic of 1848, Divided According to Nation[172]

The Population of Thessalonike and Other Demographic Information for the City in 1851[173]

Census of All Foreigners Who Arrived in Constantinople in 1850[174]

Population Census in the Ottoman Empire 1856[175]

Report on the Plague of 1835[176]

Report on an Epidemic of Smallpox and Diarrhea in Smyrna in 1841[177]

Report on the Cholera Epidemic of 1856 in Constantinople[178] "The Population of Greece by Area,[179]

Lloyds' Catalogue of Passengers, Letters, and Cargo from Every Ottoman and Greek Port[180]

Duration of Quarantine for People and Goods in the Ottoman Empire[181]

The Celebrations of Mevlit[182]

Religious Customs of Persia[183]

The Funeral Customs of the Orthodox Christians[184]

Articles and reports on inter-communal relations provide a window onto relations between the various nations that lived in the Ottoman Empire and include reports about how foreigners viewed the empire, the Greek nation, and the Orthodox Church. Examples include:

The Appointment of a New Rabbi in Smyrna[185]

171. *Ephemeris tes Smyrnes,* no.1 (April 15, 1849).
172. *Ephemeris tes Smyrnes*, no. 26 (October 7, 1849).
173. *Ephemeris tes Smyrnes*, no. 91 (January 5, 1851).
174. *Ephemeris tes Smyrnes*, no. 93 (January 19, 1851).
175. *He Hemera*, no. 56, (September 28/October 10, 1856).
176. *Mnemosyne*, no. 15 (June 15, 1835).
177. *Aster tes Anatoles*, no. 7 (November 28, 1841).
178. *Aster tes Anatoles*, no. 57 (October 5/17, 1856).
179. *Ephemeris tes Smyrnes*, no. 3 (April 29, 1849).
180. *Ephemeris tes Smyrnes*, no. 10 (June 17, 1849).
181. *Ephemeris tes Smyrnes*, no. 11 (June 24, 1849).
182. *Mnemosyne,* no. 13 (June 1, 1835).
183. *Amaltheia*, no. 361 (June 23, 1846).
184. *Elpis*, no.4 (June 6, 1841).
185. *Elpis*, no. 6 (June 20, 1841).

Great Rabbi Deposed of His Position Because of Complaints Made to the Sublime Porte by His Co-religionists[186]

The Patriarchate Forbade Mixed Marriages[187]

The Church Excommunicated Two Greeks Marrying Ottoman Women[188]

Article from the Athenian Newspaper *Athina* Ridiculing [the all-male monastic community of] Mount Athos[189]

The Enthronement of a Bishop in the Bulgarian Church of St. Stephen [reprint from the Bulgarian newspaper of Constantinople][190]

Article from the Bulgarian Newspaper-Translated into Greek from the Bulgarian – Rebutting Greek Accusations against the Bulgarians[191]

About the Bulgarians[192]

Article Praising the Sultan[193]

Sultan Gives Medals to Greeks from Greece[194]

Antagonism between Greeks and Catholics[195]

Fights between Christians and Druze[196]

Muslim Attacks Christian and Gets Punished[197]

The Drunkenness of the Ottomans is the Cause of the Killing of Christians[198]

Relations between Albanians and Vlachs[199]

Episode in Naplousa [Nablus] in Palestine between Muslims and Greeks. Prussians, English and French[200]

Easter Quarrel in Jerusalem between Greeks and Armenians in the Church of the Holy Sepulchre[201]

186. *Elpis*, no. 2 (May 23, 1841).
187. *Telegraphos tou Vosporou*, no. 401 (August 25, 1851).
188. *Telegraphos tou Vosporou*, no. 404 (September 15, 1851).
189. *Telegraphos tou Vosporou*, no. 451 (August 9, 1852).
190. Ibid.
191. *Telegraphos tou Vosporou*, no. 486 (April 18, 1853).
192. *Telegraphos tou Vosporou*, no. 489 (May 9, 1853).
193. *Telegraphos tou Vosporou*, no. 418 (December 25, 1851).
194. *He Hemera,* no. 29 (March 23/April 4,1856).
195. *Mnemosyne*, no. 14 (June 8, 1835).
196. *Mnemosyne*, no. 1 (March 9, 1835).
197. *Elpis*, no. 3 (May 30, 1841).
198. *Elpis*, no. 4 (June 6, 1841).
199. *He Hemera,* no. 30 (March 30/April 11, 1856).
200. *He Hemera,* no. 35 (May 4/16, 1856).
201. *He Hemera,* no. 36 (May 11/23, 1856).

Ottoman Fanaticism against Christians[202]

Muslims are Christian Heretics[203]

Muslim Converts Return to Christianity[204]

The Treatment of Christians in Tripoli of Syria by Muslims[205]

The Treatment of a Rich Jew in Palestine by Muslims[206]

Dispute between Orthodox and Armenians in Caesaria[207]

The Voyage of Ottoman Pilgrims from Damascus to Mecca[208]

The Circumcision Celebrations in Alexandria[209]

The Word of a Christian against a Muslim Doesn't Count in Court"[210],

Hungarian Refugee Costas in Smyrna[211]

A downside of travelling, as recorded in the press, was the risk of losing one's valuables and occasionally one's life. The location of trouble spots, areas infested with brigands, and war zones were clearly and frequently noted, and we have already mentioned several articles and reports referring to the above. Often the Greek press recorded the efforts of the Ottoman government to impose law and order, but the image of persistent violence and government impotence to stamp it out becomes inescapable when reading through the pages of the newspapers.

A small category of advertisements reveals some overlooked consequences of business travel. "Lost and Found" notices dealt with lost property usually consisting of attaché cases containing money, bills of exchange, and IOUs. The people who placed these advertisements were generally lawyers and provincial priests entrusted with the money and business affairs of people living in the provinces or abroad:

Today at 10:00 a.m., an attaché case belonging to Mr. Livanis was lost at Pemptopazaron [Perşembe Pazar]. It contained paper money in notes of 20/150 and 80 *kuruş*, various IOUs as well as a bill of Exchange for 500 Roubles issued last year by Mr. Triantaphyllos Panayiotou in favor of Mr.

202. *He Hemera*, no. 30 (March 30/April 11, 1856), no. 41 (July 15/27, 1856), no. 42 (June 22/July 4, 1856), no. 44 (July 6/18, 1856), no. 54 (September 14/26, 1856), no. 56 (September 28/October 10, 1856).
203. *He Hemera*, no. 30 (March 30/April 11, 1856).
204. *He Hemera*, no. 31 (April 6/18, 1856).
205. *Ephemeris tes Smyrnes*, no. 12 (April 22, 1849).
206. *Ephemeris tes Smyrnes*, no. 22 (September 9, 1849).
207. *Ephemeris tes Smyrnes*, no. 73 (September 15, 1850).
208. *Ephemeris tes Smyrnes*, no. 12 (April 22, 1849) and no. 14 (July 15, 1849).
209. *Ephemeris tes Smyrnes*, no. 26 (October 7, 1849).
210. *Ephemeris tes Smyrnes*, no. 60 (June 2, 1850).
211. *Telegraphos tou Vosporou*, no. 500 (July 25, 1853).

A. Despotopoulos of Odessa. The former had paid one half of the money and the payment of the other half is to be discussed at the Ticaret [Commercial Court] today. Therefore, we will donate the money in the attaché case to the person who produces it, if we recover the Bill of Exchange and the IOUs. Constantinople June 14, 1851.[212]

People seem to have responded to these advertisements, because in many cases the newspaper reported the recovery of the lost property.

We notify the person who lost his briefcase (advertisement March 29) that it was found and handed to us by the captain of a ship bound for Mount Athos. Please collect it from our offices.[213]

The above advertisements are yet another indication that the Ottoman Greek newspapers were perceived by the public as being widely read. This observation is strengthened by the fact that people also advertised in the press for news of lost relatives and friends. These notices were mostly referring to people who had disappeared during the Crimean War effort, but had not been listed as dead:

Stephanos Phakirides, brother of Ignatios, the Archdeacon of His Eminence the Metropolitan of Philippoupolis, had been working as a pharmacist in the Ottoman Imperial Army for two years, when he was sent to Erzerum and then to Hasan Kale and then on to Kars for a year. Since then, he has not sent any letters to his brother or the rest of the family in Philippoupolis, nor has he sent them any news. We ask anyone, who knows anything about him to contact, in person or by letter, the editor of newspaper *Anatole*.[214]

Apart from advertisements for hotels and restaurants the lifestyle sections included some advertisements of food and drink products placed by importers and wholesalers. Below are two examples, the second of which offers rare information about how the new crop of the potato was introduced into the Ottoman Empire:

New warehouse stores the superior and much praised wines of Santorine, in various types and prices from 100 *para*s to 4 *kuruş* per *oka*. The wine warehouse is in Pemptopazaron [Perşembe Pazar] under the Old Genoese house and opposite the head office of the Rostan steamship company, and it is managed by Frandjescos Mandjarakes. Anyone who samples these wines for a week will discover their great benefits viz. the strengthening of the stomach and the improvement of digestion. Taste and judge.[215]

212. *Telegraphos tou Vosporou*, no. 391 (June, 16, 1851).
213. *Telegraphos tou Vosporou kai Vyzantis*, no. 175 (May 24, 1858).
214. *Telegraphos tou Vosporou*, no. 632 (February 11, 1856).
215. *Telegraphos tou Vosporou*, no. 346 (August 5, 1850).

⋇

We recommend the financial benefits to be had by using the potato, not only for those who cannot afford to buy flour made from wheat sold at 40 and 50 *paras* per *oka*, but even for those who have plenty of rice [?]. This apple [from the French *pomme de terre?*] is today used internationally and replaces the other pulses [*sic*], is cheap, juicy, and fills the stomach of the poor and families with many children, and can be cooked in many ways. Let us hope that its cultivation will be introduced in the East [Anatole] as it was introduced in the Ionian Islands and recently into Greece. A sufficient number of potatoes is sold for 20 *kuruş* per *kantar* by Mr. S. Deuterevon from Kythera [Ionian Islands] in the Ionion Hotel at the Fregham Barker beach. You can buy from a half to one *kadar* each.[216]

These two advertisements clearly address two financially distinct groups of people. The fact that both advertisements were published in Ottoman Greek newspapers leads again to the conclusion that the press was perceived as reaching various strata of the population. Many other privately-run establishments that offered services to the public and advertised in the Greek press made such an assumption. They included, apart from restaurants, hotels and importers or wholesalers of foods, barber shops, photographic shops, watchmakers, and shops offering services such as grinding coffee, refining olive oil, and oil for lamps and stoves, examples of which we saw earlier.

Between 1835 and 1862 several new medicines and "admirable cures" were promoted in the Ottoman Greek press and at least until the 1850s these constituted a significant proportion of the commercial advertisements. They were mostly manufactured in France and England, and were usually concerned with indigestion, constipation, hemorrhoids, venereal and sexually transmitted diseases, and nervous disorders. The medicines were usually advertised by the pharmacists who imported them, and less often by wholesalers – importers who were not connected with the medical profession at all.

Private individuals brought various herbal cures to Constantinople and Smyrna and advertised them in the papers. For example:

Gentleman from Alexandria brought "a plant, which cures sufferers of the Candia worm."[217]

The first substance with medical properties to be advertised in an Ottoman Greek newspaper was arrowroot.[218] It was advertised in 1835 by a French pharmacist in Smyrna, M. Vicar, who sold it in his pharmacy. It was described as an American specialty for feeding babies who could not drink milk, for convalescing people,

216. *Mnemosyne*, no. 4 (March 30, 1835).
217. *Ephemeris tes Smyrnes*, no. 80 (October 20, 1850).
218. *Mnemosyne*, no. 8 (April 27, 1835).

and for those who had difficulty in digesting their food. The advertisement gave a detailed description of the properties of arrowroot and stated that "its use has just been introduced in Smyrna." Arrowroot was the first in a long line of medical substances that began to flood the Ottoman pharmaceutical market in the nineteenth century, as Western European industries explored new markets for their products. By the 1850s the unchecked import of "miracle cures from Europe," many of which were useless and sometimes even harmful concoctions, took on epidemic proportions. This prompted the Ottoman pharmacists to create a Pharmaceutical Society, which would check every new medical substance that entered the empire and decide on their suitability. Until 1858 their meetings were irregular, though they were usually held at the pharmacy of George Houmbros in Bahçekapı. By the summer of 1858 the Pharmaceutical Society was

> so inundated with applications [to license new drugs] … that from now on we have decided to meet regularly every fortnight in the same place.[219]

Other categories of professionals with specialist qualifications also chose to advertise in the press: lawyers, doctors, dentists, translators, and occasionally bookbinders, customs officers, architects, and others. Below are some examples:

> Translator: Mr. Constantine Photiades, the publisher of our newspaper [*Telegraphos tou Vosporou*] translates various documents from Turkish into our language and English, or vice versa. Those who wish to make use of his services should go to his house in the Phanar opposite the Great Phanar School. The price of translation is according to the document. Half of the money should be paid in advance[220]

> Dentist: Mr. Ioannis Seim, dentist, residing opposite the English [*sic*] Embassy in the house of Krespen, No. 52, informs his honorable clientele that he recently received from Paris a large collection of false teeth made from enamel as well as various other materials, such as gold, etc. for making bridges. He has also received other things for improving teeth from France, England, Belgium, and America. The doctor has been extremely successful in our capital, and has recently equipped himself with a lot of new machinery necessary for his profession. He hopes that the refurbishment of his surgery will attract the attention of the high society of our city. Mr. Ioannis Seim accepts every kind of dental work. With his new machinery he can make dentures of great stability and extract teeth painlessly with chloroform.[221]

---

219. *Telegraphos tou Vosporou kai Vyzantis*, no. 181 (June 18, 1858).
220. *Telegraphos tou Vosporou kai Vyzantis*, no. 80 (May 15, 1857).
221. *Telegraphos tou Vosporou*, no. 373 (July 11, 1851).

Bookbinder: We notify those of our co-nationals who are lovers of beauty, and all those who would like to see their libraries filled with smart and securely bound books, that within the printing press of Messrs. Coromelas and Paspales there is now a bookbinding service run by two young bookbinders from Athens. These artisans from Greece assure the respected public of our great city that they can bind any size of book smartly and securely and, most important, at a better price than any other bookbinder. The scarcity of good bookbinders in the city will ensure a large clientele for the two young bookbinders.[222]

Doctor: Dr. K. Th. Georgiades has the honor to inform the public that he would examine free of charge all the poor patients who come to his house in Vlah Sarayı in the Phanar. He would also like to inform all those families that honor him by calling on him that he undertakes all surgical and gynecological operations.[223]

Physiotherapist: Mr. Tucker, Professor of Hydrotherapy, who has resided in Constantinople for twenty-six years, announces that he has begun to treat people with various illnesses, either in his own home or the patient's home. Mr. Tucker uses only water for his therapies.... Mr. Tucker would like to collaborate with those doctors who are willing to send him their chronically ill patients.... He has studied Hydrotherapy for 2 years and knows all the latest techniques. In Galata, enquire at Mr. Stampa's shop; in Pera at Mr. Sample's shop, and in Aynalı at Mr. Tucker's house.[224]

Ophthalmologist: Mr. Demetrios L. Eustathiou, who gave us here [in Smyrna] such a demonstration of his abilities to cure glaucoma, cataract and other diseases of the eyes and eylids ... has moved to Magnesia (Tekin in Turkish) where he continues to treat patients.[225]

Lawyer: Mr. George A. Rodokanakes, lawyer, having successfully practised his profession in the Athenian courts, has decided to pursue his profession in Smyrna. Those who wish him to take their cases should know that he

222. *Telegraphos tou Vosporou kai Vyzantis,* no. 129 (December 7, 1857).
223. *Telegraphos tou Vosporou kai Vyzantis,* no. 107 (September 18, 1857).
224. *Telegraphos tou Vosporou,* no. 446 (July 7, 1852).
225. *Aster tes Anatoles,* no. 28 (May 1, 1842).

will accept them with eagerness, care, and honesty. Prospective clients may meet him in his house in Bahçeli Street, or in his office on the seafront in the old fish market.[226]

❧

Law practice: Recently opened by Antonios Grammaticopoulos and D. Karageorgopoulos in the Barbarescos Kervansaray in Smyrna, a Law office, trilingual in Italian, Greek, and Turkish, which will accept any commercial or political case, as well as petitions and applications in the Turkish dialect [*sic*] and translation of documents in the above three languages.[227]

There were also advertisements by organizations requesting professionals:

TO ALL ARCHITECTS. In accordance with the decision of the Governors of the school for the poor girls in Pera, there will be a competition for the building of an extension to the school in a plot of 190 *pecheis*. The lowest bidder will get the contract. We ask those who are interested to approach the Ephors of the school in the shop of Messrs. Eustratios M.Vouros and Petros Savlitses.[228]

The rise in professional and other people coming to Smyrna and Constantinople to live with their families brought a parallel rise in the supply and demand of commercial and domestic properties and land, whether for sale or rent, as is attested by such advertisements in the Ottoman Greek press. The houses advertised were usually large stone or wooden dwellings with six to ten bedrooms, several bathrooms, one or two kitchens, usually an orchard and a cistern. The measurements were given in the ancient Greek measure of *pecheis*. [1 *pechys* = 25–30 inches]. Apart from the house owners, there were other individuals willing to act as agents, usually shopkeepers. Sometimes the newspaper that carried the advertisement acted as the agent, especially if the properties were out of town. Below follow two such examples:

Mr. Hadji Petros Kalfas owns a wooden house in the Parish of Elpis in Kontoskalion. It is attached to the wall of the church and has 4 bedrooms, a large living room and a basement of approx. 200 *pecheis*. It also has a garden of approximately 100 *pecheis*. Those wishing to buy it can either approach the owner directly or go to the *muhtar* [leader] of the Romans [Orthodox Christians] or to the parish of the Armenians.[229]

❧

226. *Aster tes Anatoles*, no. 5 (November 14, 1841).
227. *Aster tes Anatoles*, no. 6 (November 22, 1841).
228. *Telegraphos tou Vosporou kai Vyzantis*, no. 129 (December 7, 1857).
229. *Telegraphos tou Vosporou*, no. 451 (August 9, 1852).

In the neighborhood of Vezneciler, between two pharmacies, there is a stone-built workshop with all amenities and a basement, ready to let. Those who wish to rent it as a patisserie or a restaurant can inquire from Mr. Ioannis Pyrloglou in Astarcı Han.[230]

The vast improvement in the quality of life among Greek-speaking Orthodox Christians, as depicted in the Ottoman Greek press, especially in the economic sphere, was aided by government initiatives intended to update the Ottoman Empire, such as the land registration program as we read in this announcement:

> The state council has decided to start the Land Registration Program. It therefore requests that the public allow access for the inspection and measurement of the interior of their houses and shops, in order that the area can be registered and that a correct description and valuation of the buildings can be made.[231]

Extraterritoriality for foreign passport-holders was also a significant factor in the improvement of the life and business prospects of those Ottomans who had managed to secure the protection of a foreign power. Extraterritoriality meant that, as far as their political and legal rights were concerned, foreign passport holders would not have to deal with the Ottoman government, but with the government of the state whose passport they were holding. The announcement below by the Greek Consulate of Smyrna in 1841 advertises the extraterritoriality rights of Greek citizens in the Ottoman Empire:

> The Royal Greek Consulate invites all Greek citizens who reside here to present themselves at this office within forty days from next Monday December 1/13 [1841]. After forty days, all those who have not registered with the Consulate will be denied the right of legal defense. Times of presentation are between 9 and 12 a.m. Smyrna November 29/December 11, 1841. The Greek Consul Th. Xenos.[232]

During the period of this study, the Ottoman Greek press suggests that a large number of Orthodox Christians took full advantage of the new opportunities arising from the Tanzimat. They included the opening of doors to government departments, the civil service, the judiciary, and the armed forces to non-Muslims. We have already examined some professions related to education, medicine, and food. But there is further evidence of the Orthodox Christian involvement in shipping, finance, commerce, trade and related professions.

Shipping has been a quintessentially Greek occupation since antiquity. Al-

---

230. *Telegraphos tou Vosporou,* no. 380 (March 31, 1851).
231. *Telegraphos tou Vosporou kai Vyzantis,* no. 164 (April 19, 1858).
232. *Aster tes Anatoles,* no. 10 (December 19, 1841).

though after the fall of Constantinople and the subsequent rise of the Venetian naval presence in the eastern Mediterranean, Greek shipping lost its prominence, it recovered in the aftermath of the Treaty of Küçük Kaynarca in 1774, which afforded full Russian protection in any ship – including Ottoman Greek ships – flying the Russian flag. This is reflected in a plethora of shipping advertisements in the Ottoman Greek press. They appear in almost every issue, soliciting passengers and cargo and publicizing new lines of operation. Shipping was the most important and efficient means of transport and about 5,000 ships arrived annually in Constantinople and a similar number in Smyrna.[233] This period also witnessed the introduction of steam into Greek shipping, which could then begin to compete with European shipping for cargo, passengers, and mail, offering regular services at a lower price. We also observe a collaboration between Ottoman Greeks and Ottoman Muslims:

> The Royal Ottoman Steamship Peyk-i Şevket begins regular trips on the 30th of November [1845], from Smyrna to Constantinople, and will depart on the 10th, 20th, and 30th of each month. Deck passengers will pay 90 *kuruş* instead of the 105 they pay at Lloyd's; the price for the other classes as well as for groups or cargo is negotiable. Whoever wishes to travel should come to the Steamship Manager in the offices of Mr. Ioannis Ahtindjis in the *kervansaray* of Dervişoğlu.[234]

Austrian Lloyd responded to the challenge by improving its service and increasing its destinations:

> We can announce to the public and the citizens of Sivas, Tokate, Şebin-karahisar, Niksar, Ünye, Fatsa, and all the surrounding suburbs, that from today Austrian Lloyd's steamships will dock in Ordu, as well as Trebizond, and therefore we advise the people of those towns to send their merchandise via Ordu, whereby they will benefit greatly since the cost of transferring their goods by land to ports further away is much higher. During the winter the steamships will dock at Bona, which is four hours from Ordu by land and [only] one hour by sea. [signed] The agent for Lloyd's in Constantinople. 6/18 June 1858.

Competition between local and foreign shipping was followed by the appearance of various Ottoman shipping insurance companies, competing for business with Lloyds and other foreign maritime insurance companies. Most of them were wiped out by heavy losses due to the Crimean War, but some of them reappeared soon afterwards as the following advertisement of 1856 attests:

233. *Ephemeris tes Smyrnes*, no. 61 (June 9, 1850).
234. *Amaltheia*, no. 355 (May 5, 1845).

I notify the commercial establishment of our city that on the 23rd of last month an insurance company for maritime risks called "Neos Triton" began operating under my management. Our offices are in Koutalianos Karavansarayı opposite Haviar Karavansarayı. This company consists of 250 shares of 1,500 francs each and some of the most solvent merchants of our city are shareholders. We also have promissory notes of 1,250,000 francs should the need arise. We promise that we shall conduct ourselves with justice, will honor our insurance agreements and avoid quarrels and disputes. We will satisfy every claim as quickly as possible in the interests of our clientele. The public will know this from the previous operations of "Triton," which dissolved its operations at the beginning of the [Crimean] war, which recently ended and which settled several claims and gave many bonuses to the shareholders. We urge the respected merchants of our city to honor "Neos Triton" with their custom and they will have prompt service, dedication, and action by the director, Mr. Dialegmenos.[235]

This particular insurance company seems to have been extremely successful because by 1861 it had increased its shares to 330 and its capital to 1,650,000 francs.[236]

Large public companies also took advantage of the Greek press. The 1850s saw the establishment and expansion of the Telegraph company, which advertised frequently in the Greek press.

The management of the Telegraph company announces that the Telegraph service in Philippoupolis is now connected with all the post offices of Europe and Turkey [*sic*] in the following languages: French, English, German, and Italian.[237]

The languages were always mentioned in the advertisements, because there was no uniform system in use by the Telegraph company for all the Ottoman telegraph services:

[I]n the new telegraphic line between Ruschuk and Trnovo, which has started communicating with all the other lines in Turkey, the language would be only Turkish.[238]

Other advertisements for the telegraph inform us about the types of service offered. This example addressing "the merchants of Constantinople" advised them

to give their correct [business] addresses to the Telegraph office as well as their home addresses so that their telegrams can be delivered at all hours.[239]

235. *Telegraphos tou Vosporou*, no. 640 (April 7, 1856).
236. *Telegraphos tou Vosporou kai Vyzantis*, no. 487 (July 19, 1861).
237. *Telegraphos tou Vosporou kai Vyzantis*, no. 115 (October 16, 1857).
238. Ibid.
239. *Telegraphos tou Vosporou kai Vyzantis*, no. 130 (December 11, 1857).

By 1857 the address was excluded from the price calculation of sending a telegram "according to a treaty signed between Turkey and Austria, unless the address is more than five words,"[240] thus reducing the price of the telegrams to that country.

Several postal services operated in the Ottoman Empire, run by various foreign states under the terms of the capitulations, which dealt with correspondence outside the empire. Correspondence or parcels had to be taken to the relevant postal service to be mailed abroad. Most post office advertisements, therefore, announced their addresses or changes of address so that people could take their correspondence and parcels to the right place:

> The management of the Greek Post Office announces that the Royal Greek Post will be transferred to behind the Ministry of Health in the house of Mr. Koumbaris from next Thursday.

The Ottoman Railway Company took advantage of the Greek press as well. Their advertisements did not concern existing railway services but gave information about new lines under development and invited investors to buy shares in the company. In 1858, for example, the Ottoman Railway Company began to develop the line from Smyrna to Aydın and in January of that year advertisements appeared tendering shares in the new line:

> OTTOMAN RAILWAY – SMYRNA TO AYDIN. From Monday the 25th [January 1858] the public will receive from the company share certificates valued at three pounds each.... The bills can be cashed at the company's bankers, Hanson and Co. Every shareholder who wishes to pay in advance the sum of 20 pounds per share, can have this put on his certificates and the whole sum will receive interest at 6% per annum. Constantinople, 18 January 1858, Robert Bidkins – agent for the company.[241]

Advertisements for shares in this line continued to appear in the press periodically until 1862.

The financial institutions that advertised in the Greek press were the stock exchange and the banks.

The Ottoman stock exchange was run by a five-member committee elected from the commercial establishment. Stockbrokers subscribed to it annually and were listed:

> The five-member committee of the Stock Exchange informs those who wish to continue their subscription this year [1858] that they have to send their brokers to the establishment of Mr. Zariphis (the treasurer), between the eighteenth of this month [January] and the first of February, in order to receive their bill of membership. Those who fail to meet the deadline

---

240. *Telegraphos tou Vosporou kai Vyzantis*, no. 120 (November 2, 1857).
241. *Telegraphos tou Vosporou kai Vyzantis*, no. 141 (January 25, 1858).

will be considered as having resigned and entrance to the Stock Exchange will not be free to them. Galata, January 3, 1858.[242]

By 1861 the stock exchange moved into its own specially built quarters and advertised for membership:

The Bankers Association, the merchants, and the accountants of our town are advised that personal memberships are now available in the newly-built Stock Exchange, in the *han* of Karaköy, for the sum of 500 *kuruş* a year, prepaid. The operations of the Stock Exchange will commence as soon as 200 people have become subscribers. The regulation of the Stock Exchange will be prepared by a committee elected by the members. Subscriptions will be made at the office of Mr. Vitervos, which is the *han* of Karaköy. In Galata 4/16 October 1861.[243]

Banks advertised in the Ottoman Greek press as early as 1842, when the first commercial bank appeared in Smyrna:

[T]he newly established bank was created by Greek and European merchants and is directed by Mr. F. Krammer. This measure ... will greatly improve the commercial transactions, although it will slightly hurt the business of some individuals, who have been carrying out the banking functions until now. Promissory notes (bona) are abolished. All bills of exchange in any currency will be exchanged at the Bank. 5% commission will be deducted, and you will receive clean currency. Thus, merchants of all classes will avoid a loss in currency and fluctuations in commission, which they have suffered before now, because the exchange rate of the currencies has been set and because the various other difficulties have been ironed out.[244]

The capital followed suit seven years later with the creation of the Bank of Constantinople:

We have the honor to announce to the public that the government of His Majesty has decided to create a bank with a capital of 25,000,000 *kuruş*, and has appointed us directors of this bank, called Bank of Constantinople. The Bank of Constantinople will prepay all Bills of Exchange taking 3% commission and will provide merchants with the necessary foreign currency for their transactions and trips abroad. The Bank will have the sole right of exchanging foreign currency. This enterprise is guaranteed by the government for all losses, interest paid and expenses, and of course by

242. *Telegraphos tou Vosporou kai Vyzantis*, no. 138 (January 4, 1858).
243. *Telegraphos tou Vosporou kai Vyzantis*, no. 510 (October 4, 1861).
244. *Aster tes Anatoles*, no. 30 (May 15, 1842).

the sum of 25,000,000 *kuruş* that has been entrusted to us by the government. The directors of the Bank of Constantinople, I. Alleon and E. Baltadjis.[245]

Lottery advertisements are a more modest category in the Greek press. Lotteries were a popular means of selling goods and property and were advertised quite frequently. Private individuals who wished to dispose of an artefact or a house would set up a lottery and advertise in order to sell tickets. Sometimes the draw would be postponed because not enough tickets had been sold. After the drawing of lots the winning ticket numbers were listed in the press:

> The drawing of lots for the gold and enamel snuffbox, which was to have taken place last Sunday, was postponed because of the illness of the person responsible. There are still some lottery tickets at Mr. François Guizi the tailors, near the Tekke of Stavrodromion and also at the Smyrna paper shop. Those who do not pay for their lottery tickets, will lose the right to take part in the draw, and if their ticket should win it will be disqualified.[246]

The Ottoman government of the autonomous principalities of Moldavia and Wallachia and the governments of other countries used the Greek press to advertise various commercial enterprises. The most common advertisements, both of the Ottoman state and the autonomous principalities, were for auctions for the right to collect the annual tithe and the rights to various government monopolies.

> Mr. Konstantinos Sevastopoulos, government agent for the *mukataa* [tax farming] of the leeches of the Ottoman lands, has the honor to inform the public that Sarim Beyefendi, director of commerce, has ordered the auction of all the *mukataa*s for the fishing of leeches. It will take place at the beginning of next year, 1842. The auction will take place inside the Royal Ticarethane [Commercial House] and those wishing to bid for any of those *mukataa*s must go there in person at the appointed time with their guarantors.[247]

჻

> The public in the capital is informed that the auction of the tithes of Cyprus, Erdekion [Turkish Erdek, Greek Artake], Adana, Afion Karahisar, Ikonion [Turkish Konya], Kütahya, and Balıkesir for the Ottoman year 1277 will take place on the 11/23rd of April at the offices of Mr. Stephanos Mavrokordatos at the Pemptopazaron, in Galata. The auctions will take place on Tuesday and Thursday of each week [until all the tithes are

---

245. *Ephemeris tes Smyrnes*, no. 8 (June 3, 1849).
246. *Telegraphos tou Vosporou*, no. 393 (June 30, 1851).
247. *Aster tes Anatoles*, no. 8 (December 5, 1841).

sold] at about 10 a.m. Those who want to know the terms of sale or further information should contact the above-mentioned office.[248]

Autonomous principalities under the suzerainty of the sultan also advertised tithe
auctions in the Ottoman Greek press:

> The government of Samos announces that the tithes of its towns and vil-
> lages will be auctioned on the 19th of May. Both locals and foreigners are
> welcome at this auction.[249]

Finally, other states also advertised similar auctions.

> The state of Greece announces that emery, which is produced in the island
> of Naxos, will be auctioned for a ten-year exploitation. The auction will
> take place on the October 4/16, 1835. All those interested in knowing the
> conditions under which the 10-year agreement of exploitation will be giv-
> en should go either to the Greek Consulate [of Smyrna] or to the *Ionian
> Press* in order to read the announcement posted outside the door.[250]

Private and state-owned land was put up for sale by private treaty or auction and
advertised in the Ottoman Greek press (two examples follow):

> The *çiftlik* [farm] called Küçük Yeniçeri, which is on the Asiatic side, be-
> tween Paşakçı and Alan Dayı and Ömerli, is for sale. This *çiftlik* contains
> various plots of arable and potentially arable land. It has a drinking water
> fountain, garden, house, storage buildings, and twenty-three small and
> large animals, namely cows, bulls, and horses. It is dependent on the *kaza*
> of Pisideia and Beykoz. Those wishing to buy it can go to the offices of
> Vyzantis.[251]

> For sale by auction: House and land owned by Demetrios Pervazis in
> the center of Beşiktaş opposite the house of Kijal ağaçı in the position of
> Havuz Bardağı. The public is informed that the auction will take place
> in two lots, as follows. The house comprises eight rooms and two recep-
> tion rooms, courtyard, kitchen etc., and a large garden of 2,700 *pecheis*
> including the grounds, where the house is built. The front of the plot is
> 72 *pecheis* and the back is 76. The auction of the land will take place in
> the Havyar Han in Galata at 11 o'clock on Monday September 18/30 and
> of the house September 25/October 7. The land and the house are *vakıf*

248. *Telegraphos tou Vosporou kai Vyzantis*, no. 458 (April 3, 1861).
249. *Mnemosyne*, no. 9 (May 4, 1835).
250. *Mnemosyne*, no.19 (July 13, 1835).
251. *Telegraphos tou Vosporou kai Vyzantis*, no. 178 (June 9, 1858).

[property endowed for religious or charitable use] and pay in total 32 *idja-le* [actual Ottoman word *icare* – rent payed to the *vakıf* or government] per year. For more information apply to the office of the undersigned in Galata, where there is also an exact plan, or to Mr. Dimitri Pervali in Kambur Han Asma Altı in Constantinople, or to the Epitrope [committee member] Mr. K. Vaikovich in Gerez Han.[252]

It was inevitable that some commercial ventures would result in failure. Another set of announcements in the Greek press recorded these failed attempts and the way they were dealt with. It also recorded the legal system of extraterritoriality, a result of the capitulations agreed by the Ottoman government.

Legal announcements comprise a group of notices usually pertaining to bankruptcies and auctions as a result of bad debt:

I have been appointed by the Office of the Wallachian Principality to take charge of the bankruptcy of Mr. P. Vokoresis, Wallachian merchant. According to article 236 of the Wallachian code of law, I invite the creditors of the above gentleman to appear within twenty days from Monday next at the Wallachian office, in person or through a representative, to declare the sum they are owed. We declare Monday 20th of November as the commencing date for the inspection of the loan documents at the Wallachian Office. Constantinople 14 October 1852, I. Xenokrates.[253]

One type of auction that occurred frequently was the auctions of ships whose owners had to surrender them as a result of debt or bankruptcy. The earliest such advertisement appeared in 1835:

On the 20th of next month [June] the brig called Theologos, sailing under captain Ioannis Sandrakalos will be auctioned. The ship, which is docked in this port [Smyrna] sails under the Ottoman commercial flag. A list of the furniture and equipment is to be obtained either on the ship or through Mr. A. A. Makres.[254]

Sometimes, ships were confiscated by only some of their creditors and then were sold to a third party. The buyer then had to advertise in the press and call on any other creditors to come forward within the time limit set by law, or they would lose their claim:

I, P. E. Inglesis, Ionian citizen, have bought from the creditors of Mr. Ioannis Nikolaides his property, the Greek brig "Patra" of 366 Greek tonnes, which he had given his creditors to pay off his debt. I also bought from

252. *Telegraphos tou Vosporou kai Vyzantis*, no. 508 (October 20, 1861).
253. *Telegraphos tou Vosporou*, no. 462 (October 28, 1852).
254. *Mnemosyne*, no. 12 (May 25, 1835).

Mr. Ioannis Eleutheriou the remaining third of the above-mentioned ship. All the purchases were agreed before the Consul of the Greek Commercial Office. I announce to all those who might have any rights and demands on this brig to come to me within the time limit set by law, otherwise their claims will be invalid. Constantinople 10/22 January 1853, P. E. Inglesis.[255]

More common in our period are announcements of the auction of a merchant's belongings following his bankruptcy:

On the 22nd of August 1861 at 5 o'clock, Turkish style, the property of the tobacco merchant Koutoupis will be presented for auction. The highest bidder will have to pay the price in paper money. Constantinople, 18 July 1861, the creditors Halil Efendi and Cleanthes S. Kandis.[256]

As no address was given for the place of auction, it is possible that auctions were held in a recognized location designated for auctions, probably the imperial treasury's auction rooms. Note also the definition of time as 'Turkish style" – a definition appearing in several advertisements. As the Ottomans counted time from dawn to dusk, assuming that dawn was at 7 a.m., then five o'clock was at 12 noon.

The Imperial Treasury would also auction properties of individuals, who had not paid their taxes:

An auction by Imperial decree will take part in the relevant place of the ministry of Finance next Tuesday, Wednesday, and Saturday. The following properties are to be auctioned: one mill called Batalumba in the district of Trikala in the province of Larissa, which belongs to the Imperial Allowance. Four stone shops in the province of Larissa. One Pharmacy in Yenişehir, province of Larissa, which belongs to the Imperial Allowance. One horse station [*menzil hane*] in Dolapdere in Tatavla, which belongs with a proper title to Mr. Alacadaci-Kevork and which will be sold by Imperial Decree for the Imperial Treasury for moneys not paid to it by Mr. Kevork. One hat shop in Uzunçarşısı of the Constantinople market also belonging to the Imperial Allowance. Those who wish to buy any of the above must come to the ministry of Finance on the appointed days escorted by guarantors recognized by the Imperial Treasury.[257]

Finally, private individuals used the newspapers to publicize private suits pending against other citizens:

Between the *vakıf* of the old customs buildings there is a site [*ferhane*] containing eight stone buildings, and two one-story houses, which belong

---

255. *Telegraphos tou Vosporou*, no. 475 (January 31, 1853).
256. *Telegraphos tou Vosporou kai Vyzantis*, no. 487 (July 19, 1861).
257. *Telegraphos tou Vosporou kai Vyzantis*, no. 524 (November 25, 1861).

to me, but were seized illegally by a certain Hüseyin, against whom there is a law-suit pending. Because I have heard that he proposes to sell this property, I am informing the public that such a sale cannot proceed, as it is illegal. Smyrna 1/13 November 1857, Christodoulos Scarpetis Manouel.[258]

In Sum

As the life of the Ottoman Greeks pours out of the pages of the Ottoman Greek press it is clear that in addition to the commercial, professional and intellectual opportunities which presented themselves to Ottoman Greeks abroad, the Tanzimat was an important domestic development not least because it established in writing the unopposed entry of Western European businesses into the empire. From the early 1830s until at least the 1860s several of its innovations, and especially the ones pertaining to commerce and trade, helped improve the quality of life of a great number of Ottoman Greeks in the Ottoman Empire.

As portrayed in the Ottoman Greek press up to the early 1860s the everyday life of the Ottoman Greeks had several aspects that were agreeable and fulfilling. Unlike the industrialized West, the quality of urban life was superior to life in small towns, villages, and rural areas. Although Ottoman Greek society was financially diverse, with some extremely affluent people, at the other end of the spectrum, there was apparently no financial hardship of the kind that existed in Western Europe at the same time. As non-Muslims were not generally expected to serve in the army, the Crimean War did not have a significantly negative impact on the Ottoman Greek economy or population, yet they were able to reap the benefits of the Treaty of Paris.

Ottoman Greek men in urban centers had an array of possible occupations to choose from, whether in the professions (for example, as a doctor, lawyer, pharmacist, architect, or teacher); in business (whether in commerce, trade, banking, service industries, the stock exchange, shipping, or agriculture); or in the civil service and judiciary.

On the other hand, Ottoman Greek women, like those in other European nations at the time, had a more limited spectrum of occupations, such as teacher, nurse, musician, photographer, hairdresser, or housekeeper. Most were content with the roles of wife and mother, and city women appear to have been sufficiently well educated and socially accepted to be able to deal with men of business on equal terms and manage their own financial affairs. This fact astonished Western Europeans and attracted some negative criticism in the Western European press, as mentioned earlier.

The debates concerning culture in the press affords insights into such issues as

258. *Telegraphos tou Vosporou kai Vyzantis*, no. 123 (November 13, 1857).

education, the Greek language, the proliferation of schools, the printing of books, the availability of better-qualified teachers and the improvement of the school curriculum. Through the extensive reports, announcements, and advertisements we follow the Ottoman Greek city dwellers' other cultural pursuits, such as the theatre, music, literature, poetry, and public lectures. They reveal that diversions were abundant in the big cities and that private clubs played an important role in the intellectual growth and entertainment of their members.

Significant improvements in the means of travel and communication helped increase knowledge and understanding of the "other," both within the empire and abroad.

But not everything was pleasant, fulfilling, and progressive for the Ottoman Greeks of the Ottoman Empire in our period. Reports from the provinces and, to a much lesser extent, the cities show that they often had to tolerate the demeaning behavior of their Muslim compatriots whether on the street, or by local government officials, or by the security forces. Even after the promulgation of the Tanzimat, the continued absence of law and order in the provinces and the weakening of the protective powers of the patriarchate exacerbated the insecurity of life and property, and the basic human rights of Christians continued to be violated. Reading the Ottoman Greek press, one senses that Orthodox Christians, and especially the Greek-speakers among them, had a cynical view towards most of their Muslim compatriots – especially those residing in the provinces. They often referred to them in the press as "ignorant" and "beasts" and although the sultan, most of the Muslim upper classes, and the Muslim intellectuals were spared such epithets, in general, in the lower strata of the population there seems to be little respect for or interaction between Christians and Muslims, with only a few exceptions.

Some Muslims were equally robust in expressing disdain for Christians, quoted in the press stating that "Christians are destined to be the slaves of the Ottomans forever." This belittling of the Christians continued unabated in some quarters, as witnessed by Sir Charles Eliot's much later account of his visit to the *konak* of the Vali of Karakeni in Ottoman Macedonia. To his great astonishment Sir Charles heard the official pronounce to his face that "all Christians are pigs."[259] A little earlier the Vali gave his views on Westernization to Sir Charles, with whom he had collaborated some time before in building a railway between Durograd and Moropolis:

> All Christians big and small know how to make money; we only know
> how to take it. You want to introduce a system in which Christians will
> be able to squeeze the money out of us and our country and keep it. Who
> profits by all these concessions for railways, harbors and quays? Franks,
> Jews, Greeks, and Armenians but never a Moslem.... In that railway I

259. Eliot 1908, 14.

helped you build … Franks travel in it, Greeks and Armenians sell the tickets and in the end all the money goes to the Jews. But what Turk wants the railway, and how much has any Turk made out of it?

Sir Charles comments in his book that he could have retorted, "exactly as much as passed into Your Highness's pockets when the concession was arranged."[260]

Sir Charles's revelations, first published in the late 1890s, suggest that Muslim attitudes remained on the whole little changed, especially in the provinces. The Christians' cynical view of the Muslims extended to their professional dealings with them. As demonstrated in the press, the conviction that, in general, Muslim officials were incapable of understanding the merits of facilitating business and trade in the Ottoman Empire for the general good made the bribing of individuals the norm and usually the only way forward.

Although considerable criticism of their Muslim compatriots and of several aspects of life was recorded in the press between 1830 and 1862, the Ottoman Greeks never openly expressed any desire to sever themselves from the empire. This contrasts with the situation during the first two decades of the nineteenth century, which saw the creation of the Greek state. It seems that for this later generation of Ottoman Greeks living in the Ottoman Empire, despite constant complaints about the relative absence of law and order, life was sufficiently fulfilling to contain any thoughts of rebellion; instead, there was forward planning, an air of creativity, and hope for a better future.

260. Eliot 1908, 12–13.

Postscript

As we reflect on the remarkable slice of social history presented in this book, we are led to a bigger question: how exactly does this episode, the flourishing of the Ottoman Greeks in the mid-nineteenth century, fit into the broader narrative of the history of the Ottoman Empire?

To put the question more precisely, was the exuberant energy of the Ottoman Greeks simply a curious but ultimately irrelevant counter-current during a long period of Ottoman decline? Or was it, on the contrary, an important harbinger of creative symbiosis between peoples of various nationalities – which served as a precursor of European developments in the second half of the twentieth century?

From one, narrow point of view, the story of the Ottoman Empire could be described as the rise, supremacy, and decline of the heavy cavalry as the chief power in war. To a certain extent this is how Western European countries viewed the Ottoman Empire from the late eighteenth century onward: an unmodernized military force in decline, unable to sustain either its conquering drive or its defence from both external and internal threats.

From the eighteenth century onward, the empire suffered a gradual loss of power and territories to Christian Europe, which by then had changed and improved its military to rely less on the cavalry and more on a disciplined and well-trained infantry, employing the latest technology for its weaponry. To reverse this trend, the Ottoman sultans relied increasingly on their Christian – mainly Greek – population to help them understand Western European progress, import Western European know-how, and run the empire in a more modern fashion.

It could be argued that if the Ottoman Empire had managed to modernize its army a century earlier, no one in Europe at the dawn of the nineteenth century would have considered it a country in decline. Nor would living conditions among its vanquished populations have improved to the degree they did under the reforms of the Tanzimat.

The Ottoman Greek press provides a window through which to view the Ottoman Empire in the middle years of the nineteenth century, at a time when the importation of social, political, and military reforms from Western Europe, also known as Tanzimat, were in full swing. The Greeks of the Ottoman Empire were the only ones among the subject peoples in the empire that had a heritage including all three components of humanism as it was introduced in Western Europe in the eighteenth century: ancient Greek political and philosophical thought, Roman law, and Christian values. As such their understanding of and reaction to the importation of Western European advancements in the Ottoman Empire throughout the Tanzimat period is valuable if we are to improve our understanding of the condition of the Ottoman state in the nineteenth century. In this respect the Ottoman Greek newspapers from 1830 through 1862 provide a corpus of sufficient magnitude to be regarded as a substantial primary source for that period.

In addition to their value as a mine of first-hand information about the Ottoman Empire, the Ottoman Greek newspapers offer an understanding of how a vanquished nation in a non-democratic country with no political rights and living under an oppressive situation, managed to devise ways not just to survive but even to thrive and occasionally turn oppression to its advantage.

On the domestic front, the Tanzimat reforms and the concomitant efforts (successes and failures) of the government to impose it on the various Muslim populations of the empire took center stage in the Greek press. The reception of the various reforms by both Muslims and non-Muslims was reported from all over the empire and commented on extensively. Among those reforms, the one with the greatest repercussions for the Rum milleti was the reform of the Patriarchate of Constantinople. The Ottoman Greek newspapers, with their day-to-day coverage, their discussion of the reception of the reforms by the various nations that formed the Orthodox Christian community, their analyses, commentaries, and even public warnings to the Ottoman government about changing the status quo ante, are a unique source for this reform.

The columns of the newspapers also followed social news with articles, commentary, supplements, and advertisements, unfurling the everyday life of the Ottoman Greeks and the other peoples of the empire before our eyes. Through the newspapers we glimpse many aspects of everyday life, from the celebration of religious holidays to the social, professional, and commercial life of the empire and especially of the Ottoman Greeks within it; from the description and sometimes criticism of the extravagant life-style of modish society and the great benefactors of the community; from the public examinations of the schools and the push for universal education, to visits to the opera and the theatre; from the creation of comfortable new hotels in the spa towns and the pleasures of mixed sea-bathing, to the introduction of steamships, the railways, the telegraph and the stock exchange; Ottoman everyday life and especially that of the Ottoman Greek community comes alive again in these pages.

In parallel with the positive aspects of life, its negative characteristics also find their place in the press, providing a balanced overview of everyday life in the empire: robberies, thefts, murders, fires, diseases, earthquakes, and the often intolerably overweening behavior of local governors, the police, and some members of the Muslim population towards the Christians of the empire.

The contents of the newspapers shatter the widespread perception that the Ottoman Empire in the nineteenth century was constantly a "sick man," kept alive only because of the failure of the great powers to agree on how to divide its dying corpse, and reveals this as a period of significant progress and improvements in the well-being of many of its inhabitants, especially in the urban areas and the islands. Rather than depicting an empire in terminal decline, or a "Greek" nation on its way out of the empire, our source provides ample evidence to the contrary. During the thirty years covered extensively by the papers, there was a surge of activity, productivity, and innovation in the empire. Also, the conditions of life for non-Muslims in the cities are shown to have improved dramatically. A rich and educated Greek middle class emerged, enjoying life in the empire and displaying no desire to leave. In fact, the evidence presented in this book suggests that the Ottoman Greeks (and to a lesser extent other members of the Rum milleti), the Armenians, and the Jews in this period held most of the key positions of financial and cultural life in the main cities, creating a financial and social boom in the whole of the Ottoman Empire.

Reading through the pages of the Ottoman Greek press it is clear that for the Ottoman Greeks, life in a multicultural society, provided it was based on equality and collaboration with the other nations of the empire and all over the world, was their preferred option.

Some prominent Greeks, like Ion Dragoumis (1878–1920),[1] looking back to the period we have covered in this book, pointed out the improvements to the life of the non-Muslim millets during the Tanzimat years. They also noted that the commercial and other opportunities that appeared at that time gave the Ottoman Greeks the possibility to obtain a position of equality to the Turks in the multicultural empire that succeeded the Eastern Roman Empire/Byzantium.

This is supported by the newspapers we have reviewed. Dragoumis' ideas of a "Greco-Turkish" state with a democratic government, shared by a number of Greeks both in Greece and the Ottoman Empire, were embodied in 1908 when he established, together with Athanassios Souliotes-Nikolaides, the Constantinople Organization (Organosis Konstantinoupoleos). This organization encouraged collaboration between Greeks and Turks for the creation of a unified "Greco-Turkish" state along European lines, and pressed for equality for all nationalities in the Ottoman Empire.

Dragoumis' ideas can also be seen as an updated version of the plan of Demetrios Hypsilantes/Selim III discussed in an earlier chapter and various other attempts by Ottoman Greeks to effect a symbiosis of equals, a later reignition of what had transpired in 1453 when only a few months after the fall of Con-

---

1. Ion Dragoumis was a diplomat, politician and writer, supporter of the demotic Greek language, and a political opponent of Venizelos.

stantinople, the Greek intellectual Georgios Trapezoutios (George of Trebizond) proposed such a relationship to Mehmed II.

The revival of such ideas in the early twentieth century found some support among progressive Turks, who were opposed to Sultan Abdülhamid II's closure of the Ottoman Parliament in 1878, an event that had brought the Tanzimat era to a halt. But any hope of a breakthrough was destroyed by the drive for the creation of a Turkish secular national identity and by the nationalist strategies pursued by the Young Turks, who wanted to create a monoethnic/monocultural state at any price.

Dragoumis' idea of a Greco-Turkish[2] state also went against the dominant view in the state of Greece embodied by Eleutherios Venizelos (1864–1936), the Cretan revolutionary and later prime minister of Greece, who hoped to unite all the Greeks of the Ottoman Empire within a larger mono-ethnic, mono-religious Greek state, a modern recreation of ancient Greece, emerging out of the ruins of the Ottoman Empire. Venizelos' ideas corresponded with the then prevailing European ideology of the nation-state and were consistent with Western European ambitions for a successor state to the Ottoman Empire with Western European links.

It is also worth reflecting on the tragic series of events that came to a horrific climax around sixty years after the booming period presented in this book. During the 1920s, millions of people either died or were permanently uprooted from their homes when the final division of the Ottoman Empire into nation-states took place, culminating in a war that ended with the creation of modern Turkey. This was done by removing the overwhelming majority of all Christians, with a few minor exceptions, from the part of the Ottoman Empire which became the state of modern Turkey. These events followed the mass extermination of the Armenians of the Ottoman Empire during World War One, when the Ottoman Empire was allied with Germany. The enormity of the operation and the decisiveness by which it was carried out gave rise to a real fear that the millions of Greeks still living in the Ottoman Empire would be next; and this was one of the reasons why, following the end of World War One, the victorious allies gave the green light to Venizelos to pursue his vision.[3] This in turn led to a further dismemberment of the Ottoman Empire with the Treaty of Sèvres (10 August 1920) as a diplomatic high point, although it proved in practice to be a dead letter. At various times, and with varying levels of enthusiasm, Britain, France, Italy, and Greece (which provided the main military and naval forces) were lined up against the Ottomans.

The end of this war sealed the tragic fate of millions of people in both Greece and the new state of Turkey, who were either killed or forcefully deported according to their religion, either to the state of Greece (the Orthodox Christians) or the new state of Turkey (the Muslims). The harsh pragmatism of the Treaty of Lausanne (July 24, 1923), which ended this final break-up of the Ottoman Empire, endorsed the enforced exchange of populations between Greece and the emerging state of Turkey on religious terms. The readiness with which both Venizelos and Ataturk accepted and signed it shows that both leaders had realized that multicultural empires were a thing of the past and that the concept of a mono-cultural nation-state was the only realistic way forward. The Treaty of Lausanne granted immunity from prosecution for all crimes against humanity committed by the Ottoman side, between 1914 and 1922, most notably the Armenian genocide. Many, like Hans-Lukas Kieser, have criticized the treaty as "tacitly endorsing comprehensive policies of expulsion and extermination of hetero-ethnic and hetero-religious groups."[4] Despite its immense cruelty and whitewashing of serious crimes, the Lausanne treaty established the state of Turkey and became the blueprint for other, more recently created, nation-states such as India and Pakistan; and, perverted as it might seem, for the past hundred years it has helped maintain peace between the neighboring states of Greece and Turkey.

The violence and loss of life in the two world wars and related struggles of the first half of the twentieth century were unprecedented in human history. They exceeded in brutality and magnitude the invasions of the Germanic tribes that conquered the western part of the Roman Empire and destroyed its civilization. However, the aftermath has been a pleasant surprise. Instead of further centuries of "dark ages," Europeans collaborated to create the European Union, a partnership of nation-states, in which they included the defeated perpetrator of the worst blood-bath in history as an equal partner. The EU is a voluntary union of nation-states that share the same humanist values: ancient Greek political and philosophical thought, Roman law, and Christian morality. In this union even the most prodigal of sons could be accepted as equal as long as they understood their mistakes and repented.

Is the EU the perfect political configuration? Not by a long way. However, it represents an attempt to mitigate the worst aspects of human behavior and the worst forms of collective cruelty. While oppression is part of human history, it often seems a universal condition that "the strong will do what they can and the weak will suffer what they must."[5] By adhering (not always with success) to its humanist values, the EU has gradually managed to mitigate this cruel cycle of violence through imposing the rule of law and political rights that are accessible to all irrespective of sex, color, race, religion, or wealth, and by providing a safety net of support for the weakest members of society.

4. Kieser 2010.
5. Thucydides 5.89. Translation by C. F. Smith, in Loeb Classical Library 110 (Cambridge, MA: 1921).

As their newspapers show, the Ottoman Greeks believed that their world was evolving in a liberal direction – towards a multi-national commonwealth in which different people of different cultures could co-exist, underpinned by the rule of law and freedom of expression. But they failed to persuade their Ottoman partners, and sixty years later, in the period 1914–1923, this failure had catastrophic results for all the inhabitants of what was then the Ottoman Empire.

But tragedy did not have the last word: in 1981, six decades after the expulsion of the Greeks from their ancient homes in Asia Minor and the other parts of the Ottoman Empire, the Republic of Greece became a full member of the European Economic Community, later the European Union. Many of the Greek diplomats and public servants who prepared the way for the accession treaty were descendants of those Greeks who had been forced to leave the Ottoman Empire. Thus, it could be said that the heirs of the Ottoman Greeks did finally achieve their dream of living in a multi-ethnic collaborative society, governed by humanist values.

Hegel famously believed that we never learn from history and this could often be said to be the case. But on the rare occasions that we have the courage to look objectively at our past and the wisdom to learn from it, the result is a giant leap towards the attainment of a better existence for us all.

It seems apposite to end with this quote from the editor of *Amaltheia* of Smyrna written in 1847:

> [N]ations do not live by memories of the past and hopes for the future alone, but … it would be preferable for them to accept their present condition and strive to improve it without violent changes and destruction.[6]

6. *Amaltheia* 428, April 11, 1847.

Bibliography

Aboona, H. 2008. *Assyrians, Kurds and Ottomans: Intercommunal Relations in the Periphery of the Ottoman Empire*. Amherst, NY.

Akson, V. and D. Goffman. 2007. *The Early Modern Ottomans*. Cambridge, UK.

Allen, E. W. 1930. "International Origins of the Newspapers: The Establishment of Periodicity in Print." *Journalism Quarterly* 7 (December): 310 ff.

Altbolz, J. L. 1989. *The Religious Press in Britain 1760-1900*. Westport, CT.

Anastassiadou, M. 1997. *Salonique, 1830-1912, une ville Ottomane à l'Age des Réformes*. Leiden.

Angelopoulos, G. 1865. *Ta kata ton Aoidemon Patriarchen Konstantinoupoleos Gregorion V´*. Vol. 1. Athens.

Antoniades, E. (ed). 1846. *Dike tou Kyriou Iona King Enopion tou Ariou Pagou*. Athens.

Ari, O. 1975. "The Mass Media Communication in Izmir." In *Social Change in Izmir*, edited by Bozkurt Günenç. Ankara.

Aristarchi, D. (Bey). 1874. *Législation ottomane*. Vols. 1–3. Constantinople

Aristarchis, D. 1876. *To Voulgarikon zetema kai ai neai Plektanai tou Panslavismou en Anatole*. Athens.

Arslan, A. 2004. *O Ellenikos Typos sto Othomaniko Kratos opos katagraphetai mesa apo ta Eggrapha tes Epochis*, translated by Chr. L. Pampalos. Athens.

Aspinall, A. 1946. "The Circulation of Newspapers in the Early Nineteenth Century." *Review of English Studies* o.s. 22, no. 85 (July): 29-42.

———. 1949. *Politics and the Press, 1780-1850*. London.

Athanasiou, C. 1988. "Oi Hellenes tes protes diasporas sten Ouggaria (1544–1920). Tote... 34:6–13.

Balta, E. 2003 *Miscellaneous Studies on the Karamanlidika Literary Tradition*. Istanbul.

———. "Karamanlidika Press (Smyrna 1845-Athens 1925)." In *Beyond the Language Frontier: Studies on the Karamanlis and the Karamanlidika Printing*, edited by E. Balta. Istanbul.

———. 2013. "The First Family Periodical in the Ottoman Empire: A Karamanlı Magazine in Smyrna (1849-1850)." *Journal of Turkish Studies* 39 (December): 212-13.

Baykal, E. 2019. *The Ottoman Press (1908-1923)*. The Ottoman Empire and its Heritage, vol. 67. Leiden.

Binark, I. 1977. "Türkiyede matbaanın geç girişi sosyal psikolojik sebepleri." VII Türk Tarih Kongresi'ne (11-15 Ekim 1976) Ankara, in *Türk Kütüphanecilği*, volume 26, no. 1.

Fedalto G. 1973–1978. *La Chiesa Latina in Oriente*. Vols. 1–3. Verona.

Borzecka, M., S. Plaskowicka-Rymkiewicz, and M. Lacecka-Koecherova. 1971. *Historia Literatury Tureckiej*. Warsaw.

Boyar, E., and Fleet, K. 2010. *A Social History of Ottoman Istanbul*. New York.

Bulwer-Lytton, Sir Edward. 1833. *England and the English*. London.

Burmov, T. 1902. *Balgarogratskata Tsarkova Razpriya*. Sofia.

Byzantios, S. 1851. *Constantinoupolis*, Vols. 1-3. Athens.

Cantemir, D. 1743. *Histoire de l' Empire Ottoman*. Paris.

Carr, E. H. 2001. *What is History?* Basingstoke.

Cassels, L. 1966. *The Struggle for the Ottoman Empire 1717–1740*. London.

Chassiotes, G. 1881. *L'Instruction publique chez les Grecques*. Paris.

Christides Serraios D. 1862. *Oi Didaskaloi tes Constantinoupoleos*. Constantinople.

Christopoulos, P. 1993. *Ephemerides Apokeimenes sten Vivliotheke tes Voules (1789–1970)*. Athens.

Christovitz, G., and S. Karatheodori. 1860. *Minutes of the National Assembly in the Telegraphos tou Vosporou kai Vyzantis*. Constantinople.

Cioeta, D. J. 1979. "Ottoman Censorship in Lebanon and Syria 1876–1908." *International Journal of Middle East* Studies 10, no. 2 (May): 167–86. doi:10.1017/S0020743800034759.

Clogg, R. 1979. "An Attempt to Revive Turkish Printing in Istanbul in 1779." International Journal of Middle East Studies 10, no. 1 (February): 67 –70. doi:10.1017/S0020743800053320.

———. 1996. *Anatolica, Studies in the Greek East in the Eighteenth and Nineteenth Centuries*. Hampshire.

Collins, I. 1959. *The Government and the Newspaper Press in France, 1814–1881*. Oxford.

Collins, L. 1985. "Vizantis and the Bulgarian Church Movement in 1860. In *Anglo-Bulgarian Symposium July 1982*, School of Slavonic and East European Studies, 65–87. London.

———. 1993. "Book Burning, the First Braila Revolt and Other Matters Relevant to Bulgarian History, Covered by the Greek Press of Athens, 1839–1841." In *Proceedings of the Second Anglo-Bulgarian Symposium in Blagoevgrad, September 1985*, School of Slavonic and East European Studies, 11–24. London.

Cruickshank , J., ed. 1969 *French Literature and its Background*. Oxford.

Dalrymple, W. 2005. *From the Holy Mountain*. London.

Daskalakis, A. 1930. *La Presse Néo-hellénique*. Paris.

Demaras, K. Th. 1962. "To Keimeno tou Rossoagglogallou." *Hellenika* 17:188-201.

Devereux. R. 1963. *The First Ottoman Constitutional Period*. Baltimore.

Didot, A .F. 1826. *Notes d'un voyage fait dans le Levant en 1816 et 1817*. Paris.

Dimakis, J. 1977. "The Greek Press." In *Greece in Transition*, edited by J. Koumoulides. London.

Dragoumis, I. 1907. *Martyron kai Heroon Aima*. Athens.

Drinov, M. 1971. "Istoricheski pregled na Balgarskata tsarkva ot samoto i nachalo do dnes." In *Sobrani SachincniyaI*. Vol. 2, edited by Marin Drinov. Sofia.

Droulia, L., and Y. Koutsopanagou, eds. 2008. *Encyclopaedia tou Ellenikou Typou*. Instituto Neoellenikon Erevnon, Ethniko Idryma Erevnon. Athen.

Droulia, L., ed. 2005. *O Ellenikos Typos 1784 Os Semera, Istorikes kai Theoritikes Proseggiseis*. Instituto Neoellenikon Erevnon, Ethniko Idryma Erevnon. Athens.

Eisenstein, L. 1979. *The Printing Press as an Agent of Change*. Cambridge.

Eliot, C. 1908. *Turkey in Europe*. London.

Eliou, Ph. 1983. *Koinotiki Agones kai Diaphotismos: He Periptosis tes Smyrnes (1819)*. Athens.

Ellegard, A. 1957. *The Readership of the Periodical Press in Mid-Victorian Britain*. Göteborg.

Emerson, J. 1826. *Journal de mon séjour parmis les Grecs*. Paris.

Emery, E. and M. Emery. 1978. *The Press and America, An Interpretative History of the Mass Media*. New York.

Emin, A. 1914. *The Development of Modern Turkey as Measured by Its Press*. Columbia University Studies in History, Economics and Public Law. Vol. 59. New York.

Enepekides, P. 1965. *Symvolai eis ten Historian tou Hellenikou typou kai Typographeion tes Viennes*. Athens.

Erdem, H. Y. 1996. *Slavery in the Ottoman Empire and Its Demise, 1800–1909*. London.

Erskine, T., 1st Baron. 1793. *Declaration of the Friends of the Liberty of the Press*. London.

Ersoy, O. 1959. *Türkiye'de Matbaanin Girişi ve Ilk Basılan Eserler*. Ankara.

Evangelides, T. 1936. *He Paideia epi Tourkokratias*. Vol. 2. Athens.

Falierou, A. 2006. "Les rédacteurs et le lectorat d'une revue grecque d'Istanbul: Vosporis (1899–1907)." *International Journal of Turcologia* 1, no. 1: 39-54.

Farah, C. 1977. "Censorship and Freedom of Expression in Ottoman Syria and Egypt." In *Nationalism in a Non-National State*, edited by W. Haddad and W. Ochsenwald, 151–94. Colombus.

Fortna, B. 2011. *Learning to Read in the Late Ottoman Empire and the Early Turkish Republic*. London.

Frangakis-Syrett, E. 1987. "Greek Mercantile Activities in the Eastern Mediterranean, 1780–1820." *Balkan Sudies* 28:73–86.

Gedeon, M. 1893. *Paideia kai Ptocheia par Hemin kata tous Teleutaious Aionas*. Constantinople.

———. 1908. *Eggrapha Patriarchika kai Synodika peri tou Volgarikou Zetematos 1852–1873*. Constantinople.

———. 1922. *Patriarchikes Historias Mnemeia*. Athens.

———. 1932. *Aposemeiomata Chronographou 1800–1913*. Athens.

———. 1939. *Istoria ton tou Christou peneton 1453–1913*. Athens.

Gerov, N. 1852. *Nyakolko isli za Balgarskiy Yazık*. Constantinople.

Ginis, D. 1967. *Katalogos Hellenikon Ephemeridon kai Periodikon 181 –1863*. Athens.

Göçek, F. M. 2005. 'The Legal Recourse of Minorities in History: Eighteenth-Century Appeals to the Islamic Court in Galata." In *Minorities in the Ottoman Empire*, edited by M. Greene, 47–69. Princeton.

Gondicas, D., and C. Issawi, eds. 1999. *Ottoman Greeks in the Age of Nationalism: Politics, Economy and Society in the Nineteenth Century*. Princeton.

Gough, John, and Muriel Gough. 1978. *An Introduction to Nineteenth-Century France*. London.

Greene, M., ed. 2005. *Minorities in the Ottoman Empire*. Princeton.

Groç, G., and J. Çağlar. 1980. *La Presse Francaise de la Turquie de 1795 à Nos Jours*. Istanbul.

Hadjinikolaou, L. K., *O Missionarismos kai Protestantismos eis tas Anatolas* (Athens 1837)

Hanioğlu, M. Ş. 2008. *A Brief History of the Late Ottoman Empire*. Princeton.

Harris, M., and A. Lee, eds. 1986. *The Press in English Society from the Seventeenth to the Nineteenth Centuries*. London.

Helladios, A. 1714. *Status Praesens Ecclesiae Graecae*. Altdorf.

Herd, H. 1952. *The March of Journalism: The Story of the British Press from 1622 to the Present Day*. London.

Hitchins, K. 1996. *The Romanians, 1774–1866*. Oxford.

Ingram, E. 1992. *Eastern Questions in the Nineteenth Century, Selected Essays by Allan Cunningham*. Vol. 2. London.

Ioannides, S. 1873. *Homeros*. Smyrna.

İskit, S. 1937. *Hususi ilk Türkçe gazetemiz Tercümani ahval ve Agâh Efendi*. Ankara.

Ivanov, Y. 1912. "Gratsko-Balgarski Otnosheniya Predi Tsarkovnata Borba," In *Sbornik v Chest na Professor L. Miletich*. Sofia.

Kalapothakis, D. 1928. *A Short History of the Greek Press*. Cologne.

Karabines, F., and K. Vaphas, K. eds. 1851. *Elenchos tes Kakodoxias tou Pseudo-apostolou Iona King*. Athens.

Karadjas, S. 1958. *Smyrnes Tragodies*. Athens.

Kariophylles, G., ed. 1863. *He Anaskevi*. Athens.

Kitromilides, P. 1994. "Religious Criticism between Orthodoxy and Protestantism: Ideological Consequences of Social Conflict in Smyrna," in *Enlightenment, Nationalism, Orthodoxy*. Aldershot, UK.

Kitsikis, D. 1963. *Propagande et pressions en politique internationale, La Grèce et ses revendications à la Conférence de la Paix 1919–1920*. Paris.

———. 1978. "Grande idée et hellénoturquisme. Essai d'interpretation nouvelle de l'histoire néo-grecque." Actes du IIme Congrès International des Etudes Sud-Est Européen, 1970–Athènes. Association des Etudes Sud-Est européen. Vol. 3.

———. 1990. *Synkritike Historia Hellados Tourkias ston Eikosto Aiona*. Athens.

Köksal. Y. 2019. *The Ottoman Empire in the Tanzimat Era: Provincial Perspectives from Ankara to Edirne*. London.

Koloğlu, O. 1981. *Takvim i Vekayi*. Ankara.

———. 1985. "Türkçe – dışı Basın." *Tanzimat'tan Cumhuriyet'e Türkiye Ansiklopedisi* 1: 94–98. Istanbul.

———. 1986. *Miyop Çörçil Olayı*. Ankara.

———. 1989. *İlk Gazete İlk Polemik*. Ankara.

Konomos, D. 1964. *Eptanissiakos Typos, 1798 –1864*. Athens.

Konortas. P. 1998. *Othomanikes Theoriseis gia to OIkoumeniko Patriarcheio. Beratia gia tous prokathemenous tes Magales Ekklesias (17os - arches 20ou aiona)*. Alexandria

Konstantinides, A. 1930. *Hellenike en Aigypto Demosiographia 1830 –1930*. Alexandria

Koraes, A. 1983 *Epistolai*, edited by N. Damalas. Athens.

Koss, S. 1981–84. *The Rise and Fall of the Political Press in Britain*. 2 vols. London.

Koukou, H. 1984. *Ioannis Kapodistrias o Anthropos – o Diplomates 1800–1828*. Athens.

Koumanoudis, S. 1880. *Katalogos Ephemeridon 1821 –1880*. Athens.

Koumarianou, A., ed. 1971. *O typos ston Agona*. Vols 1–3. Athens.

Koumoulides, J. T., ed. 1977. *Greece in Transition,* London.

Kunzle, D. 1973. *The Early Comic Strip: Narrative Strips and Picture Stories in the European Broadsheet from c. 1450 to 1825*. Berkeley.

Kyriakides. E. 1892. *Historia tou Sychronou Hellenismou.* Reprinted in 1972. Athens.

Lacroix, F. 1839. *Guide du Voyageur à Constantinople et dans ses Environs.* Paris.

Lady Marks, M. 2005. "Oi Hellenikes Ephemerides tes Othonomanikes Autokratorias (1830-1862)." In *O Hellenikos Typos 1784 eos Semera: Historikes kai Theoritikes Proseggiseis,* edited by L. Droulia, 434–42. Athens.

Laios, G. 1957. *Oi Adelfoi Markides Pouliou.* Athens.

———. 1960. "Eggrapha peri tes protes ephemeridos en Vienne." *Probleme der Neugriechischen Literatur.* Vienna.

———. 1961. *O Hellenikos Typos tes Viennes 1774–1821.* Athens.

Lappas, T. 1959. *Roumelioticos Typos 1821–1880.* Athens.

Lee, A. J. 1976. *The Origins of the Popular Press in England, 1855–1914.* London.

Lewis, B. 1966. *The Emergence of Modern Turkey.* Oxford.

Linton, D., and R. Boston, eds. 1989. *The Newspaper Press in Britain.* London.

Machiavelli, N. 1985. *The Prince.* Translated by H. C. Mansfield. Chicago.

Madden, L., and D. Dixon. 1975. "The Nineteenth Century Periodical Press in Britain." Supplement to the earlier version of *Victorian Periodicals. Victorian Periodicals Newsletter* 8, no. 3 (September): 95–112.

Mansfield, P. 2010. *The History of the Middle East,* 3rd ed. London.

Mastoridis, K. 1999. *Casting the Greek Newspaper.* Thessaloniki.

Mavrogenis, G. E. 1899. *Historia ton Ionion Neson 1797–1815.* 2 vols. Athens.

Mayer, K. 1960. *Historia tou Hellenikou Typou.* Athens.

Mazarakis-Ainian, I. 1970. *Ta Hellenika Typographeia tou Agonos.* Athens.

McCarthy, J. 2001. *The Ottoman Peoples and the End of Empire.* London.

McMurtrie, D. C. 1943. *The Book: The Story of Printing and Bookmaking.* New York.

Michalopoulos, F. 1940. "Mia Agnostos Ephemeris tes Hellenikes Epanastaseos." *To Vema,* July 21.

Michaud, J. F. and J. J. F. Poujoulat. 1834. *Correspondence d' Orient 1830–31,* Vol. 3. Paris.

Minçoğlu, N. 1860. *Apantesis eis ton Logon tou kyriou Karatheodori.* Translated from Bulgarian. Constantinople.

Misaelides, E. 1988. *Seyreyle Dünyayı.* Edited by R. Anhagger and V. Gunyol. 2nd ed. Istanbul.

Moran, J. 1973. *Printing Presses: History and Development from the Fifteenth Century to Modern Time.* Berkeley.

Moreau, O. 2007. "Service Historique de l'Armée de Terre, archives unitaires Françaises à Vincennes." In *L'Empire Ottoman à l'Âge des Reformes; les hommes et les idées du 'nouvel ordre' militaire 1826–1914,* 354–55. Paris.

Moschopoulos, N. 1931. *La Presse dans la Renaissance Balkanique.* Athens.

Moscoff, C. 1988. *Historia tou Kinematos tes Ergatikes Takses*. Athens.

Nikolaides-Philadelpheus, C. 1874. *Homeros*. Smyrna.

Nikov, P. 1929. *Vazrazhdane na Balgarskiya Narod. Tsarkovno-Natsionalni Borbi i Postizheniya*. Sophia.

Nüzhet, S. G. 1931. *Türk Gazeteciliği*. Istanbul.

Oikonomos, C. 1841. *L'histoire de Smyrne*. Paris.

Oikonomou, I. 1962. *Epistoles Diaphoron 1757–1824*. Athens.

Oikonomou, S., ed. 1871. *Oikonomos, C., Ta Sozomena Philologika Syggramata*. Athens.

Olson, K. E. 1966. *The History Makers*. London.

Özdalga, E. 2005. *Late Ottoman Society: The Intellectual Legacy*. London.

Papageorgiou S. 1975. "He Typographia sten Athena sta prota Othomanika Chronia." *Eranistes* 12:53–72.

Papalexandrou, C. 1972. *Frouria Eleftherias*. Athens.

Paranikas, M. 1867. *Schediasma peri tes en to Helleniko Ethnei Katastaseos ton Grammaton apo tes Haloseos tes Constantinoupoleos 1453, mechri ton Archon tes Henestoses 19 Hekatontaeteridos*. Constantinople.

————. 1885. *Historia tes Evaggelikes Scholes Smyrnes*. Athens.

Persignac, Comte A. de. 1907. "Les Gaîtés de la Censure en Turquie." *La Revue* 67, no. 2 (April): 384–94, 521–37.

Philimon, I. 1859. *Dokimion Istorikon peri tes Hellenikes Epanastaseos*. Vol. I. Athens.

Pouquevill, F. C. L. 1827. *Voyage en Gréce*. Paris.

Quataert, D. 1999. *Consumption Studies and the History of the Ottoman Empire 1550–1922*. New York.

————. 2003. "Ottoman History Writing and Changing Attitudes Towards the Notion of Decline," *History Compass* 1, no. 1 (August). https://doi.org/10.1111/1478-0542.038.

Read, D. 1961. *Press and People, 1790–1850*. Westport, CT.

Roberts, R. J. 1967. *The Greek Press at Constantinople in 1627 and Its Antecedents*. London.

Rocos, G. D. 1983. "He Hellenike Typographia sten Mikra Asia." *Diavazo* 74:24–31.

Rosen, G. 1860. *Geschichte der Türkei 1826–1856*. Leipzig.

Runciman, S. 1968. *The Great Church in Captivity*. Cambridge.

Russell, B. 1994. *History of Western Philosophy*. Reprint. London.

Sakali Lady Marks, M. 1998. "Osmanlı-Rum Basınında Türk/Müslüman İmajı." Tarih Eğitimi ve Tarihte "Öteki" Sorunu, Haz. [edited by] A. Berktay and H. C. Tuncer, 54–55. İstanbul.

Sakali, M. 1997. "The Image of the Turks/Muslims in the Ottoman Greek Press 1830–1860." *Balkan Studies* 38, no. 1 (January): 123–34.

Sammarco, A. 1930. *II Regno di Muhammad Ali negli Documenti Inediti Italiani.* Vol. 8. Rome.

Schoell, R., and G. Kroll, G., eds. 1928. *Corpus juris civilis* III. Berlin.

Şemşedin Sami. 1983. "Lisan ve Edebiyatımız." In *Origins and Development of the Turkish Novel,* edited by A. Ö. Evin, pages 181 and following. *Minneapolis*

Shattock, J., M. and Wolff, M., eds. 1982. *The Victorian Periodical Press.* Leicester.

Shismanov, I. D. 1894. "Constantin G. Photinov, Negoviyat Shivat, i Negovata Dynost." In *Sbornik za narodni umotvorenya, nauka i knishnina.* Isdava Ministerstvoto na Narodnoto Prosveshchenie, kniga XI. Sofia.

Skiadas, N. 1920. *Les Armeniens et l'imprimerie.* Istanbul.

Smith, A. 1979. *The New Societies: An International History.* London.

Sokolov, I. 2013. *The Church of Constantinople in the Nineteenth Centuryı.* [Translated from the Russian as published in Moscow in 1904. Bern.

Solomonides, Ch. 1959. *He Demosiographia sten Smyrne 1821–1922.* Athens.

Solomonides, S. 1893. *Hemerologion Amaltheias.* Smyrna.

Stamatopoulos, D. 2003. *Metarrythmise kai Ekkosmekeuse.* Athens.

Stavrides, V. 1991. *Historia tou Oikoumenikou Patriarcheiou.* Athens.

Sturdza. M. D. 1983. *Les familles de Grèce, d'Albanie et de Constantinople. Dictionnaire historique et généalogique.* Paris.

Sugar, P. P. 1994. *E Notioanatolike Europe kato apo Othomanike Kyriarhia 1354–1804.* Athens.

Teoman, E. 1951. *Istiklal Harbinde Türk Ortodoksları.* Istanbul.

Todorov, N. 1960. *La genèse du capitalisme dans les provinces Bulgares de l'Empire Ottoman au cours de la première moitié du XIX siècle.* Etudes Historiques. Sofia.

———. 1982. *He Valkanike Diastasis tes Epanastaseos tou 1821 (He periptosis ton Voulgaron).* Athens.

Torunoglu, B. 2012. *Murder in Salonika 1876: A Tale of Apostasy and International Crisis.* Piscataway, NJ.

Tsapanidou, A. 2018. "Hellenes Polemioi kai Therapontes tou Soultanou sten Constantinoupole too 19ou Aiona." In *He Constantinoupole sten Historia kai ten Logotechnia,* edited by C. A. Menaoglou, 517–38. Athens.

Tsoukalas, G. 1859. *He Voulgaroslavike Symmoria kai he Triandria Autes.* Constantinople.

Ubicini, M. A. 1856. *Letters on Turkey.* London.

Union Catalogue of the Periodicals in Arabic Script 1828–1928 in the Libraries of Istanbul. 1986. Research Centre for Islamic History, Art and Culture, Organisation of the Islamic Conference. Istanbul.

Vakalopoulos, A. 1961. *Historia tou Neou Hellenismou*. Salonica.

Vakalopoulos, K. 2008. *Ion Dragoumis Martyron kai Heroon Aima-Anatomia tes Hellenikes Pragmatikotetas*. Athens.

Valetas, G., ed. 1949. *Anonymou tou Hellenos: Hellenike Nomarchia etoi Logos peri Eleutherias*. Athens.

Valetas, G., ed. 1971. *O Armatomenos Logos, oi Antistasiakes Didaches tou Nektariou Terpou Vgalmenes sta 1730*. Athens.

Walsh, Rev. R. 1836. *A Residence at Constantinople during a Period Including the Commencement, Progress and Termination of the Greek and Turkish Revolution*. London.

Watson, G., ed. 1969. *The New Cambridge Bibliography of English Literature*. Vol. 3. Cambridge.

Wilberg, F. 1902. "Ta typographeia tou Anglou syntagmatarchou Leister Stanhope, 1824–1826." *Armonia* 3:178–89.

Yazıcı, N. 1991. "*Vakayı-i Misriye üzerine birkaç söz.*" *OTAM* 2:267–78.

Zachariadou, E., ed. 1996. *Ten Turkish Documents*. Athens.

Zepos, J., and P. Zepos. 1931. *Jus graeco-romanum*. Athens.

Index